LILLEE & THOMMO

LILLEE & THOMMO

THE DEADLY PAIR'S REIGN OF TERROR

IAN BRAYSHAW

hardie grant books

Published in 2017 by Hardie Grant Books, an imprint of Hardie Grant Publishing

Hardie Grant Books (Melbourne)
Building 1, 658 Church Street
Richmond, Victoria 3121

Hardie Grant Books (London)
5th & 6th Floors
52–54 Southwark Street
London SE1 1UN

hardiegrantbooks.com

All rights reserved. No part of this publication may be reproduced, stored in a retrieval system or transmitted in any form by any means, electronic, mechanical, photocopying, recording or otherwise, without the prior written permission of the publishers and copyright holders.

The moral rights of the author have been asserted.

Copyright text © Ian Brayshaw 2017

A Cataloguing-in-Publication entry is available from the catalogue of the National Library of Australia at www.nla.gov.au

Lillee & Thommo
ISBN 978 1 74379 259 9

Cover design by Blue Cork/Luke Causby
Typeset in 11.5/18 pt Sabon by Kirby Jones
Statistics by Lawrie Colliver
Cover images courtesy of Getty Images
Printed by McPherson's Printing Group, Maryborough, Victoria

The paper this book is printed on is certified against the Forest Stewardship Council® Standards. FSC® promotes environmentally responsible, socially beneficial and economically viable management of the world's forests.

Viv Richards, reflecting on his foray as a young man into boxing: 'Fighting was hard, but not as hard as facing Dennis Lillee and Jeff Thomson.'

THE CONTRIBUTORS

In gathering material, the author was grateful to interview many players, an umpire, a longstanding cricket correspondent and the son of a legendary cricketer. Thank you to the following who contributed:

Ian Chappell – *Australian captain*
Greg Chappell – *Australian captain*
Geoff Howarth – *New Zealand captain*
Mike Brearley – *England captain*
Rod Marsh – *Australian wicketkeeper*
Dennis Amiss – *England batsman*
David Lloyd – *England batsman*
John Wright – *New Zealand batsman*
John Inverarity – *Australian batsman*
Ross Edwards – *Australian batsman*
Bruce Laird – *Australian batsman*
Robin Bailhache – *Test umpire*
John Woodcock – *London* Times *Cricket Correspondent*
Jeremy Cowdrey – *son of Sir Colin Cowdrey*

CONTENTS

PART I. DESTROYING ENGLAND   9
1 Prelude in Adelaide   11
2 The Road to Brisbane   16
    The phoney war   16
    Are you ready?   20
    Payback time   24
    A sticky wicket   27
    Gentlemen ... play   28
    Assessing the damage   42
3 The Road to Perth   44
    The false start, then the falter   45
    A big decision   55
    'I'd love to'   58
    Smectite and Little Roy   63
    Recommence hostilities!   67
    Impressions   74
    What about those bouncers?   78
4 Carnage Countrywide   89
    So close, so far, for Amiss and England   89
    The captain's head   94
    A bad serve   102
    The spirit of the game – and broken spirits   109
    Batsmen weren't the only ones bruised   114

5 Off to the World Cup	122
Here we go again	127
Change at the top	134
PART II. DESTROYING THE WEST INDIES	**137**
But first …	139
Up, down, out	141
A fast reaction	152
Disaster – and triumph	156
'It's impossible to bowl faster'	161
Question mark	178
The great divide	181
That one day	184
The quickest	188
Together again	194
PART III. BREAKING THE PARTNERSHIP	**199**
Ups and downs	201
'A captain's dream, a batsman's nightmare'	208
A study in contrasts	225
The fear, the laughter	239
The numbers	244
The final dance	248
Partnership broken	253
Limited overs, limited joy	255
One last time	258
Statistical Analysis	261
Acknowledgements	271

PART I
DESTROYING ENGLAND

Dennis Lillee, Max Walker and Jeff Thomson celebrate after Australia won the first Test match between England and Australia at Edgbaston, Birmingham, 14 July 1975. Australia won the match by an innings and 85 runs. (Photo by Ken Kelly/Popperfoto/Getty Images)

ONE

PRELUDE IN ADELAIDE

THE *OLD* Adelaide Oval. Flanking the western side of the ground, the rust-red iron roof of the Sir Edwin Smith, George Giffen and Mostyn Evan stands; on the eastern side, concrete terraces concealing the Victor Richardson Gates, and in between and to the north, The Hill and the famous Edwardian scoreboard. Above the lot, imperiously looking down upon the glorious scene, St Peter's Cathedral.

Out in the middle, the traditionally batsman-friendly pitch is surrounded by an outfield as pure and true as the putting greens at the not-too-distant Royal Adelaide Golf Club. Adding to the ground's uniqueness and charm, the players' dressing rooms: side-on to the wicket, rather than the usual end-on. This position offered resting players a sleepy view across the ground and beyond to the Adelaide Hills. For the next man in, however, it gave a distorted view of the pace of the bowling he was preparing to face; it conspired to make a fast-medium bowler look really quick!

Few more than 1000 people were present at the ground on 25 October 1974 – not surprising, given it was a week day and rain clouds hung low over the flat city. Although it was just another day's play in the time-honoured Sheffield Shield competition, it was a very special day in the larger context of Australian cricket. Dennis Lillee would be back in action at the head of Western Australia's attack, testing the strength of his back after a season missed through injury. The rain clouds fulfilled their promise, and when the day's play was eventually called off, with not one wicket fallen, Lillee returned to the dressing room, pleased to find his body intact. He sat down, already planning a more robust workout the following day.

Before being struck down by a crippling back injury, Lillee was one of the world's premier fast bowlers. Back injuries are notoriously fickle and prognoses uncertain, so there was considerable interest in Lillee's return. So much interest that his captain, John Inverarity, took an unusual step. 'We didn't want Dennis to be distracted, so we arranged a media conference, to be held at our motel the day before the game.' The idea was to offer the media open slather – so that they would leave Lillee alone once the game started. Leave him free to let his bowling do the talking.

Day two of the game dawned fine and sunny. It was a Saturday, so Adelaide's boilermakers and bankers, its builders and barristers, were free to attend. The crowd swelled to 5000 – more than would attend the entire four days' play of other games that season. Among those at the ground that day was a very special group: the touring party of the Marleybone Cricket Club (MCC), as the English team was quaintly known in all but test matches. The very batsmen who would have to see off the fury of Lillee – if his back was up to it. They had just arrived Down Under and had booked a session in the nets, which were laid out on turf behind the Mostyn Evan Stand. As Lillee warmed to the task, a group of men in whites appeared up the concrete steps that led to the grandstands from the practice area. It was the MCC players.

Dennis Amiss: I was one of the England players who left the nets in Adelaide to watch Dennis that day. He bowled off a short run and still looked a good bowler. The action was still there. We just thought, 'If he's going to bowl off a short run we might be able to handle that'.

The man himself was aware of this special *audience*. 'I noticed that a number of the English players wandered over from the nets when I opened the bowling. I also saw that they walked away fairly swiftly, after watching only a few balls. They clearly thought this new-look Dennis Lillee was going to be no threat to them at all.' In fact, England's captain, Mike Denness, is reported as saying: 'He was not employing the high kick and jump, which he had used just before delivery ... neither did he look as quick as before.'

That may have been an accurate observation from that day, but was it really a sign of what was to come? According to one of Lillee's teammates, the deception, if you could call it that, had worked.

> **Ross Edwards:** Dennis was bowling downhill at the time, not too quick because it was his first game back after injury, and you could almost see the smile on the Poms' faces, because it appeared from this little cameo that he wasn't going to be a major force in our attack for the Test series. He could only bowl medium pace ... his back was broken ... da-da, da-da-da-da.

The author stood in the slips in Lillee's comeback games and, along with others, found the task particularly difficult. Lillee was testing his back off a short run, which meant the slips cordon had to stand closer to the action than was the case when he was working at full tilt. That proximity to the batsman was fine – until Lillee squeezed out the occasional *effort* ball – and then those in the cordon needed the extra couple of metres' distance from the batsman to get their hands in place to have any chance of making the catch.

Lillee packed his bags after that game, which his team had won by two wickets, happy that step one had been negotiated safely. There was a very warm vibe in the WA camp. Their main man had sent down a total of 28 overs, taken seven wickets and, most importantly, had emerged unscathed. In both innings he dismissed the South Australian and, more importantly, Australian captain, Ian Chappell – which couldn't have done his chances of national selection any harm. On to Melbourne then. His return at the hallowed ground was 27 overs and four wickets. In Sydney he upped the workload to 45 overs for four wickets. Finally to Brisbane, 34 overs and four more wickets. All of these eight-ball overs, as was the way in those days in Australia. A fair workload for a fast bowler on the comeback trail.

That month on the road for his state side had been a serious test of Lillee's back. He had sent down a total of 134 overs – more than a thousand deliveries in match conditions – producing 19 wickets. A wicket every seven overs.

Feeling his way back, operating mainly off a shortened run, bowling within himself. There promised to be a week's rest, then the first Test against England in Brisbane. Would the champion make it back after a heartbreaking twenty-one months in rehabilitation?

TWO

THE ROAD TO BRISBANE

The phoney war

CRICKETING BLOOD courses through Greg Chappell's veins. Those gates at the Adelaide Oval are named after his grandfather, Vic Richardson, who captained Australia on the 1935–36 tour of South Africa. His blood passed to his son, Martin, who fathered Greg and his brothers, the older Ian and the younger Trevor. Martin had been an Adelaide club cricketer who went close to state selection.

Starting his cricket in South Australia, Greg had been lured north to Queensland, the bait being the captaincy of the state team. In his first season there he almost led the state to its first Sheffield Shield title in 1973–74, only to be denied by NSW tearaway quick Jeff Thomson in the season's last game. And, as Mike Denness's Ashes touring party worked their way around the country, with tour games in Adelaide, Melbourne,

Sydney and Brisbane, Greg Chappell deployed his shrewdness and hatched a plan: to leave the English bats guessing about this fellow Thomson, who he had likewise lured north.

The tourists would play Queensland in the week leading up to the first Test in Brisbane. Chappell managed the situation to a nicety. He tells how it unfolded:

> **Greg Chappell:** I thought 'This bloke is going to be a sensation and the less they see of him now the more sensational it's likely to be'. So I decided to use him sparingly in the lead-up game – and definitely not a lot against their best top-order batsmen – just to keep him up our sleeves for the Test match.
>
> Before the game I took Thommo to one side and told him to just keep it under wraps, that the England players had no idea what he was capable of – and that there was no point in showing it to them too early.
>
> I told him he'd be bowling a few overs here and there, to get a bit of rhythm ... but not to go flat out. Just to keep himself comfortable, so that he would be ready to go in the Test the following week. He wasn't happy about not being allowed loose, but I said to him, 'Mate, these wickets don't count – but they *will* count in the Test match. Let's surprise them then'.

Indeed, captain Mike Denness wasn't overly impressed by what he saw of Thomson. He is reported as saying, 'for a couple of overs he was sharp, but then he cut back and the feeling was that he was quick but wayward. Most of us found it a little difficult to pick up the ball, because when the arm goes back it is hidden behind the body, and could not be seen again until just before delivery. At that time we were very open-minded about the threat he posed'.

Denness was not alone in his opinion.

Dennis Amiss: We were aware that Thomson had played one Test against Pakistan, but that's about all we knew about him. When we saw him for the first time, in the game against Queensland, he only bowled a couple of overs at a time. We could see he had some pace, but, really, he was all over the place. So, with some doubt about Dennis Lillee's fitness, returning after a long period out, we thought if we could keep those two out we'd have a chance. But we had no idea what was coming.

David Lloyd: Dennis, we knew, was coming back from a serious back injury and it was touch and go as to whether he'd be up for the Tests – maybe for one or two at the end of the series. So we were looking at the likes of Colley, Gilmour, Dymock and Walker.

However, we knew little about Jeff Thomson. Only that he'd played one Test match and not taken a wicket for plenty of runs. For a while before we left on the tour we actually thought the bowler they were talking about was Alan 'Froggy' Thomson, who played for Victoria and had a very strange delivery style.

The misunderstanding was understandable in the pre-internet days, especially given the bowlers shared a surname and both had unique actions. The Englishmen had seen 'Froggy' Thomson before, in four Tests while touring here in 1970–71. Thomson has the distinction of taking the first wicket in international one-day cricket: Geoffrey Boycott, caught hooking, by Bill Lawry.

> **David Lloyd:** When we played Queensland in the week before the first Test, Jeff Thomson looked okay but didn't do very much. Despite his rather brash promise on television, that he could bowl 'much quicker', nobody really took much notice.

> **John Woodcock:** Thomson we weren't particularly worried about. But maybe we were deceived by his performance in the game for Queensland leading up to the Test. On a previous tour we'd seen Ian Meckiff in the state game against Victoria and we thought he threw the ball. The thinking was 'Don't say anything about him [his action], because he's not very good' – but it turned out he wasn't flat out in that game!

It seemed that Greg Chappell's little ruse was working a treat – despite the fact that Thomson had told a television audience in the week leading up to the Test match that he could 'bowl a lot faster than that'.

Are you ready?

FOR IAN CHAPPELL, who would lead the Australian team in its six-Test quest for cricket's Holy Grail – the Ashes – the waters were a little muddy as he prepared to leave Adelaide for Brisbane and game one. Would Dennis Lillee's back stand up to the rigours of his explosive craft in the heat of competition and high summer? And what about this bloke Jeff Thomson, whom he'd seen make an abortive beginning to a Test career two summers before?

Ian Chappell: When I arrived in Brisbane, as soon as I'd put my gear down in my room at the motel, I rang Rod Marsh's room and said, 'any beer in the fridge, mate?'

'Yeah.'

'I'll be right over.'

So I cracked a beer. I knew WA had played Queensland a fortnight before and was keen for information.

'What's Thommo like?'

'Oh, Christ, he's bloody quick!'

Bacchus went on to explain. 'I got a few, but being a left-hander I was lucky because he was going across me. I was able to get some away over the slips, but he quickly worked that out and bowled me one that was more leg stump, coming at me. If it wasn't for the handle of the bat, I'm not here to talk with you. I'm dead. It hit the handle of the bat, right in front of my face. Mate, he *is* quick!'

I grinned and said, 'That's just the news I was hoping to hear'.

That was a resounding tick for Thomson, but Lillee still needed the selectors' approval – and he admits it wasn't much fun waiting to find out. 'I thought I'd bowled well enough, but I was afraid the selectors would be thinking "will he last for a full Test match?" I was really thrilled when I heard the news that I was in. It was like starting my career all over again.

'But now I knew that I'd reached the time when I'd have to make a big decision: when the ball was thrown to me, should I continue to bowl with something in reserve or should I give it all – because a Test match will always deserve a player's all. Sitting in my motel room that night I made the decision. I had to give it everything I could; I'd revert to bowling fairly quickly.'

For Lillee there was another thought. 'It was amazing that Thommo and I actually did get together for that game. He had failed in his first Test and then was dropped for the entire time I was out with my back injury. For the selectors it was a gamble for me to play at all, just as it was a bit of a surprise when they picked Thommo.'

The national selectors – Phil Ridings, Sam Loxton and Neil Harvey – had not changed during that time. What had changed was that the NSW selectors gave Thomson only one game throughout the 1973–74 season despite the fact his last match had been a Test – and the one they gave him was the last one of the season. He could hardly be picked for Australia if his state selectors considered him not good enough for NSW.

Lillee may have doubted his capacity to return, but others had more faith.

Greg Chappell: I was always reasonably confident that Dennis would be able to come back successfully. He had such a strong, indomitable will. Then I saw him bowling with his redesigned action when WA played Queensland in Brisbane a fortnight before the Test. I faced him for a while and realised, firstly, that he hadn't lost his competitive instincts!

He wasn't the tearaway bowler that he had been, probably bowling at about eighty per cent effort, but he still hit the bat very hard and now had the great ability to change his pace up. What he had also gained was a greater degree of control. With the manic running style of his early game he was all over the place at times – when it clicked he was quick, when it didn't click it wasn't so quick and would generally go down leg side or wide of off stump.

The new version enabled him to just home into an area where most batsmen didn't want the ball to be consistently pitching: a line coming down just outside off-stump ... the corridor of uncertainty. If he could stand up for the six Tests he was going to be a handful.

Dennis Amiss: We had seen what Dennis could do in England in 1972, but after that he'd suffered some real back troubles and we believed he, himself, wasn't quite sure whether he'd make the series or not. Obviously a very fine bowler, but what he would be able to deliver in the series was totally alien to us.

John Inverarity: I knew there was no person with greater determination ... but, would he make it back? I didn't know. However, the single factor about Dennis, which stood him apart from the best of the rest, was just one word ... *will*. With him, if there was a contest there was only going to be one winner.

David Lloyd: It seemed to us to be odds-on that Dennis wouldn't make it. You just sensed that it would be a bonus for Australia if he got one or two games in the series. After all, this was a really serious injury. But the real determination and discipline of the man meant that, in fact, he *would* get back. Very few in my experience have been able to achieve that.

The cricketers' minds were filled with doubts about themselves and their opponents. One of the umpires had his own doubts – Robin Bailhache admits that before he departed for the game he hadn't a clue where the Gabba was. The South Australian, who would wear the white jacket for the first time in a Test, had risen to the top so quickly that almost everything about this very important game was new.

Robin Bailhache: It was my debut Test match and I only learnt that I was to stand in it on the Sunday

> before the game. I honestly didn't know where the Gabba was – and I'd never even met Tom Brooks, my fellow umpire for the game. More importantly, I had never met four or five of the Australian players, including Jeff Thomson.

Bailhache and Brooks would stand in all six Tests of the series. As they walked out for day one of the opening encounter, on Friday 29 November 1974, they had no idea what was coming. Neither did the English batsmen.

Payback time

AUSTRALIA'S 1972 tour of England was a bitter-sweet affair. A hard-fought series was marred by the Fusarium Test, the fourth of five in the series, at Headingley, the suburban ground in Leeds. The tourists had arrived in Leeds level in the series after a loss at Old Trafford, a win at Lord's, on the back of Bob Massie's extraordinary 16-wicket haul on debut, and a draw at Trent Bridge. To their dismay the wicket being prepared had no grass whatsoever. The reason, they were told, was because of an attack by the *fusarium* fungus.

England called left-arm spinner Derek Underwood into the side, to combine with Ray Illingworth's off-spin – and in the two innings Underwood claimed a total of 10 wickets for 82 runs. Defeated by nine wickets, the Australians felt cheated. Thanks to that outcome, they had lost the chance of regaining the Ashes. The word 'fusarium' stuck in the collective craw of a group that had intended to prove false its tag of 'worst touring Australian side ever' by taking the urn back home Down Under with them.

Six members of that team – the Chappells, Lillee, Rod Marsh, Ross Edwards and Doug Walters – would play in the nations' next encounter, in Brisbane. For these men the memory of the disappointment – in particular of the Leeds Test – remained a bitter pill still stuck in their gullet.

Greg Chappell: It wasn't something we talked about, but being beaten, particularly over the *Fusarium* wicket, it did sit badly with us. Looking back, we learnt so much on that tour. About ourselves - about what it took to win a series. It made us stronger, more determined and we would soon realise that it was a lot more fun winning than losing.

To be fair, we did learn a lot from Ray Illingworth and his team. They were a good side and Illy was a shrewd captain, though not overly aggressive. He would attack you when you first came in and if you settled he would go back into a very defensive mode and make runs hard to come by. We were never going to be so defensive, but there was a lot we learnt about tactics and strategies.

Before the final Test at The Oval in that series there was a fair bit in the English media about the fact that we were gone. That we had dropped our bundle. On the night before the game we had a team meeting and the manager, Ray Steele, got up and produced the cutting of a story about how we were going to lie down and get run over.

Then his voice boomed out: 'Pig's bloody arse we will!'

> Next Ian spoke. 'Two-all's going to be looked at pretty favourably ... but three-one would be a bloody disaster ... and could affect the careers of many of you in this room.'
>
> It was to be a six-day Test. Fortunes fluctuated for five days and come the morning of the sixth day it could have gone either way. When Rod Marsh and Paul Sheahan got the winning runs ... it was just a great, great feeling and I think that was the making of that team. We came home with a fair bit of belief and realised that if we could just keep playing five days of good cricket we'd win more than we'd lose.

In fact that final day at The Oval was the first day's play in an overseas Test match to be telecast live in Australia, and the scenes as Marsh and Sheahan galloped across the ground to join the celebrations with their teammates, having successfully chased the 242 runs required for victory, are etched into the memories of all who saw them.

Just over two years on and the word 'Fusarium' remained burnt into the memories of five Australians about to embark on an arduous journey: six Tests Down Under against the Old Foe, with a chance to regain the Ashes. And now it was the Englishmen's turn to battle a dodgy wicket. Payback time!

A sticky wicket

EVERY GAME of cricket, be it a hit-out in the park or a Test match, deserves the best possible conditions for play. Sadly, the Gabba in 1974 fell way short of expectations. The wicket prepared for the series opener just wasn't up to Test match standard. Which is perhaps not surprising, given that in a bizarre set of circumstances its final preparation was performed by the Lord Mayor of Brisbane.

For those who know the vagaries of the weather in the Queensland capital, it would come as no shock that in the week leading up to the Test rain had fallen heavily. Progress with the wicket intended for the big game was such that Alderman Clem Jones, a long-serving administrator of the Queensland Cricket Association, took it upon himself to remove the curator and take over the reins, about ten days before the game. Here's the England team's slant on it all, written by the legendary cricket scribe, E.W. Swanton: 'When Mike Denness and his side went to the ground on the Wednesday morning, two days before the Test, the pitch to their astonishment was a morass of black mud. They left the acting-curator and reigning Lord Mayor of Brisbane, clad in a yellow safety-helmet, flattening it, roughly speaking, with a heavy motor-roller.'

Further, from Michael Melford in the *Daily Telegraph*: 'Civic duties and curatorship do not easily blend'. The Lord Mayor, a down-to-earth, determined character, admitted as much himself when he confessed that the Test wicket was 'a bit crook at one end'. The England batsmen would soon agree – 16 of their 20 wickets fell at the Stanley Street end. Alderman Jones suggested the unevenness would 'enable the fast bowlers to get the ball to rear right up'. And although the England bats would agree with that, they would disagree with his rider: 'Because the wicket is so soft underneath it will only rear up slowly'.

In the end Jones discarded that muddy strip in favour of the wicket that had been used in the Queensland–Western Australia Shield game a fortnight earlier. These capers didn't escape the notice of the England camp. One Englishman vividly remembers the curator.

> **David Lloyd:** He was in flip-flops and T-shirt, rolling the Test wicket. An hour and a half later, I'm nudging [team manager] Alec Bedser at a Lord Mayoral reception, saying, 'Isn't that the same geezer who was looking after the wicket?'

Alderman Clem Jones was Brisbane's longest-serving lord mayor – and the Gabba's shortest-serving curator. His next job was as the chief administrator for the reconstruction of Darwin, after it was levelled by Cyclone Tracy on Christmas Day 1974. And he left a lasting legacy to the cricketing world: his name. The Australian pace bowler Terry Alderman is known to all and sundry as 'Clem'.

Gentlemen ... play!

A BALL HAD yet to be bowled in the series and the England selectors, led by the taciturn Alec Bedser, who was also the team manager, had to consider a list that was three men down. David Lloyd had broken a finger fielding, while bowler Geoff Arnold had a strained shoulder and fellow paceman Chris Old an injured hand.

One could argue they were five men down. Opening bat

Geoff Boycott was named in the original touring squad but shortly afterwards made himself unavailable for the tour, citing unspecified personal reasons. Some said he did not want to play under the captaincy of Denness. Others said he was afraid of Australia's pace, but his self-imposed exile would last until 1977. Paceman John Snow, who had done so well on the 1970–71 tour, likewise was missing from action.

England went in with three pace bowlers – Bob Willis, Peter Lever and Mick Hendrick – seam-bowling all-rounder Tony Greig and spinner Derek Underwood. Australia would rely on three pace bowlers – Lillee, Thomson and Max Walker – plus spinner Terry Jenner and with back up from spare-parts bowlers Doug Walters and Greg Chappell if needed.

From the outset the trump cards promised to be Lillee and Thomson, who, according to Lillee, at that time barely knew each other. 'We had played together in the one Test in 1972–3, plus against each other a couple of times after that, when we'd exchanged cursory nods. But we got on straight away once we were in the same team again. You could never fail to get on with Thommo, because he was just the easiest-going guy of all time.'

That was demonstrated when they met up in Brisbane. Thomson was enjoying a scotch at the bar. After all, he had told the media that he was 'training on whisky'.

For Lillee, as he looked at a six-Test program, there was the serious matter of being able to get through without further injury problems. 'It was always in my mind that my back could go at any time. Then there was the *new* action. I didn't know if it was going to work, whether it was going to be successful.' Lillee had modified his action, thanks to a program of training in running technique. Gone were the flailing arms and galloping legs ... the new model was silky smooth, with far less energy expended.

There were some questions in Thomson's mind, too. 'Between the last time I played for Australia and this time, what if it went wrong? But I was ready to go. Super fit and bowling at the fastest of my career. I had a lot to prove. Against Pakistan two years before, I was raw and thought I was lucky to be there. This time I knew no other bloke was better than me.'

Time for action! Ian Chappell won the toss – or more accurately the visiting captain Mike Denness called incorrectly – and chose to bat. He and his brother provided half-centuries. It was slow but sure progress on an uneven wicket not at all conducive to flamboyant strokeplay. Australia was finally dismissed for 309 – a respectable total in the circumstances. A tick after two o'clock on the second day, the crowd of 15,957 sat up and took notice as the Australian XI entered the field.

When it came time to decide who would take the new ball, as far as the skipper was concerned seniority held sway.

> **Ian Chappell:** I gave the ball to Dennis first, downwind, and told 'Tangles' [Max Walker] he'd be into the wind. Thinking he could swing it about a bit. Halfway through the first over I said to myself, 'Ian, you're a bloody idiot ... you've got a really fast bowler here, you've got to give him the new ball'.
>
> So I gestured to Tangles, 'Hold on mate' – and signalled to Thommo to loosen up. I don't think he did

anything, but give me a 'yeah, sure mate' wave. Anyway, he came in and bowled like the wind from the very first ball. His first over was quick ... I was standing beside Rod Marsh as the ball thudded into his gloves. He tossed it to Greg at second slip – and wrung his hands.

'Something wrong, pal?' I asked.

'Christ, that hurt,' said Bacchus, 'but I love it!'

Dennis Amiss: Brian Luckhurst and I went out to open the innings. Well, there's Dennis measuring out his long run. I remember saying to Brian, 'What's he doing? Maybe he'll break down. Come on, let's get stuck in'. Mind you, the wicket wasn't great. A little bit corrugated and up and down with bounce. Australia had, in fact, done well to get 309 on it.

The first three balls from Thommo I've done the old English thing – you know, started to get onto the front foot, get behind it and push it back down the wicket. Those balls just whistled past my head. Subsequently, I've said to friends, 'Those first three balls give you an inkling of what was to come for us on the rest of the tour'. And we had to look forward to having him and Dennis for, not five Tests, we had them for six!

Even bowling into the wind Thommo was lightning fast. And, being so strong he could get incredible bounce, especially with the new ball.

The ferocity and incredible speed generated by the bowlers did not go unnoticed by the umpires.

Robin Bailhache: When it started it was fearsome. It was all new to me – and I copped this! Tom Brooks was a great help to me, but he had his hands full himself. Did I ever feel for the batsman? Quite often. Where I was standing was quite safe, but being down the other end? It actually worried me at times, because I didn't want to be around when somebody got really hurt.

The Australian fieldsmen were likewise alive to what was happening.

Ross Edwards: Dennis came out and bowled quick – that gave the Poms a bit of a surprise. Then in his first over, bowling uphill, there was this Thommo bloke, sending them down much, much quicker than Lillee. You should have seen the Poms' eyes. You could see them looking out from the dressing room, the big white orbs of their eyes. Thommo bowled lightning quick. I think the series was all over after his first over. They were absolutely shellshocked.

Richie Benaud, that doyen of cricket commentators, said at the time that the English bowlers had deliberately bounced the Australians on the first day. And, Benaud added, the Australians just might retaliate.

Luckhurst was the first to fall, caught by Marsh off Thomson for 1, as the opener played a ball off his hips into the keeper's gloves. His opening partner fared little better.

Dennis Amiss: At one stage I got hit on the end of the thumb with a hot one from Thommo and it lobbed over Doug Walters' head in the gully (not his normal place, in the covers ... they didn't really need anybody there!) and I got down to the other end. What a relief! Then the umpire called 'over' – and the first ball of the next over Dennis hit me on the thumb again. The same place; broke my thumb.

But the Australians were not finished hitting Amiss yet. Thomson got another one to rear and it caught his hand again, this time flying to gully, where Terry Jenner completed the catch. Amiss had made 7, and four of those were a snick through slips. Thomson now had two wickets for four runs. 'There was no respite,' Amiss later said. 'They were in your face the whole time.'

That dismissal brought to the crease the England captain, Mike Denness. He had an early taste of what was in store when he was hit on the collarbone by a steepling flier from Thomson. 'Of course it hurt,' the England captain is reported as saying, 'but you couldn't show any signs of distress against the Aussies because they will always smell blood.'

Perhaps rattled by the extreme pace, Denness was soon making his way back to the pavilion, out lbw to Max Walker, not offering a shot. England 3–33.

Down the other end John Edrich was trying to make the most of the fact that he had survived an early chance, fending off a ball at the body that just eluded Ian Redpath at short leg. Keith Fletcher was next in. His batting lacked composure. He slashed a wide Thomson ball over slips for four, and heaved another one in the air over mid-off for another boundary. His resistance wasn't to last – a shortish ball from Lillee at the body, but not a bouncer, was played on to the stumps. Lillee had his first wicket. England 4–57.

That brought Tony Greig to the middle – to the boos of the crowd. Greig was cast as the villain – and looked the part with his turned-up collar – for in Australia's first innings Greig had bounced Lillee, eventually dismissing him with a short one. Lillee had marched off the field furious.

Umpire Robin Bailhache remembers it well:

> Thommo hardly said 'boo' in the game, but Dennis occasionally had a few words. Like in the first innings, when Tony Greig had him caught behind off a bouncer. If there had been any friendship between the two before that it went flying out the window. The words Dennis said to him as he walked off aren't printable. And when Greig came in to bat, Dennis bowled two of the shortest and widest balls I've ever seen ... clear over Greig's head, over Rod Marsh's head and down for four byes.'

Greig was the man Lillee had been waiting for. Which Greig knew. He later told journalist Philip Derriman:

> If you went in while Lillee was bowling, he was somehow able to make you feel as you walked to the wicket that you were the one he had been waiting to

bowl to all day. He made you feel he had too many fieldsmen, that everything was loaded in his favour. You felt intimidated by the presence of the man before he bowled a ball to you.

Lillee went back to his long run. His first ball to the lanky blonde bat was a wild short one down leg side – a foretaste of what was to come.

> **Ian Chappell:** Greigy really did get up Dennis's nose. He was signalling fours when he had snicked the ball over the slips. He would do this right under Dennis's nose and he was getting really pissed off with this.

Greig and Edrich stayed together until stumps, but with the Australians rested – and rehydrated – overnight, it started again quickly on the third day, an extremely hot one. Edrich, who had batted manfully to be 40 not out overnight, was the victim. Lillee struck the first blow hitting the 36-year-old veteran on the gloves – the result, a broken index finger. Thomson completed the double act, a rearing delivery snapped up by Ian Chappell in the slips.

Greig was dropped on 42, slashing at a short one off Lillee, which did the quick's frame of mind no good. And Greig resolved to make the best of his good fortune.

> **Greg Chappell:** In terms of being flat out, Dennis got up there. Especially after he'd been stirred up by Greigy. He got a bit angry and let a few go. In this

second incarnation he was as quick as he ever was, but he was much more dangerous with it because he could direct it where he wanted it to go. Like, when he bowled a bouncer it would hit the mark. Actually, we made a bit of a mess of it in the first innings. Particularly Dennis, who went on a bit of a bouncer barrage. Mainly he went after Greigy and tried to pin him to the sightscreen. And I'm sure that's why Greigy had bowled bouncers at Dennis, because he wanted Dennis to have a go at him. As for Thommo, he didn't have to drop it that short to get it up ... and bowling bouncers wasn't part of his game.

Dennis Amiss: Greigy put on quite a show of taunting the Australian bowlers, signalling boundaries and offering some commentary – on the way to compiling a wonderful century. In a way I think Dennis fell for it and for a while his rhythm was astray because he was straining at the crease.

Greig turned on a devil-may-care century, bringing it up with successive fours off Lillee. Frustration showed as four byes from a wild bouncer followed. Lillee took it out on Bob Willis, who copped a crushing blow to his box, taking his breath away. Eventually Lillee got his man, caught by Marsh while slashing, but victory was Greig's. He arrived to boos, and left to applause.

It was Walker who cleaned up the tailenders, ending with the most wickets, four, while Doug Walters, as ever, broke an annoying bottom-order partnership with his first ball, claiming Derek Underwood, whose 25 in a 58-run partnership with Greig got England back on kilter. Thanks to Greig's heroic 110 England got to within 44 of the Australian total, making a game of it.

Chappell declared shortly before stumps on the fourth day, with a lead of 332. The amateurishness that marked the pitch preparation was repeated when the heavy roller broke down, costing the Australians two overs at the Englishmen. Three Thomson bouncers to Amiss brought a talking-to from umpire Bailhache – and when the batsmen were offered the opportunity to end proceedings because of bad light, they gladly took it.

Thomson and Lillee went straight to work on the final day. Lillee struck first, as Luckhurst tried to guide one through slips. His three runs gave him four for the match.

That meant Edrich joined Amiss at the crease – one with a broken finger, the other a broken thumb.

What is it like, batting with a thumb that has been struck? First the damaged thumb becomes engorged with blood, tightening its fit inside the snug-fitting glove. More pain. Then just gripping the bat handle while taking stance sends nasty signals up to the brain. Would the batsman give up the routine of tapping his bat on the ground while he waits? Doing so means more pain, so the answer might just be 'yes'. Finally, no matter how sweetly bat meets ball there's a jar that races through the injured digit, up the arm, through the shoulder and neck, to the brain. Oh, and what about that fear factor? Fear of receiving another blow right on the same spot? A good fast bowler will most definitely have this in mind. Thomson did. Noting Edrich was unable to hit the ball with any force, Thomson had only one fielder in front of the wicket. Thomson bowled Edrich with a ball that was simply too quick. As Edrich departed, he pulled off his glove to inspect the damage. Besides the broken index finger, his thumb was ugly and badly swollen.

Out came Denness. Thomson got one up quickly to hit him straightaway.

> **Mike Denness:** In those days, I used to wear a gold St Christopher pendant, and it was only when I got back to the dressing room that I found the ball had literally embedded the pendant in my chest. For any bouncers aimed at your head, you had to rely on your reflexes, or, for those brave enough to take on the hook shot, you had to be prepared to lose your front teeth.

A good length delivery flew over Denness's outstretched bat – and his sharp intake of breath said it all. A steeper from Thomson had Amiss caught behind. A soaring good-length ball brought a look of disbelief from Fletcher.

It was time for destruction. Thomson tore the heart out of England, captain Denness caught in slips sparring at a riser. Enter Tony Greig.

> **Ian Chappell:** Before we went out for the second innings I said to Dennis and Thommo, 'Hey listen you two silly

bastards, is there any danger that we could actually get Tony Greig out, rather than trying to kill him?' And that's when Thommo came up the with the sandshoe crusher. He had a bloody good yorker. Not only was it quick, but it used to duck back in to the right-hander.

Greg Chappell: When Greigy came out in the second innings I went up to Thommo and said, 'This bloke's standing up and holding the bat in the air ... give him one of your best yorkers ... just hit him on the foot ... if it doesn't get him out it'll break bones'. Next ball he hit him flush on the left foot and it ricocheted straight into the stumps.

Lillee chipped in with a second wicket, Peter Lever, whose spirit was broken by the short balls. Thomson did the rest, stopping on the way to rap two more players on the hand – Underwood, who top-scored with 30, on his right non-bowling hand, and Mike Hendrick.

When Thomson ripped one through the defence of Hendrick, it was all over. England out for 166. For the home side, victory by 166 runs. Australia's first win against England at the Gabba since the 1958–59 Ashes series. For the visitors, the stark reality that their batting was brittle against the Lillee and Thomson tornado. The rampaging Thomson finished with 6–46 from 17.5 overs. That made 9–105 for the match. When he played his last Test, eleven years later, those figures remained his best for a Test innings and his best for a Test match.

Australia v England 1974-1975
The Ashes – 1st Test – Woolloongabba, Brisbane
29, 30 November & 1, 3, 4 December 1974

Australia 1st Innings

I R Redpath	b Willis	5
W J Edwards	c Amiss b Hendrick	4
I M Chappell*	c Greig b Willis	90
G S Chappell	c Fletcher b Underwood	58
R Edwards	c †Knott b Underwood	32
K D Walters	c Lever b Willis	3
R W Marsh†	c Denness b Hendrick	14
T J Jenner	c Lever b Willis	12
D K Lillee	c †Knott b Greig	15
M H N Walker	not out	41
J R Thomson	run out	23
Extras	(lb 4, nb 8)	12
Total	All Out (92.5 overs @ 3.33 rpo)	309

England Bowling 1st Innings

Bowling	O	M	R	W	ER
R G D Willis	21.5	3	56	4	2.56
P Lever	16	1	53	0	3.31
M Hendrick	19	3	64	2	3.37
A W Greig	16	2	70	1	4.38
D L Underwood	20	6	54	2	2.70

England 1st Innings

D L Amiss	c Jenner b Thomson	7
B W Luckhurst	c †Marsh b Thomson	1
J H Edrich	c I M Chappell b Thomson	48
M H Denness*	lbw b Walker	6
K W R Fletcher	b Lillee	17
A W Greig	c †Marsh b Lillee	110
A P E Knott†	c Jenner b Walker	12
P Lever	c I M Chappell b Walker	4
D L Underwood	c Redpath b Walters	25
R G D Willis	not out	13
M Hendrick	c Redpath b Walker	4
Extras	(b 5, lb 2, w 3, nb 8)	18
Total	All Out (80.5 overs @ 3.28 rpo)	265

Australia Bowling 1st Innings

Bowling	O	M	R	W	ER
D K Lillee	23	6	73	2	3.17
J R Thomson	21	5	59	3	2.81
M H N Walker	24.5	2	73	4	2.94
K D Walters	6	1	18	1	3.00
T J Jenner	6	1	24	0	4.00

Australia 2nd Innings

I R Redpath	b Willis	25
W J Edwards	c †Knott b Willis	5
I M Chappell*	c Fletcher b Underwood	11
G S Chappell	b Underwood	71
R Edwards	c †Knott b Willis	53
K D Walters	not out	62
R W Marsh†	not out	46
T J Jenner		
D K Lillee		
M H N Walker		
J R Thomson		
Extras	(b 1, lb 7, w 1, nb 6)	15
Total	5 wickets declared (85.0 overs @ 3.39 rpo)	288

England Bowling 2nd Innings

Bowling	O	M	R	W	ER
R G D Willis	15	3	45	3	3.00
P Lever	18	4	58	0	3.22
M Hendrick	13	2	47	0	3.62
A W Greig	13	2	60	0	4.62
D L Underwood	26	6	63	2	2.42

England 2nd Innings (target 333)

D L Amiss	c Walters b Thomson	25
B W Luckhurst	c I M Chappell b Lillee	3
J H Edrich	b Thomson	6
M H Denness*	c Walters b Thomson	27
K W R Fletcher	c G S Chappell b Jenner	19
A W Greig	b Thomson	2
A P E Knott†	b Thomson	19
P Lever	c Redpath b Lillee	14
D L Underwood	c Walker b Jenner	30
R G D Willis	not out	3
M Hendrick	b Thomson	0
Extras	(b 8, lb 3, w 2, nb 5)	18
Total	All Out (56.5 overs @ 2.92 rpo)	166

Australia Bowling 2nd Innings

Bowling	O	M	R	W	ER
D K Lillee	12	2	25	2	2.08
J R Thomson	17.5	3	46	6	2.58
M H N Walker	9	4	32	0	3.56
K D Walters	2	2	0	0	0.00
T J Jenner	16	5	45	2	2.81

Assessing the damage

LILLEE AND THOMSON had taken 13 of the 20 England wickets to fall, nine to Thomson and four to his partner in speed. But perhaps more important, the pair had bruised, both bodily and mentally, the prime of the opposition's batting line-up, and the tailenders too. Virtually everyone who had batted had come away with the battle scars to prove it.

The great Australian all-rounder Keith Miller wrote of Thomson's pace and hostility: 'He frightened me with some of his nasty, rising deliveries ... and I was sitting 200 yards away'. Lillee agreed. 'At the time I didn't realise just how quick he was, but you knew that it was extremely fast given the way the ball reared off a good length – and, perhaps more enlightening, was how the batsmen reacted. In their desperate attempts to get out of the line of fire, you could see that their whole being was in survival mode.'

> **Ian Chappell:** At the end of the game, when Thommo had bagged a total of nine wickets and was instrumental in us having a big win, Rod Marsh was asked, 'is Thomson the fastest bowler in the world?' Rod thought about it and said, "Well that's a big question ... but I'll tell

you what he is ... he's the fastest into-the-wind bowler in the world!' That was the thing about Thommo. Because he didn't do much in his run-up he could go just as well into the wind. His own description of his action – 'I just shuffle up and go WHANG, mate!' – is a perfect fit. The wind made so little difference to the outcome.

A hand injury had meant young England opener David Lloyd hadn't been available to play in the first Test of the series. From the relative safety of the other side of the boundary, he came to a different conclusion.

> **David Lloyd:** I would say that there wasn't a massive impression made in our dressing room – because we thought we might have got the rough end of the pitch. The thinking of the team after the game was, 'okay, we're one down and we were on the receiving end of the conditions ... we can't do anything about the elements that produced this'.
>
> One positive, though: the real Tony Greig shone through in adversity – 'I'm not going to go down without a fight ... and if there's one coming down with my name on it I'm not going to be defending'. He worked out a shot to the short-pitched ball – over the slips and down to third man. That shot in today's game is run of the mill, but in that era there was a stigma about it ... like, the batsman's running away. Greigy took the game on and there haven't been many England players prepared to do that. After him there've been Ian Botham, Andrew

Flintoff and Ben Stokes. They're all the same. 'I'm going to take it on.' And they're all all-rounders.

That's how it may have looked to Lloyd from the dressing room, but to one English correspondent it looked different from the press box.

John Woodcock: The bowling of Lillee and Thomson was terrifying. They were so fast – and there were no helmets in those days. I'm not sure if our players were not more mentally injured than physically injured … we should have had a red cross on the side of our plane going to Perth.

For the dishevelled tourists, there was a lot of soul-searching – and planning – to be done before they fronted up to Lillee and Thomson again. They had to cross the vast continent, to Perth – the fastest and bounciest wicket in the world.

THREE

THE ROAD TO PERTH

The false start, then the falter

THE WAY Dennis Lillee and Jeff Thomson slipped into such a strong marriage, after a very short courtship, a casual observer would have been excused for thinking they'd been betrothed for eons. Yet the relationship got off to a shaky start. That was in the second Test against Pakistan at the Melbourne Cricket Ground, starting on 29 December 1972. Lillee was well established at the time, but this was to be Thomson's debut – and a flash-in-the-pan one at that.

He was carrying a serious foot injury when his name was read out the first time for national honours. 'I could hardly walk on it', Thomson later said. 'It was a big decision for me to make, whether to let on about my foot. If I'd pulled out of the game I might never have played for Australia again. I made the wrong decision.'

Ian Chappell: Thommo probably shouldn't have played. He came into the game with a broken bone in his foot and only told me about it on the night of the fourth day, when Pakistan needed 290 to win on the last day. To that point I had been thinking, 'Hmmm, 290 ... that'll be all right ... we've got Lillee and Thomson'. Then Thommo comes and gives me this news.

I said, 'Mate, you could have told me that before'.

Thommo's reply was typically frank. 'I wasn't going to tell anyone ... I wanted to play.' In one way that was good – you want blokes who are so keen to play.

Thomson staggered through the game, bowling 17 overs without taking a wicket and conceding an even 100 runs in the first innings. That was followed by a wicketless two overs for 10 runs in the second. After such a shaky debut, Thomson, the fast bowler with so much promise, would have to bide his time for almost two years. But that one fraught appearance against Pakistan had left an impression on his captain.

Ian Chappell: I remember Ian Redpath saying after the game (which we ended up winning), 'We've found a good one in this game ...'

I said, 'Yeah, Thommo ...'

And he said, 'No, Max Walker (who also had made his debut)'.

I replied, 'Mate, you can go wander around the beaches of Melbourne and you'll find a whole pile of medium-fast bowlers ... but go searching right around Australia and try to find someone who's quick and you won't find too many'.

Because Thommo had played with that injury, I really didn't know how quick he was, otherwise I would have told Redder, 'In fact, you won't find *any*!'

Instead, I said to him, 'You can have Max Walker and I'll take Thommo ... thanks very much'.

Don't get me wrong, Tangles [Max Walker] was a pretty good bowler, but he profited from bowling at the other end to Lillee or Thomson. Much in the same way Bob Massie, when he took those 16 wickets in his Test debut at Lord's in 1972, benefited from bowling at the other end to Dennis Lillee, who took the other four.

Meantime, subsequent to that one Test when Lillee and Thomson first came together, the older and more experienced partner had run into injury problems of his own. Back troubles arrived on the radar screen during the next and final Test of the same series against Pakistan. Unaware of just how serious the problem was, Lillee made himself available for the tour to the West Indies shortly after. He played the first Test at Kingston, Jamaica, failed to take a wicket – and that was it for him.

While in the Caribbean his back trouble was diagnosed as stress fractures of the lower lumbar vertebrae and he limped home at the end of the tour to begin treatment. Initially that meant being immobilised, first in a plaster cast that ran from his buttocks to the top of his chest, to give his injured back complete rest. That restriction lasted for six very uncomfortable weeks. Lillee's relief at the removal of the cast was shortlived – next he was instructed to wear an aluminium-ribbed webbing harness for a further six weeks. At least this contraption was removable.

A period of cautious movement followed, under strict medical supervision. Then light exercises, some stretching and running. Lillee had suffered injuries before – but nothing that had threatened his future as a fast bowler. His mental anguish was palpable. But then the human movement experts from the University of Western Australia stepped in, led by the late Dr Frank Pyke, himself a former first-grade cricketer who bowled left-arm fast-mediums.

Lillee was not far into a comprehensive rehabilitation program implemented by Dr Pyke when he arrived at a decision that was extremely tough for a man who had been walking tall among the world's best quickies: to give himself the best chance of a complete recovery he would stand out of the 1973–74 first-class and international season. By this time he was 24 years of age and had the world at his feet, with the promise of many good years ahead. It had to be the *right* decision. So, Lillee threw himself into the prescribed work, with a gusto that amounted to total commitment ... and more. And the author, who lived a couple of kilometres away in Perth's south-eastern suburbs, was recruited as a training partner.

Dr Pyke had set a series of isometric exercises – in which muscles work against each other or a fixed object – which were designed to strengthen and support the damaged area by building up the back and stomach muscles. This program was aligned with a rigorous general fitness campaign. With Dr Pyke's isometrics, the plan was for Lillee to move to a position of maximum extension – say, getting as close as possible to touching his toes (either standing or sitting on the floor) – at which point his training partner would hold him in that position while Lillee pushed back against what was meant to be an immovable barrier.

To begin with, that worked well. The author found providing the necessary resistance for the full set of exercises was a doddle. But as the weeks went by, Lillee's strength grew to the point that it would take two of his teammates to hold him down. The author has a vivid recollection from the Western Australian team's eastern states tour at the beginning of Lillee's comeback season, 1974–75. It was isometric-exercises time in the team motel and there was no second partner available. So, desperate to ensure that he could hold the resistance point, the author set himself in a rigid straight position ... with his feet against the wall and his hands on his mate's back. And was just able to hold on!

For the young speedster, those months in the late winter of 1973 and beyond were a step into the unknown. He had complete faith in Dr Pyke, but there were so many questions going through his mind. As he said at the time, 'I thought I'd be able to bowl fast again – but how long would I last? Would I bowl one over, maybe two overs and then break down again? Would I do well enough to get back in the Test side only to collapse in agony during my first over?' As to all the questions ... in time they'd be answered in full.

All the while he was maintaining the punishing isometric exercises and all the traditional Lillee strength work, plus stretching and running. Mondays were work days, when the author would join in a serious run through a nearby pine forest, followed by a full battery of the isometrics, which Lillee was also doing regularly with the experts at the University of Western Australia.

Not far into it all there was a setback, when pain returned in his lower back. Devastated, Lillee hurried in to see his orthopedic surgeon, who assured him this was merely muscular. He backed off for a couple of weeks, then resumed the workload.

The 1973–74 season was not a complete waste. While the rehab program continued to roll on, the champion quickie took on the job as captain-coach of the Perth Cricket Club – for whom Dr Pyke had once opened the bowling.

Lillee waded into the role, keeping the promise he made to his medical support group to resist the temptation to bowl. This stood firm for the first half of the season, while he applied himself to two new facets of the game: batting responsibly and calling the shots as captain. It was a maturation process, and Lillee was passing with flying colours. The club responded to his down-to-earth methods and, for a real rabbit with the bat for state and country, he was an outstanding success in this sphere.

Then came a big decision in the New Year. He would resume bowling, but only off a short run and *never* applying too much pressure to his back. He blossomed into an all-round bowler, learning how to be very effective without the weapon of express pace. He quickly learnt the value of being able to control line and length, while putting polish on his developing skills in moving the ball through the air and off the wicket. All these acquisitions would stand him in good stead when Father Time caught up with his body and he could no longer rely on pace as his number-one asset.

Lillee finished the season having bowled 227.4 overs of mainly just above medium-pace, capturing 48 wickets at 15.89. He compiled 654 runs – the most of anyone in the competition – at an average of 43.60. As captain, he led Perth to the minor premiership, but lost the grand final. As coach, he led Perth to the Club Championship, for best team performance across all four grades. No wonder he was named the Perth competition's Club Cricketer of the Year. He had set out to 'work no wonders, just to build up a bit of team spirit and let that do the job'. He ended up leading by inspirational example.

Jeff Thomson did not need the same sort of rehabilitation to fix the foot injury that marred his first Test – it healed itself. But the amazing thing is, just like Lillee, he spent the summer of 1973–74 languishing in District cricket, on the other side of the continent, in Sydney.

When the team for New South Wales' first Shield game was announced for that season, Thomson's name was missing. He was far from impressed. 'My last game was a Test match', he said. 'I was good enough to play for Australia then. Now I didn't even make the Shield side. That was a grand how'd ya do!'

The weeks rolled by and still Thomson couldn't find a way into the State side. Dave Colley, who played three Tests in England in 1972, played in that NSW team and has his opinions as to why Thomson missed out.

> **Dave Colley:** This was largely because of the balance of the team. Steve Bernard had a hold on the down-wind position and Gary Gilmour and I were the up-wind bowlers. Both of us also making runs at the right time. Then, backing the three of us were Doug Walters and Kerry O'Keeffe. The team was going well and there just wasn't a place for him. I remember Stan Sismey was the chairman of what you could describe as an older group of selectors and I think that while they appreciated Thommo's ability, they just didn't want to play around with the combination. You know, if it's not broken why try to fix it?

Thomson's anger at being overlooked by the state selectors was released on a weekly basis when he turned out for his club side, Bankstown–Canterbury. He regularly let it rip – often against players ill-equipped to handle his terrifying pace. He bowled a bouncer at Manly Oval that cleared the wicketkeeper by a big margin and crashed into the boundary fence for four byes – leading to speculation that he was capable of bowling one so big that it would go for *six* byes.

Those who were present at Bankstown Oval for the game that season when Mosman's batsmen faced a Jeff Thomson bubbling over with fury, still shudder at the memory.

Dave Colley: We were considered to be the silvertails, while Bankstown were the fibros. Real rough and tumble characters who had plenty to say on the field and were basically out to kill anybody from the North Shore. What didn't help that day was the decision of our captain, Barry Knight, an ex-England player, to drive to the ground in his Rolls Royce – and to park it right next to the Bankstown dressing room. He explained this by saying he was hopeful of stirring Thommo up so much that he might lose his radar.

It was a slightly under-prepared grade wicket. A kid called Greg Bush comes in after we've lost a couple of quick wickets and Thommo bowls a ball that I'll never forget ... it came off a good length and hit the young fellow flush under the eye. He fell forward onto the wicket and there was blood pouring out of every orifice. It was a horrible mess. Right on the crease. Thommo took no notice, just went back to his mark. The kid had to be carried off and spent about a month in hospital, having his face reshaped. Thommo never had the courtesy to even visit him.

So, who's next in but me – and at Barry Knight's suggestion I'm wearing my New South Wales sweater! Again to provoke, because I was one of the players keeping Thommo out of the state side. I had never taken centre in a pool of blood. It was a very disconcerting feeling. I just knew that I was the one they were after and they were absolutely getting stuck into me. I said to myself, 'You can't dog it ... you've got to get back and across and do your best'. Apparently I did get back and across, but I was about a second too late and he knocked the leg stump out of the ground. I've got to say I've never been so relieved in my life. It was a frightening experience.

So when Thomson was to say when preparing for the 1974–75 Ashes that he liked to see 'blood on the pitch', he was talking from experience.

Like Dennis Lillee playing in the Perth District competition, Thomson wreaked havoc. He finished the season with 47 wickets at an average of 13.23. Forever holding a grudge, he vented his spleen on a Saturday afternoon at club grounds around Sydney. As the season wore on it became an open secret around the traps that he was considering moving to any other state that might offer him greater opportunities than he was receiving at home.

> **Dave Colley:** I know Thommo was very dirty about being overlooked by the state selectors ... understandably, I suppose. It stayed that way until early February [2 February], when they called him up for the Gillette Cup [one-day] semi-final against Western Australia in Sydney. I remember WA's opener Graeme Watson after one particularly quick delivery from Thommo turning around and giving us a look that said 'I think I'd rather be somewhere else'. The ball had raced past him, then blown its way through Brian Taber's gloves and gone down for four byes.

Then came the final Sheffield Shield game of the season, a week later, against Queensland at the SCG, and he was picked to play. Thommo bowled really fast and took ten wickets for the game and that was when Greg Chappell moved heaven and earth to get him to move north to play for Queensland. As a group we had mixed feelings. Yes, we'd lost a really fast bowler to another state and that meant we'd have to face him twice each season – but then not at all in the nets. For Gary Gilmour and me, too, his departure meant our place in the state side was cemented.

For Lillee and Thomson, that 1972–73 Down Under tour by Pakistan held unhappy memories. And the following summer was a real test of their character – as one stood out and the other simply couldn't get in, until the very end. By another quirk of fate, both men would return to Test match action in the same game.

A big decision

PICTURE, IF you will, the scene. The England leadership and selection panel gathered around a table in the team's Perth hotel, to consider the parlous situation: Alec Bedser, team manager and chairman of selectors; assistant manager Alan 'A.C.' Smith; captain Mike Denness; and senior players John Edrich and Tony Greig. You can imagine their furrowed brows.

At the head of the table sat Bedser, a big, broad man whose large hands made a cricket ball look like a bantam's egg.

Bedser was a hero of post-war England teams, particularly remembered for his success against the mighty Don Bradman during the 1948 tour of England. It was the farewell tour for Bradman, who had plundered England attacks for twenty years. Working to a plan, Bedser dismissed the Australian champion in all four innings of the first two Tests. At a special dinner in Adelaide many years later, the quietly spoken Englishman explained to the author the 'leg trap' he and England had applied. 'We knew that Don liked to get off the mark with a push into the on-side', he said. 'So we set two men in a catching position behind square and one in front and bowled leg stump … It worked, for a while.'

As chairman of selectors, Bedser was in control of proceedings in the Perth hotel – for what was, in modern management terms, a crisis meeting. Memories of the carnage of Brisbane lay just behind the furrows, in the forefront of each man's mind. Bedser, conducting the meeting in his no-nonsense manner; the wispy Smith, who had played six Tests in the sixties as a true all-rounder – batsman, wrong-foot medium-pacer and wicketkeeper – sitting back and waiting for developments; Denness, a quietly spoken Scot, thoroughly decent but perhaps not the strongest man ever to lead England; the tough-as-steel John Edrich; and the flamboyant, outspoken Greig.

Making a bad situation for this group even worse, two of the most stout-hearted members of the England batting line-up had to be ruled out of the Perth Test. Dennis Amiss was nursing a broken thumb and Edrich a broken index finger. Add to that reality, the fear among the group seated around the table that the Lillee–Thomson Brisbane blitz had rendered some of the others less than confident going to the fast and bouncy Perth track.

You can almost hear Bedser presiding. 'Gentlemen, perhaps we need to consider reinforcements.' Around the table, heads nodding, eyes down. It seemed, as it does in war, an admission of weakness, but it was also a necessity. 'We don't have much time. Let's reconvene in a couple of hours. A very big decision has to be made. Do we ask Lord's to send someone out, and, if so, who?' The meeting breaks up.

Another senior member of the touring party remembers what next unfolded within the group.

> **Dennis Amiss:** Mike Denness, as captain, came and spoke to the senior players about this probability. After some really clear thinking, Alan Knott and I were both adamant that if somebody were to come, the best man for the job was Basil D'Oliveira. The others present at this little gathering sort of went along with that. A little more discussion and we were unanimous in our thoughts.
>
> We could see it was between Basil and Colin Cowdrey. However, the thought in our group was that 'Kipper' [Colin Cowdrey] was at the end of his career and probably wouldn't handle it as well as Basil, who was comfortable against the quicks and was still a good player. Plus, 'Dolly' was a good back-foot player – and a hooker – which would both be handy attributes against Lillee and Thomson on the bouncy Perth track.

Obviously we didn't get our way. And I don't know what happened. I never really got to the bottom of it with Mike (who died in 2013). But my assumption is that Alec Bedser and A.C. Smith walked over Mike. At the time Alec was looked upon as a great man, who had enjoyed success against Australia – and he could be quite forceful. Maybe it was that, I don't know. But certainly Mike didn't get his way.

We knew that Colin had been a great player. One or two of us had played with him, plus we'd seen him score his hundreds. But he hadn't played a Test for three years or so. Mind you, Dolly was a year older, but he'd played his last Test a year later than Colin. When we were told it was to be Colin, we thought, 'This is the decision ... we've got to get on with it. Let's hope he can help us combat this fearsome duo'.

David Lloyd: Young players like me weren't involved in the decision. But you had to ask the questions – about Colin's age and the fact that he wouldn't have picked up a bat for a while. Having said that, the decision was well received by the group ... 'Good old Kipper ... the weather'll be nice ...'

'I'd love to'

THE PANTHEON of post-war English batsmen hosts no shortage of batting gods – Len Hutton, Denis Compton, Peter May, Tom Graveney, Ken Barrington and Ted Dexter –

but pre-eminent among them was Colin Cowdrey. After he played what appeared to have been his last Test for England – against Pakistan at Birmingham in 1971 – his decorated Test career read: 109 Tests (having become the first in history to play 100) for 7459 runs, including 22 centuries, equalling the England record set between the wars by the great Walter Hammond.

Sometimes batsmen with statistics like that are unattractive accumulators, grinding out milestone after milestone. The description applied perhaps to Len Hutton or Ken Barrington – but most definitely not to Colin Cowdrey. He oozed class from every pore of his cricketing body. He was all style and elegance, appealing to allcomers, from the dyed-in-the-wool purist to the lager-loving fan in the outer or on the terraces. Much in the latter-day style of David Gower and Mark Waugh, he would caress, rather than hit, the ball when essaying one of a fine array of scoring strokes.

And he had consistently gone in high up the order for his country, absorbing the brunt of new balls being fired down at real pace, by the likes of South Africa's Peter Heine and Neil Adcock and the fearsome West Indian duo of Wes Hall and Charlie Griffith. Possessing a solid technique and courage in the face of fire, Cowdrey had plenty of avenues in which to score runs – and a cheery demeanour to go with it.

Cowdrey had played out the 1974 season in the County competition with Kent. He had scored 1000 runs in each of his past three seasons for the club and was settling into a comfy chair at home to consider the winter ahead – and, perhaps, his future in the game – when the phone rang. It was

Mike Denness, his captain at Kent – calling long-distance, from Australia.

Denness began by relaying the news – Amiss and Edrich had been ruled out of the second Test through injuries sustained in the first encounter. Then, in his soft Scots burr, Denness popped the question to Cowdrey: would he be prepared to come out to Australia and lend a hand? With little thought given, and typical understatement, Cowdrey replied, 'Yes, I'd love to'.

It was a monumental task. After all, Cowdrey was only a few days short of his 42nd birthday. His first visit to these shores pre-dated television. Alec Bedser had even been a *teammate* then. It was more than three years since he'd appeared in a Test match ... and it was eleven weeks since he'd last wielded a bat, in making 16 for Kent against Derbyshire at Folkestone. One of Cowdrey's sons recalls the occasion in vivid detail. Let him tell the story.

> **Jeremy Cowdrey:** I remember Dad was rather shocked to get that call from Mike ... though I think he was quite proud that he'd been considered the one for the job. The extraordinary thing about it was that at the time he was in complete relax mode, way off thinking about playing cricket. He was spending most of his time in an armchair, watching 'Match of the Day' and cricket highlights.
>
> He knew it wasn't going to be a tea party, far from it, but he was completely calm about the whole thing. I recall him saying, 'This should be rather fun'. And that's

how he treated it, I'm sure. There was no asking Mum – or anybody. He just felt he had to go. He lived for cricket and had to answer the call. And he wasn't remotely worried that he'd get his head knocked off ... whereas the rest of us were!

Obviously there was a bit of a hurry to pack his bags and get away. But he had promised the local cricket club, Limpsfield, that he would be the guest speaker at their annual dinner that night. Even though he was to leave for Australia the next morning! He said he just had to go. 'I've got this quite good joke, I must go and tell it', he said. While he was giving the speech that night, about every twenty seconds he'd duck – or sway his body around – and say, 'Sorry, but I'm just getting in the mood'. This brought the house down. They all knew what he was about to take on.

He was a great theoriser and I recall him watching the highlights from the first Test – with our bats struggling – and he kept saying, 'Why don't they keep still ... and stop ducking about'. And he would be talking about how he would play these guys: 'No backlift at all for the first three or four overs, keep your head still and make sure to defend your stumps ... the runs coming don't really matter.' Then, unbelievably, just like that he had the chance to try it for himself. He had 100 per cent confidence in his technique.

In those days there wasn't anything much in the way of padding to protect the batsman's body. So, he hurriedly fashioned something of his own, to cover the chest area. He cut out pieces of padding and got my mother to sew them into place on an undershirt. The plan was that if he was to be hit, he could better take the blow because of the padding. And he said he'd rather be hit than caught fending off a short one.

An old man, in cricketing terms, preparing to travel to the other side of the planet and take up the cudgels for Queen and country. Reaction from Down Under was somewhat less calm.

> **Greg Chappell:** I thought it was madness. That everyone had taken leave of their senses … and that 'Kipper' was crazy to have acceded to the invitation.

> **Ian Chappell:** I was pretty sympathetic for Kipper. I mean, it seemed like a ludicrous decision, given his age and the fact that he was coming out of winter. And, where's he going to play his first Test? In Perth … against Lillee and Thomson! But I guess it said a lot about the guy, that he accepted. I'm sure there'd have been a lot of Englishmen who'd have told Mike Denness to go and jump in the lake.
>
> But when you think of it, that decision was in line with English thinking in those days. If there was any trouble they'd always go for an experienced player. Whereas at that time Australia would be more likely to go looking for a good young player.

John Woodcock: I'm not sure that Colin would have seen much of the Brisbane Test – highlights only – so he couldn't *really* have known what he was letting himself in for. I was staying at the Weld Club in Perth and not long after he flew in I received a late-night call, asking could he come around for a few frames of snooker. He was battling to get over jet lag and couldn't sleep.

The enormous task ahead of the veteran was made worse by the fact that his hurried flight to Perth was stymied by a nineteen-hour delay in Bombay (now Mumbai). This meant he would arrive too late for the MCC game against Western Australia. Instead he had to settle for nets practice, facing anybody he could cajole into bowling to him, seeking to become accustomed to the light and the pace of the Perth wickets. Just, it seemed, to get a good feel of a bat in his hands again.

All these years later, the decision to call upon a man of Colin Cowdrey's age and stage – and his decision to say 'I'd love to' – remains one of cricket's most extraordinary stories. And if he had a good joke for the lads at Limpsfield, he had a better one for the inevitable question from the Australian media about how he would handle the pace of Lillee and Thomson. 'I can't believe they are as fast as Gregory and McDonald in the twenties, and I played them.'

Smectite and Little Roy

WORD HAD spread far and wide over the years since a short, stocky, taciturn man by the name of Roy Abbott took over as curator at the WACA Ground – and finally succeeded in putting his own stamp on the wicket block. Abbott's fabled reign at the ground began in 1951 and he went to work on the existing surface, finally achieving his goal of making it the fastest and bounciest strip in the world.

Roy was a typical gardener type. He cared for every blade of grass on the ground – and when the Western Australian squad took fielding practice out near the middle, there he'd be in his khaki shorts and sandals, faded cap askew, making sure we didn't venture anywhere near the bowler's run-up for the coming game. He was known to all as 'Little Roy'. His deputy, who would spend a lot of time riding the motorised roller on the wicket, was 'Big Roy'. Roy Price was just that, a very big man, who was even more stingy with his words than his boss.

If there was one peculiarity about Roy Abbott it was his *walk*. For his size he was a long strider. The gait had a gentle rhythm about it. But there it was, every time: whereas most people's hands would face inwards as they swung through, his right hand (only his right hand) would turn backwards. Bob Massie, a marvellous swing bowler for Western Australia and country, happens to be an excellent mimic – and had the Little Roy hand-flapping walk down to a nicety. Eccentricities aside, though, Roy was a dedicated groundsman who quite rightly earned himself a little slot in the echelons of those who made a significant contribution to the game. After all, he was responsible for the liveliest 22 yards in the business.

As with most grounds, the nature of his wickets was determined by the unique nature of the soil available for its creation. The WACA Ground clay was collected from the banks of the Harvey River, about 100 kilometres south of Perth, and delivered each year by the truckload. The main component of Harvey River clay is smectite, which has the characteristic of setting very hard. Hence the WACA's extraordinary bounce, which would see short-pitched deliveries from very fast bowlers steeple over the wicketkeeper's head and even, occasionally, reach the boundary after the first bounce.

The secret to Abbott's success with the Harvey River clay was his ability to cultivate good grass cover within the clay. Even though mown short and flattened by a heavy roller, this grass would remain alive for most of the four days of a first-class game. A benefit, for pace bowlers at least, was that the grass cover meant the ball would not be seriously scarred by contact with the pitch, offering the swing merchants the chance to maintain the shine to enable them to move the ball through the air. For batsmen, a plus factor was the very reliable bounce derived from an Abbott surface. The ball lands at a certain length, and you knew what its height would be when it reached you.

Oddly enough, when Roy Abbott and his team prepared the wicket for the first-ever Test match at the ground – an Ashes clash in December 1970 – the outcome was not a typically lively WACA strip. In fact on day one, when England batted, the surface played more like a day-three, even day-four, WACA track. England marched along to 397, Australia replied with 440 and the game ended in a tame draw.

Almost exactly twelve months later there was another international match in Perth, this time Australia pitted against a Rest of the World XI – cobbled together after a planned tour by South Africa was cancelled in the apartheid years. This was more like the WACA pitch we all knew so well – one where the pace and bounce were good on day one, but hotted right up on day two when the clay had dried out. Australia had first use of the wicket and reached 349 in comfortable fashion. What happened the next day was extraordinary.

The visitors' batting line-up, including India's Sunil Gavaskar, Pakistan's Zaheer Abbas and the West Indies' Rohan Kanhai, Clive Lloyd and Garry Sobers, came face to face with Dennis Lillee producing fire and brimstone on a very helpful surface. Lillee had arrived at the ground feeling unwell. Indeed, after four overs he told captain Ian Chappell he wanted a spell. His figures at the time were 2–29. Chappell urged him to go 'a couple more' and the result was six more wickets for no runs in the space of fifteen deliveries – and final figures of 8–29. The World team was out before lunch for a meagre 59, following on to be dismissed for 279. Lillee's match figures were a stunning 12–92.

You can only imagine the wry grin creasing the face of Roy Abbott as he went about tidying up the wicket block after the game had ended. He carried on supervising things at the ground until his retirement in 1980, but before that date he made many more crackerjack WACA Ground wickets including the one he marked out for the second Test of the 1974–75 Ashes series.

Recommence hostilities!

WHEN THE crowd settled into their seats on the opening morning of the Perth Test, there was a feeling of heightened tension in the air. The day was cloudy and cool. Ian Chappell again had the choice and elected to bowl. 'I sent them in to bat,' he said, 'purely on the basis that they were so hammered mentally from Brisbane that I thought we had the psychological edge ... so let's sort of bang it home.'

Brian Luckhurst might have been feeling good when he went out to open the batting. Cricketers love returning to the site of their success, and four years earlier he had also opened on day one, at Perth's first Test – sharing a 171-run partnership with Geoff Boycott. Luckhurst made 131 that day, which would remain his highest Test score. If he *was* feeling good, it didn't last long – Thomson struck him a painful blow on the top hand in his first over. He was the first to fall, caught out cutting Max Walker, for 27, 24 of which were boundaries, most of them slashed behind square, as is so often the case in Perth.

The portly figure of Colin Cowdrey walked onto the arena, to generous applause from the crowd, a cheeky tilt to the navy blue England cap atop his cherubic head. His portliness was accentuated by the sizeable homespun chest guard he was wearing. Not long after his arrival in the middle, the English veteran reportedly ventured to say to Thomson, 'I don't think we've met ... the name's Cowdrey'. Thomson remembers it slightly differently: 'I handed my hat to the umpire, revved up and just wanting to kill somebody, when Kipper walked all the way up to me and said, 'Mr Thomson I believe ... it's so good to meet you'. And I said, 'That's not going to help you, Fatso, now piss off'.

Then the Aussie paceman and his partner Lillee proceeded to offer up a red-hot welcome for the courageous veteran.

> **David Lloyd:** I really didn't know Colin and there I was out in the middle when he came in first drop. And there *he* was, asking *me* questions ... you know, 'What are they like?' I talked about Thomson's slingy action and how when he gets into his delivery stride the ball's hidden and you don't have a sight of it, whereas Lillee, you know him and you can see the mechanics of the action and you can see the ball early.
>
> I suggested to him that I take Thomson, who would be angling across me as a left-hander ... you take Lillee. I tell you it was tough out there. The other thing that's worth mentioning is that there were eight-ball overs and as many as five bouncers an over. We very rarely had team meetings on that tour, but one thing that did come out was, 'Don't look at the scoreboard ... runs are not the key ... after an hour we might be 15 or 20 ...' Because if you're not a hooker and all these bouncers are coming at you, you're not scoring. After a couple of overs from Thomson, Colin and I met in the middle of the pitch and he said to me, 'It's rather fun, isn't it!' To which I replied, 'Well I've been in funnier situations than this!'

The author was at the ground that day and had to admire both the technique and the courage of Cowdrey. He adopted a back-and-across movement in response to the two speedsters, as he had hypothesised to his son on his couch back in Kent, which made a lot of sense on the very lively WACA Ground strip. And he took blow after blow on the body, rather than offer a shot and risk an edge to balls that were climbing off a length. Those blows must have inflicted serious pain, yet he never flinched.

> **Greg Chappell:** He wasn't going away. He stood in there and they were thumping either into his chest or the splice of his bat. Mind you, he was wearing some innovative chest protection ... I think he brought half a sofa with him.
>
> **David Lloyd:** Colin was wearing this chest guard – and *he* made it! It actually resembled a bed pillow, which made him look miles bigger. All of a sudden other lads were doing some stitching here and there.
>
> **Dennis Amiss:** Yes, Bernard Thomas, our team physiotherapist, set about stitching padding into these jackets – made out of pillow material.

With Lillee and Thomson firing the ball in non-stop helter-skelter, and Max Walker providing stout support, it was little more than a matter of survival for the England batsmen. And, following team instructions, the run-rate was of secondary importance. Lloyd and Cowdrey moved the scoreboard along slowly, until Thomson evoked an edge from Lloyd and Greg Chappell accepted in the slips cordon. Mike Denness said that when the left-hander got back to the dressing room, 'his body was quivering ... his neck and the top half of his body were shaking, suffering from the effects of never having to move so quickly in all his life'.

It is hard to conceive of an attack having such a withering effect – which makes Cowdrey's effort of withstanding the assault for more than two hours all the more meritorious. He had scored 22 with three boundaries when he moved too far across to Thomson and lost his leg stump. Lillee was impressed by the veteran's effort. 'It was a courageous performance, though he was well padded with a thick chest guard. This gave him the confidence to let go a lot of the short-pitched deliveries that were causing all the trouble to his teammates.'

> **Greg Chappell:** He acquitted himself remarkably well. A gutsy effort. Showed his competitive nature, too.

> **Ian Chappell:** Kipper did pretty well. He didn't make a lot of runs, but he hung around for quite a long time. On one occasion he tried to pull a Thommo delivery and it hit him in the body, which was pretty well padded up. I went up to him from first slip and said, 'Are you all right?' He said, 'Ian, I'm a bloody old fool trying to pull this guy!'

Dennis Amiss: We couldn't help but admire the way he came out to Perth, had a few nets and went straight into it against two of the greatest fast bowlers of all time. Some of that genius – and that greatness – that he'd shown during his career came out.

Robin Bailhache: He showed a ton of guts. Especially on that Perth track. They attacked him and hit him time after time on the body, but he took it. That was courageous.

The tourists struggled to post 208, and were dismissed shortly before stumps. Lillee and Thomson took two wickets each. Thanks to a steady century by Ross Edwards, enjoying his home-ground pitch, and a dazzling Doug Walters century in the final session of the second day, completed with a six on the last ball of the day, Australia took a lead of 273 in the first innings. Again, runs were at a premium when England batted a second time.

David Lloyd: You'd think, 'I've batted a long time and I haven't got very many … you just weren't scoring … more surviving.
    To make matters worse for me, if that was possible, in the second innings I was hit bang on the protector by one from Thommo. I was trying to defend, but the ball found its way through. I was wearing the popular type of protector of the day, a pink plastic thing, which was split down the middle. They tried to revive me, but in the

end I was carried off – and resumed the next day. I lose my voice every December!

The stats bear out Lloyd's memory: over the two innings he scored 84 runs, having faced a mammoth 305 deliveries. A very brave and determined performance in a team under siege. As for the indomitable Cowdrey, he was advanced to open in the second innings, compiling over the two innings 63 runs from 197 balls ... many of them crashing into his body as he fought valiantly to avoid offering a pop-up chance from a short-pitched delivery.

> **Ross Edwards:** What did I think of Cowdrey's effort in that game? They were two of the most courageous innings I've ever seen. Because Thommo hit him from head to toe. I remember seeing him in the change rooms afterwards and he had these big black weals all over the left side of his body.

Thomson cut a swathe through the England middleorder, dismissing Greig, Denness, Keith Fletcher and Cowdrey in compiling figures of 5–93. In the midst of that piece of mayhem Doug Walters, a country lad renowned for his dry wit, put a rather harsh perspective on the plight of the England batting.

> **Greg Chappell:** After one of them was dismissed we were standing around in a group, waiting for the next batsman to come out. Then Freddie [Walters], who

was facing the pavilion, said, 'Oh, don't tell me!' We all looked around and one of us asked what he meant. 'Don't tell me', he said, 'that we've got to put up with *this* bloke ... for a couple of balls!'

By this stage Jeff Thomson was the talk of the cricket world. So much so that during the Perth Test a Sydney newspaper flew a senior reporter over to interview him and write a special feature story on the new wonder boy. But Thommo didn't like the press.

> **Greg Chappell:** Didn't trust them one bit! So he kept refusing to see this reporter. Well, after the game I was in a bath at the back of the dressing room, and Thommo was in one of the showers, when our twelfth man came in with a message for Thommo. 'There's this reporter outside who says he's been trying to talk to you for four days ... he's got to go and catch a flight ... wants to know if you'll give him a couple of minutes.'
>
> Thommo says, 'Okay, bring him in'. So *he's* in the shower, *I'm* in the bath and the reporter walks in. After a little small talk he says to Thommo, 'Well, how would you describe your action?'
>
> 'Oh, heck ... I just shuffle up and go WHANG'. Which is exactly what he did. It was 14 paces – it didn't seem that long – and he just tiptoed up, got side-on and went 'WHANG'.

Chasing a desultory 21, Australia won by nine wickets with a day and more to spare. England was in disarray, again. Luckhurst could not field on the second day thanks to his bruised hand, and batted No.7 in the second innings. He would never play for England again. Keith Fletcher would be dropped for the next Test. Lloyd had suffered a blow the like of which no batsman has ever known. Cowdrey's torso and back were a mass of bruises. Amiss and Edrich had missed because of their injuries from Brisbane. To rub salt into the wounds, top score was off-spinner Fred Titmus – who was 42, a full month older than Cowdrey. At the end of the debacle, commentator Richie Benaud said, 'It was a great disaster for England. I haven't seen a more pathetic batting display from an England side for many a year'.

Thomson was flying, England was dying – and still Lillee had taken no more than two wickets in an innings. And there were four more Tests to play.

Impressions

FOR IAN CHAPPELL and his team it was a dream start to a series, victory in the first two Tests taking them close to their fervently held ambition of regaining the Ashes. Chappell had reason to be extremely happy, particularly with the performance of his attack. The Twins of Terror had bagged 24 wickets between them in the first two encounters, stamping their authority on the hapless England batsmen, few, if any, of whom were showing any signs of relishing the challenge.

Ian Chappell: Looking back on it, going into that series I thought that anything Dennis did wouldn't surprise me. I knew him well enough. He gave it everything he had and had great belief in himself. But in the first two Tests, no matter how many overs he bowled he couldn't get past two wickets in an innings.

There were a couple of reasons for this. One, there was a little bit of uncertainty in his mind about how his body would stand up – to the point that I had the feeling he thought every delivery could be his last one. Also, there was in him a bit of an angry man that wasn't there before. Because I think he knew he wouldn't go through all the rehabilitation work again if he broke down. Once he became certain he was going to be around for a lot longer, that changed.

Plus, I think he wasn't sure about where he stood now that Thommo was doing so well. Thinking he had to prove himself – like he was the old gunfighter going into battle. But after a while he realised that Thommo was actually helping him. All of a sudden batsmen were almost trying to get down his end, away from Thommo. He saw this as a bonus for him.

On the other hand, I must admit that Thommo was a very, very pleasant surprise. Particularly in the second innings in Brisbane. He was bloody quick and he bowled pretty accurately.

Mike Brearley: I remember watching the first two games on highlights – the first time in England that we could watch highlights packages when the team was playing away. I watched Lillee and Thomson working on the Brisbane wicket, which was a bit up and down ... and then there was Perth, which was just *Perth*.

They seemed lethal. They were very, very quick. So much so that my Middlesex batting colleague Mike Smith said he'd sit on the floor behind the sofa with a large gin and tonic when watching Thommo bowling on television! It was some of the most ferocious bowling I've ever seen. Comparable, I suppose, to Hall and Griffith before, and to the West Indians soon after.

John Woodcock: I wasn't particularly surprised at the impact Lillee and Thomson had in those first two Tests. Though we were surprised that Lillee showed up so well from the start of the series. We thought he would take more time to overcome the back injury that had put him out of the previous summer.

As British television personality – and cricket tragic – Michael Parkinson wrote in the London *Telegraph*, 'Lillee and Thomson were the fire and brimstone of fast bowlers. Like all the best practitioners of their craft they tested the very limits of an opponent's nerve and technique'.

One Australian certainly had his eye on them.

Greg Chappell: What effect did Dennis and Thommo have on the England batsmen? They were absolutely shell-shocked after Brisbane. There were a few who didn't get behind too many after that. They were staying leg-side of it and I had a picnic in the slips. In Perth I took seven catches.

Those seven catches were a record high in a Test, and, as it happened, one of the previous record-holders Greg Chappell dislodged was his grandfather, the aforementioned Victor Richardson.

There is a real psychology to batting – and overcoming fear is a big part of it. First you have to come to terms with the fear of failure. There's a very fine line between being out and staying in – one millimetre's error and your day, and maybe your career, is over. Did you get an edge on it, or did you play and miss? There's the luck of the dice: when you're in a bit of a form trough, decisions have a way of going against you, which can be hard to deal with, that in turn presents its own challenge.

But when you are up against fast bowling there's also the *fear factor* – the awareness that being struck by a rock-hard projectile coming your way at speed can seriously hurt. And not just hurt – it can seriously injure. Competitive quickies like Lillee and Thomson play on this. They aim to hit, they aim to hurt ... they aim to take the ground by intimidation.

Never mind the fact that beyond the fear factor, both bowlers had the ability to bowl a wicket ball as though out of thin air. In Lillee's case, by persistent control of line and length plus canny movement of the ball through the air and off the wicket. In Thomson's case, through sheer pace.

What about those bouncers?

THE MAN leading Australia had an early inkling that things could get nasty. Ian Chappell made a business trip to England during the northern summer of 1974, where he found there were clear indications of plans afoot in the England camp to throw down the gauntlet to the Australian batting line-up ... with a bumper war.

> **Ian Chappell:** Part of my work there was a press confidence at Headingley, where England were playing Pakistan. One of the first questions was, 'Will Dennis Lillee come back?'
>
> I said, 'Look, mate, I'm not a medical person, so I don't know, but I'll tell you one thing ... if anybody can come back from that sort of injury it'll be Dennis. I know how hard he's working, but I'll also tell you that if he does come back it won't be as a medium-pacer'.
>
> The guy went on, suggesting that Dennis wouldn't be the same ... to the point [when] I interjected and said, 'Mate, if you're looking for a headline go ahead and write it – but you won't be doing it on one of my quotes. I repeat, he'll only come back if he can bowl fast'.
>
> Next question. 'How quick is Jeff Thomson?' 'He's pretty bloody quick, mate.'
>
> 'Oh yeah, but he wouldn't be as quick as Dennis Lillee in 1972.'
>
> 'I wouldn't bet on that ...'
>
> 'No, he couldn't be as quick.'

Again I cut in. 'You obviously also have a headline you want to write, but I'm telling you he's quick. He's a different type of bowler to Dennis, but he's bloody quick.'

As I walked away from that press conference I thought, 'I know what England are going to do ... They're going to bring a whole pile of quicks out and they're going to bounce the shit out of us'. Then I thought, 'That's fine ... we've got a few blokes who can hook ... and this time, as distinct from 1970–71, we probably will have a couple of guys who can give it back'.

Chappell had fresh in his mind the bombardment of Australia's batsmen, by John Snow in particular, when England toured Down Under in 1970–71. On that tour things simmered until the Sydney Test, when feelings boiled over. A short-pitched delivery by Snow hit tailender Terry Jenner in the head, causing him to retire hurt. When the Englishman went to fine leg he was pelted with rubbish by the crowd and manhandled. His captain, the dour Yorkshireman Ray Illingworth, responded by taking his team briefly from the field. Australian journalist R.S. Whitington, himself a former first-class player, wrote of one Snow spell: 'It resembled one of those old-time bombardments on the World War I Western Front.'

Ian Chappell: When I saw the balance of their touring party – five quicks and two spinners – I thought, 'Yes, this is on ... they're going to bounce us'. And they did. The first innings in Brisbane they bounced us a helluva lot. But it didn't last.

I think initially they saw what they expected from Dennis, who actually got quicker as the series went on. But once they saw how quick Thommo was they very smartly cut back on the headhunting. I remember talking to Tony Greig, years after we'd both retired, and he said that after Brisbane he was finding it very hard to get any of the England quicks to bowl a bouncer. In the end, he was pretty well the only one bowling them.

How did this so-called 'bumper war' start? There was an incident when Dennis was batting in the first innings in Brisbane, when Tony Greig bounced him and got him out. We could tell as Dennis walked off that he was furious. I saw trouble on the horizon and found something I had to do in the dressing room. It seemed all the other guys did, too. Suddenly the room was full.

Dennis came storming in and bashed his bat into a metal locker, made a helluva racket. Then he realised we were all in there, looking on, and he stood up and wagged his finger and said, 'Just remember who started this' ... pause ... 'but we'll fucken finish it'.

Greg Chappell: Yes, they did start it. Firstly, they didn't think Dennis would be any good – and they thought it was all bullshit about Thommo, that it was just the Australian media pumping this bloke up. So, they didn't think we had much and when we batted first they got into it. Greigy was the main offender – and it didn't help matters that he chose to bounce Dennis, eventually getting him out off a short one. That was it. War had been declared and Dennis, in particular, wasn't going to let it go.

All these years later, one of the Englishmen confirms what the Australians believed.

> **Dennis Amiss:** We had decided that there was a number of compulsive hookers in the Australian line-up and it was our plan to get in short to them. But Greigy upset Dennis, when he bounced him and Knotty ran up and caught him. It didn't worry Greigy, that he was winding up Dennis and Thommo, but I remember Keith Fletcher and I approached him and said, 'It's all right for you, mate ... but what about us?'

Being a fast bowler, Lillee naturally defended his right to fire them in short. 'A bouncer is like a yorker – a genuine fast bowler's weapon. I always thought a couple of broken ribs were a batsman's fault, not mine. I also thought bouncers should be bowled only to those capable of handling them, but I have to confess I didn't always follow those noble words.

'In Brisbane I felt I was still fast enough to bowl bouncers and frighten batsmen. What I did not want was to hit someone on the head. I didn't like guys being badly hurt and it was a relief to me when helmets came in.'

At this juncture it bears repeating that the 1974–75 series came before use of the helmet! Yes, Colin Cowdrey came Down Under with a hand-made piece of chest protection. And, yes, other England batsmen soon followed suit. David

Lloyd talked of attaching a book to his thigh pad for extra protection. You'd want *War and Peace* – not that there was any peace for the batsmen. But as for the helmet, the inside-leg thigh pad, the elbow guard and the 'formal' chest guard? They were a batsman's accoutrements of the future.

It was revealed long afterwards that, during the series, Greig had considered becoming the first batsman to use a helmet in Test cricket. Legend has it that Mike Denness was approached by a man offering head protection that looked more like a motorcycle helmet which, in fact, became one of the forerunners of the helmet as used by batsmen today. Apparently, Greig was in favour of wearing one, but was advised not to, the fear being that 'to Lillee and Thomson it would be like a red rag to a bull'.

These days, batsmen carry a lot of protection in their aptly named 'coffin'. There were always pads, gloves (not always effective) and a protector. Now they also pack a helmet with a face guard, plus two thigh pads (one for the outside of the leading leg, one for the soft inside of the back leg) and chest and arm guards. Talk about knights in shining armour. Even with all that, batsmen are still vulnerable as they wait for a fire-breathing monster to unleash a guided missile: 156 grams of cork, string and leather, coming at you at near 160 kilometres an hour – or if you prefer, 100 miles an hour, from less than 22 yards away.

The author remembers when the thigh pad became an accepted piece of protective equipment, in the 1960s. At that stage it was no more than a piece of foam plastic or rubber with a couple of straps to hold it in place. Western Australia was playing against New South Wales in Sydney, when John Benaud came out to face Lillee without a thigh pad. A few of us winced at the thought. Inevitably he was hit flush on his left thigh and was hopping around in great pain when the obvious question was posed. He puffed, 'If I don't have one it makes me watch the ball closer'.

Silly boy, you might say. But there was a similar mindset afoot a few years later, when the helmet was new to the game. While protecting the head seemed to make sense, many batsmen, the author included, were of the opinion that to suddenly start wearing one was tantamount to admitting you were afraid; and this was no way to go about your business in a pursuit that so depended on a positive mindset. So, in hindsight rather foolishly, many seasoned first-class batsmen in Australia were slow to take up the helmet.

This was in the knowledge of just how dangerous batting against serious fast bowling can be. The author witnessed four players hit in the face while batting on the bouncy WACA Ground pitch. They were WA's Len Pavy, Victoria's Ray Jordon and Max Walker and the New Zealander Bob Cunis. In each instance it was a sickening sight. All four suffered broken jaws. When Walker hit the deck there was a real fear out there in the middle that he might have been killed. Big Max lay motionless on his front for some time, blood oozing out onto the wicket near the crease.

While coach of Kent in the English County competition, the team's captain and best batsman, David Fulton, suffered a setback from which he would never recover, thanks to a flaw in helmet design. Fulton was practising against a bowling machine firing balls down short when one found its way through the grille and badly damaged an eye.

Helmets are still not infallible. Witness the tragic incident at the Sydney Cricket Ground in 2014 when Phillip Hughes died after being hit by a short one.

During the Brisbane Test and again in Perth the debate raged as to whether the Australian bowling was fair.

The charge was led by the English writers. Clive Taylor, in London's *Sun*, opened up a report on the first Test with the words, 'Is nobody in authority in Australian cricket going to speak up and condemn Lillee's philosophy?'

'Last night on television,' Taylor wrote, 'Dennis Lillee, in a discussion clinical in its detail, pointed to parts of the body he aimed to hit when he was bowling short at a batsman. Today he was warned by umpire Tom Brooks for bowling bouncers at Peter Lever and Derek Underwood. Australian captain Ian Chappell had declared last summer that he would not tolerate a bowler under his command deliberately bowling to hit a batsman. Now they boast of their efficiency at it'.

Former fast bowling great Fred Trueman went one better, suggesting that Lillee should be banned for his tactics. Writing in the *Sunday People*, Trueman said, 'Lillee should be banned for his behaviour in the series. His attitude towards batsmen is comparable to an animal that has another one cornered. During my long career I never went on the field with the intention of crippling another player. The Australian umpires and Lillee's own captain must share the blame for these antics. But our board should tell the Australians that we in England will not tolerate it'. These were words reminiscent of the furore that surrounded the tactics of Harold Larwood, in particular, in the Bodyline series of 1932–33.

Not that the English press were all of one mind.

> **Johnny Woodcock:** I wasn't aware that there was too much short-pitched bowling by Lillee and Thomson. The word 'intimidation' came into the law – but what they did in that series was not intimidating.

For a contrasting perspective, let's go to Frank Tyson, a fellow fast bowler whose whirlwind deliveries destroyed Australia on the Ashes tour here in 1954–55, earning him the nickname 'Typhoon'. At the time he was reputed to be the fastest bowler the game had ever seen, on the back of match figures of 10–130 at the SCG, and 9–95 at the MCG.

Tyson watched the 1974–75 series from the ABC commentary box, where the warm, mellifluous tones of his English voice endeared him to Australians, who had been his adopted countrymen since he moved here in 1960. In *Test of Nerves* (Wren Publishing, 1975), his book on the series, noted in calm reflection as opposed to the harried, daily reports of the journalists, he wrote:

> The whole issue of short-pitched deliveries was inflamed by statements which both Lillee and Thomson were unwise enough to make in books and magazines. Statements that were tantamount to, and admission of, attempting intimidation.

The bouncer is a legitimate weapon which should be used to prevent batsmen exploiting the perfection of the modern wickets and playing forward to every non-lifting delivery – even though they are short of a length. It is a legitimate tactic to entice the batsman who likes to hook. But it can never be justified as a weapon intended to hurt or maim.

The Australian superiority in the series boiled down to the fact that their fast bowlers were better and quicker than their English counterparts and able to make the ball lift more sharply from just short of a length.

Thomson, one felt, was never quite sure of when he was going to bowl a bouncer. His slinging action lent itself not only to exceptional speed and ability to make the ball rear unexpectedly but also to a great inconsistency in length and direction.

There were occasions when Lillee fell from grace in my eyes. In the first four Tests he often dropped the ball unnecessarily short of a length. In fact, he and Thomson frequently gorged themselves on overs which contained at least three bouncers. Even more unfortunately, they were allowed by the umpires to play at this bouncer brinkmanship.

Tyson carefully distinguishes between bouncers to batsmen and tailenders; between bouncers intended to maim or not; between one an over and three an over. His point about the umpiring is not contested by one of those self-same umpires, although there is a point of difference.

Robin Bailhache: It did turn out to be a bouncer war. And if I'd known what I knew later – and if the laws of the game had been what they later became – I would not have allowed it. As it was, the two umpires through the series came from different backgrounds. Tom had been a fast bowler and he tended to be a bit more tolerant.

And yet, the Englishmen were getting injured by being hit on the hands, not the head.

Greg Chappell: The amazing thing is, Thommo hardly bowled a bouncer. He didn't need to bowl them. In fact, if you were a batsman you'd be hoping that he *did* bowl one because it would go way over your head, whereas length balls would rear up and hit a batsman in the chest.

I discouraged him from bowling bouncers in games playing for Queensland. But I do remember one in Perth ... to Bruce (Stumpy) Laird, who'd just under-cut him for six. Well, when Thommo bounced him, the ball wouldn't have hit another Stumpy standing on his head. I realised keeper John Maclean was never reaching it and ran behind him from first slip ... just got a finger on it and then it hit the middle of the sightscreen. I've never seen anything quite like it.

Thommo didn't need to use that delivery because he bowled like he was six foot ten, so much did balls rear off a length. Actually he stood six foot one, and in the delivery stride got high up on the toes of his right foot – and when he planted his left foot he came right up over the top of it. He just bowled *taller.*

Helping even more was the fact that he was not only very strong, but also very flexible. I recall when he was in his forties being at a party with him, when he sat on the floor and took his right leg and put it on his right shoulder, then repeated it with his left leg.

Speaking after the series and before the Australian team left for England to play in the World Cup and to defend the Ashes, Ian Chappell said he would place no restrictions on bouncers bowled by Thomson and Lillee. He said, as ever he did and would, that that was the job of the umpires.

'Lillee and Thomson are no different to any pace bowlers I have seen in my life', he said. 'They can't be blamed for the faults of the batsmen. It annoys me intensely that the impression is being circulated that they are the only two pacemen in the world who are menacing batsmen with bouncers. I see them as a legitimate part of our attack's process kit.'

The men whose opinions counted most, of course, were the umpires.

> **Robin Bailhache:** There was criticism of the aggressive tactics of Lillee and Thomson. But even today, with the laws about short-pitched bowling changed, an umpire couldn't do anything about it – because a lot of it wasn't above shoulder height.

FOUR

CARNAGE COUNTRYWIDE

So close, so far, for Amiss and England

THE TWINS of Terror had destroyed England's batsmen, and in the two weeks between the second and third Tests the MCC went to Adelaide for a three-day match, hoping to restore confidence and re-establish techniques.

Dennis Amiss was back in the team in Adelaide, recovered from the hand injury that had kept him out of Perth. Amiss looked good in posting a couple of half-centuries – 73 in the first innings, 57 in the second. No fast bowler took his wicket. Once it was Terry Jenner, the other time Ashley Mallett, Jenner's fellow Australian Test spinner. On the positive side of the ledger for the tourists, they were able to stiffen the batting line-up for the next Test by bringing back stalwarts Amiss and John Edrich, after the injuries that had kept them out of the Perth debacle.

Amiss had often walked out with Geoff Boycott to begin an England innings. Two solid right-handers, each with an eye for technique. Boycott was an unabashed perfectionist and that was a word occasionally cautiously applied to Amiss, though he was much more at home with taking a calculated risk in the pursuit of a boundary. He could score freely on both sides of the wicket, and was renowned for considered placement of the ball through the extra cover and mid-wicket regions.

He landed in Australia with his sights firmly set on beating Bob Simpson's world record of 1381 for the most Test runs scored in a calendar year. Stout of build and deep of resolve, he had compiled 1253 runs from six Tests in the Caribbean, plus three Tests each against India and Pakistan at home during the northern summer. For his other efforts throughout the year, three centuries on tour in the West Indies – 174, 118 and 262 not out – then two massive home centuries against two nations – 188 against India at Lord's and 183 against a Pakistan attack boasting Imran Khan, Sarfraz Nawaz and Intikhab Alam – he was named one of *Wisden*'s Cricketers of the Year.

But everything changed in Australia.

> **Dennis Amiss:** I kept nicking them into the cordon. You knew that if you could stay there long enough you'd be a chance to go on with it. But they could always bowl a jaffer that would get you, so you never got to thinking, 'I'm on my way now, nothing can stop me'.

Mike Denness, who could not take a trick, lost the toss again in Melbourne. Ian Chappell, thinking as he had in Perth, put England in. Amiss opened. The powerfully built right-hander had three Tests Down Under before the calendar clicked over in which to make his assault on the record. When injury put him out of Perth, that made it two Tests. In Brisbane he had scored 7 and 25. So when he got to Melbourne, he still needed 97 runs for the record.

There were more than 77,000 people at the MCG that Boxing Day. But they didn't get to see much of Dennis Amiss. Lillee was in his pomp at the MCG, the game's biggest stage, for the biggest day on cricket's calendar. Sporting his trademark black mane, shirt buttoned low and gold necklace glittering in the sunshine, he produced his jaffer – a searing off-cutter that caught Amiss's outside edge. He was out for 4, caught in the slips by a diving Doug Walters. A staunch 90 in the second innings, was better – but, as well as ending 10 runs short of a century, he was three runs short of establishing a new calendar record.

The five Tests that Amiss played in the series amounted to one sad tale of woe: that 90 was his only half-century. It made up to more than half of his 175 tour runs, over eight innings, at 19.44. His series would end in ignominy: his final three innings of the tour were ducks at the hands of Lillee. If the Terror Twins had done this to the man who had taken all before him that year, imagine the blow not only to his confidence, but to his teammates' as well.

Amiss just could not find a way to score.

Dennis Amiss: Tony Greig and Alan Knott both had some success against Thommo. You go from a very tall player to one quite short – and they both stayed leg side of the ball. From that position they could play the cut shot, often over the slips.

Actually, I remember before leaving for Australia, [former Test opener] Arthur Milton said to me, 'When you're up against good fast bowling there, stay leg side of it, get the pace and the bounce and get in'. After watching Greigy and Knotty in Brisbane, I tried in the nets to develop the ability to stay leg side – but I found that when I did that it was difficult to get back into the line of the ball. It was just alien to me to do it.

Talking about Lillee and Thomson in later years, Amiss admitted his despair: 'Many a time I walked out to the middle in a Test match knowing it was virtually a waste of time carrying a bat. I knew it would not so much be used to make strokes as to fend the ball off my body'.

Nobody would blame Amiss for losing his way against the blitzkrieg unleashed on the England line-up in 1974–75. He wasn't alone in failure. Far from it. However, that said, his record overall against Australia was abysmal. It started with his first effort – a pair in 1968. Time and again he fell foul of a patient attack just outside off stump, with seven ducks in 21 innings against Australia … eight times Lillee was his master. That was the only flaw in an otherwise excellent career. In 50 Tests, Amiss hit 11 centuries and scored 3612 runs at 46.30 – a very good average for Tests in those days. But Thomson and Lillee did him over.

Lillee was there at the end of the Boxing Day Test as well as its opening. England made 242 in its first innings, Colin Cowdrey again playing the rock. First he and David Lloyd, then he and Edrich cut their backlifts, stemming the desire to score runs. Cowdrey faced 171 deliveries in scoring 35 runs, Edrich 124 for 49. Lillee took two wickets – *again!* – and Thomson four. Australia trailed by one run on the first innings and when Tony Greig added his 60 to Amiss' 90 the home side was set a target of 246 to win.

Australia's target got down to 14 with two overs remaining and Australia seven down. Underwood bowled a maiden to Lillee. Lillee fell trying to hit his nemesis Tony Greig right out of the ground in the last over and a draw was registered.

Just as much as Australia, England had fallen slightly short of victory, hampered in its pursuit by the loss during the game of bowler Mike Hendrick to a hamstring injury that ended his series. Injuries and form meant that both England's batting and bowling line-ups changed in *every* Test. To make matters worse, Fred Titmus bowled with a limp in the last innings. He had been struck a fearful blow by Thomson on the right knee while batting. Titmus had jumped outside the line of off stump and raised his bat. It appeared he must have lost sight of the ball – so its impact must have come as a shock. He hit the ground writhing in pain. He went down and could not get up. But Australia would have soon have a much bigger scalp on its plate.

The captain's head

ENGLAND CAPTAIN Mike Denness dropped himself for the fourth Test, starting in Sydney four days later. In the 97 years of England sending sides overseas, this had never happened, nor has it happened since. A sign of what was to come was perhaps there when Denness batted at No.7 in the one-day game (which England won) on New Year's Day, which followed immediately after the Boxing Day Test.

Denness explained his decision thus: 'It's in the best interests of the side that I should stand down'. True, he'd scored only 65 runs from six innings, but really? It was not a move that would strengthen a squad battling to hold itself together.

Playing on Denness's mind was his own inability to cope with the searing pace of Thomson, Lillee's aggression and Max Walker's guile. In later years he admitted he had wondered as early as Perth whether he should be in the side.

He was not the only one. Some members of the press had been calling for him to quit. The eccentric Henry Blofeld was one, writing in the New Year: 'If Denness were to bat against this Australia side until Christmas I would not back him to make a hundred'. Christopher Martin-Jenkins wrote in *Ashes to Ashes*, his book on the series, that Denness's shortcomings against fast bowling had been 'as so many of us expected, found out'.

Denness had long had his doubters – his absence from the Test side after his debut in 1969 until December 1972 was widely believed to be because then captain Ray Illingworth did not rate him. Nor did fellow Yorkshireman Geoffrey Boycott, who had so coveted the captaincy.

Some teammates too had their doubts. Keith Fletcher, who had been dropped after Perth and would replace Denness for Sydney, wrote that some doubted his captaincy and 'felt he should not have been in the side in the first place'. Fletcher thought his act was 'a sign of weakness'.

That opinion was not unanimous – Tony Greig said the decision 'showed a courage that deserved admiration'. In later years, Dennis Amiss said, 'It takes a certain moral courage for a man to stand up and admit that he is not mentally and physically equipped to play for his country at Test cricket'. Amiss added that he himself was 'not brave enough' to make that decision.

Denness later told the story of a letter he received from a member of the public. It was addressed to 'Mike Denness, Cricketer', and the letter read: 'If this letter reaches you, the Post Office think more of you than I do'.

Denness was more circumspect about another letter he received, from John Inverarity, who praised him for his conduct and leadership. Many years later, in 2001, Inverarity enjoyed being at Kent with Denness, using a period of sabbatical to have a brief stint as the County club's coach. During that time he was able to confirm his belief, established as an observer during the ill-fated 1974–5 tour, that here was a good man.

> **John Inverarity:** I was a secondary schoolteacher at that time and was always on the lookout for an opportunity

to inculcate good values into my students. The way Mike Denness carried himself during the storms his men battled through on that tour encouraged me to look beyond the carnage wrought by Dennis Lillee and Jeff Thomson. I came away most admiring the pluck and decency of the England captain.

In much the same way I developed a healthy admiration for Alistair Cook [who captained England for five years before resigning the position in 2016]. Through much of his tenure Cook came in for criticism, from fans and media alike, but he never wavered. Though often ridiculed, he kept his composure – and there's not many you could say that about. I felt the same way about Mike Denness.

As extraordinary as Denness's decision to drop himself was, it was, in a sense, a mark of the man. The author worked closely with Denness during the author's term as coach of the Kent County Cricket Club in 2002 and 2003. At that time the former England captain was chairman of the club's Cricket Committee – wielding a firm, yet not too firm, influence on the group. He was a consultative leader in that role, very quietly spoken and showing little of the brogue of most of his Scots countrymen.

Bedser, the elder statesman of English cricket and chairman of the selectors, who had rolled Denness on preferring Cowdrey to D'Oliveira, accepted the decision. Denness later wrote in his memoir *I Declare* that Bedser thought the decision wrong.

The author concluded from his many conversations with Denness during his time at Kent that he was a man of stout conviction, a proven leader through outstanding exploits in County cricket. A person who would not easily be swayed from his convictions; primarily interested in the greater good, in no way driven by ego, just wanting the best for his men and, as a consequence, his team. Regarded in this latter light, it is easier to understand why he dropped himself for the fourth Test. He thought it would be better for the team.

The decision would live with him for the rest of his life. It did not escape mention in his obituaries when he died in 2013. Just as the memory of Greg Chappell's storied career will forever be stained by the decision to ask his brother, Trevor, to send down an underarm ball in a one-day final, so will the memory of Denness's days in the game be marked by the staggering decision of a captain to drop himself. Chappell says he knows he'll never live his decision down ... Denness equivocated about whether he had made the right decision.

He wrote about how he felt watching the Sydney Test as a spectator in the dressing room: 'It is difficult to describe how I felt. It was probably a mixed feeling of despair, sadness and frustration. If I had had my leg in plaster or my arm in a sling, it would have been different, but I was fully fit.'

The amazing thing is that Denness, like Amiss, was one of *Wisden's* five Cricketers of the Year for 1974. He had made two centuries in the English summer against India, had one to come against Australia, 188 not out in the sixth Test, then another, 181, against New Zealand in the series that followed. Those four centuries were all he ever made.

Australia, led by Thomson and Lillee's ferocious attack, were not just winning – they were destroying England's best.

John Edrich replaced Denness as captain. He had no better luck calling the toss. Again Ian Chappell got to choose, and this time he chose to bat first on a track that looked to offer something for the quicks. Resolute New South Wales opener Rick McCosker – replacing Wally Edwards, whose three Tests and 68 runs would be the entirety of his Test career, which preceded many years as an administrator – made his debut and acquitted himself well with a patient 80 as his team amassed 405. Again there was a tiff between Lillee and Greig. The Englishman once more bounced Lillee, hitting him on the left elbow, prompting Bill Lawry in the commentary box to say Greig had hit the wrong elbow. With Lillee in severe pain and barely capable of holding the bat, Greig sent another one fizzing past his face. Ashley Mallett was then struck on the hand twice by bouncers from Graham Arnold, at least one of which hit his right hand, and he could not bowl in England's first innings.

Lillee was far from impressed. 'Feelings ran high when we came out to bowl,' he said, 'and I must admit I really let myself go for the first time that season'. For the England openers that day, it was very hard work.

> **Dennis Amiss:** I remember the first ball Dennis bowled that day went sailing over my head. I turned and looked

at Marshy, about thirty yards away ... he jumped way in the air and tried to fingertip it but it went straight over him and into the sightscreen on the half volley. I looked at 'Bumble' [David Lloyd] at the other end and I reckon he'd gone white!

Colin Cowdrey, who had turned 42 on Christmas Eve, recalled feeling the brunt of the slingshot superstar. 'Thommo bowled me three balls on the trot which were unbelievable. The first reared up and hit the bat handle. The second was a bit short and I tried to turn it to leg, but it hit me on the arm. I played back to the third ball but it came at me. I had to fend it off, only to see it fly off a glove for a catch at short leg. I doubt if I had ever faced three such difficult deliveries, three such nasty ones, in a row in my whole career.'

An angry, fired-up Lillee certainly cranked up some speed in that first innings. His barrage carried all the way through, hitting Derek Underwood on the chest then bowling a bean ball at Willis. Lillee apologised, but the England quick did not look mollified, throwing his bat. Thomson got in on the act too – a vicious ball hit Fletcher's gloves, deflected onto his forehead and carried all the way in the air to cover, such was the speed of the ball. He was dismissed shortly after. Strangely, the worst injury was to an Australian fielder. McCosker was struck a shocking blow on the forehead while fielding at short leg. It only got worse for him in the second innings, when a Thomson full toss on leg stump was smashed by the batsman straight into his groin.

Daily Express cricket correspondent Crawford White wrote, 'The "bash the Poms" campaign escalated with the partisan crowd turning into a soccer-type mob at its worst. Lillee was urged on by the notorious Sydney Hill pack as he bombarded England batsmen with his angriest and fastest bowling of the series'.

Under the headline 'Test of temper', White said the fourth Test erupted 'into one of the nastiest, most bad-tempered days of cricket I remember'.

Both White and Peter Laker, of *The Daily Mirror*, described the umpire's warning to England's Tony Greig about bumpers as 'a sick joke'. Laker wrote, 'To those of us who have winced at the unrestrained savagery Lillee and his hunting partner Thomson have poured on the uncomplaining English heads this winter, this was the sickest joke of all'. Adding, 'in one evil-tempered tantrum shortly before lunch yesterday Lillee dragged the fourth Test and its remnants of this bitterly physical Ashes series to the brink of total warfare'.

For all the fireworks Lillee's return was once again just two wickets – and Thomson's four. Australia had earned a first-innings lead of 110 and when Chappell declared the second innings at 4–289, the overall lead was 399. England made a promising start. For once Amiss was able to dig in and he and Lloyd took the score past 50.

Dennis Amiss: I was going along well, best I'd played in the series ... leaving it outside the off stump, not feeling for it. Bumble and I put on a few, then he got out and

> Kipper came in. He walked up to me and said, 'What's going on?'
>
> I said, 'Well, Kipper, if it's really short it's over your head ... it's that sort of a wicket, we've just got to get in'. I could see what he was thinking. Then I got out and the first ball he received from Lillee was at bouncer length and he ducked ... but the ball didn't get up and hit him straight in the ribs. The 37 I made in that innings felt like 150!

Amiss earned those runs, taking one crushing ball square in the middle of his back when he turned away from a bouncer. Even the one that got him out hurt too – a short one from Thomson struck his hands before flying off for yet another catch in the slip cordon.

Amiss's dismissal brought Edrich to the crease. His doughty 50 in the first innings, from 177 balls, had been a captain's effort, and he was hoping to back up in the chase for victory. But the captaincy was cursed. The first ball he faced ripped into his rib cage. He crashed to the ground. He could not get up unaided. Visibly struggling, Edrich was led away and taken to hospital, where X-rays revealed broken ribs. 'I've always admired Edie as a courageous and very competent player,' Lillee said, 'and I was not surprised, but very relieved, when he came back later in the innings and batted very well'. In fact, Edrich, back from hospital, was the last man standing when his team fell for 228, way short of the victory target. His courage was never in doubt.

And still Lillee was unable to break the sequence of taking two wickets in each innings, while Thomson returned six for the game and Walker four. After four Tests the scoreline read: Thomson 30, Lillee 16. If that was something to celebrate, it wasn't the reason there was such jubilation in the Australian dressing room. The Ashes had been regained! Lillee said it was a delectable feeling. 'It was a great moment; the culmination, if you like, of all that we'd been working towards since Ian Chappell had taken over the captaincy in 1971. It's no secret we had a few celebratory drinks that night – Sydney town has never been the same since!'

A bad serve

A TRADITION in those heady days of cricket was the arrangement to break up the five allotted days of a Test match with a rest day. This quaint practice was a time for the game at hand to be put to one side and, for some, to have a restful time recuperating, maybe taking a look around the city in which the game was being played. The author recalls, during the Perth Test of this series, arranging a private boat trip for a few England players to Rottnest Island, a short haul off Fremantle. When it came to the Adelaide Test, players from both sides would be invited to a splendid function at the Yalumba winery in the Barossa Valley. It was quite a special day for all who enjoyed an invitation. And in this particular year the rest day would provide an unexpected – and very positive – outcome for the England party. The confluence of events in their favour began when the first day of the Test was washed out, following an overnight deluge.

Ian Chappell: There was no play, so a few of us went out for a game of tennis on the grass courts at the back of the Adelaide Oval grandstands. Thommo was one of those who came down for a hit. And when it came to a casual game of tennis, he served like he bowled: just flat out ... with him, everything was a hundred miles an hour.

All participants survived that onslaught and the Test match began on the scheduled second day. Sent in to bat in conditions that favoured the deadly accurate spin of Derek Underwood, Australia worked very hard to post a score of 304, thanks to a solid contribution from the bottom half of the Australian order.

Underwood took the first seven Australian wickets. Then Lillee came out to bat, with Greig at the bowling crease. Coming off his looping, arcing, long-strided run, Greig pinpointed a bouncer straight at the quick's head. Only desperate evasive action with the bat saved the batsman. Greig immediately followed up with another equally well-aimed bouncer, and a wild agricultural hook from Lillee resulted in a top edge over Alan Knott's head for four. Greig would not give up, nor be dominated. Nor Lillee – a third slower short one was dispatched over mid-wicket for four more. When Bob Willis took the second new ball he wasted no time bouncing Lillee, who top-edged another one.

It was more of the same when England batted. In the first over of the second day of play Lillee dismissed Amiss, caught behind again for a duck. Lillee followed up with the wicket of Lloyd for 4, and the same story played out. Denness had returned to the side, replacing Edrich, who was nursing his broken ribs, and when Thomson had him caught behind after a sparkling 51, Lillee shook Thommo's hand – his 32 wickets were the most taken by a fast bowler in an Ashes series.

When Lillee had Greig caught behind by Marsh he finally had more than two wickets in an innings – and didn't he celebrate, skipping and hopping down the wicket. He then took more joy in sitting Fletcher on his backside as he evaded a bouncer aimed at the batsman's head. By this time the normally mild-mannered Adelaide crowd had started up the 'Lill-ee, Lill-ee' chant, more synonymous with the rowdy MCG. Lillee ended up with four wickets and Thomson three as England were skittled for 172. The lead of 132 had become 404 by the time Chappell declared at five down, Underwood adding four wickets to his seven from the first innings. However, in making that declaration Chappell had to take into consideration the fact that he would be one bowler down.

> **Ian Chappell:** On the rest day most of the boys went up to the Barossa Valley. I didn't go, but that night I got a call saying I'd better come to the hotel, Thommo had buggered his shoulder. I went in to the hotel and there he was, his arm in a sling.
>
> I said, 'What's happened, Thommo?'
>
> Sheepishly he replied, 'I'm a bloody idiot'.
>
> 'Why? What have you done?'
>
> 'We went up there and I played tennis ... and I was trying to serve one flat out and the bloody thing's gone.'

That was the end of Thomson's series. Thirty-three wickets in four and a half Tests, claimed at the wonderful average of 17.94. You just wonder how many he would have ended up with.

Thomson was within easy striking distance of the record numbers of wickets in an Ashes series: the 36 taken by leg-spinner Alfred Arthur Mailey for Australia in the long-ago 1920–21 season. Just to put in context how distant that feat was, Mailey had learned of his selection in the Australian team for that series by reading it in a newspaper while cleaning a water meter under a coolabah tree next to a chicken coop.

For Thomson himself, no real regrets. As with everything in his life to that date, it was *hard* and *fast*. 'I served the ball fast, as I usually do, and felt a terrible pain in my shoulder', he said. 'I dropped the racquet and went straight to the specialist who diagnosed a pulled tendon and torn muscles.'

Richie Benaud suffered the same injury to his bowling shoulder in 1960. He feared for Thomson – saying that his own shoulder was never the same again.

That was that. Thomson was out of the game and out of the series – not available for the final Test, at the MCG. In his absence in Adelaide, Lillee and Walker did the business. In what was now something like a broken record, Lillee had Amiss out in the first over. Unable to counter a rising ball outside off stump Amiss was yet again caught by Marsh. Lillee added a second four-wicket haul thanks to Mallett taking a trademark left-handed blinder to get rid of Cowdrey and Jenner at fly slip catching a flashing Denness. When

Lillee had Fletcher lbw on the fourth morning, the game was all but over, although the redoubtable Alan Knott put up sterling resistance, bringing up his century from a Lillee bouncer that he put over the slips for four. Lillee gave him another one for good measure, with the same result. But the Australians were not to be denied, winning by 163 runs inside barely three and a half days. England still had not topped 300 in any of their 10 innings.

There would be no Jeff Thomson for the finale at the MCG and, as it turned out, virtually no Lillee. He had feared not being able to make it through the series because of his back injury – but it was not his back that was his problem. He bowled just six overs in the only innings England required, before he broke down with a bruised foot.

Lillee's six overs produced just one wicket … guess who? Dennis Amiss, lbw 0. Amiss's tour ended in ruins. The Englishman was glad to be out of the tour, but recalled a heckler, that game, in the MCG outer, trying to get under his skin.

> **Dennis Amiss:** I was fielding on the boundary in Australia's first innings and there was this guy taunting me … 'Lillee's going to get you … Lillee's going to get you …' Well, I tried to humour him, but it made no difference. And wherever I went on the field he followed me. In the end I went up to Mike [Denness, the captain]

and asked him if I could come up into the slips. He looked at me and said, 'No, you're not good enough'.

England bowled Australia out for a miserable 152 after Chappell won the toss, this time choosing to bat on a wicket that showed signs of rain damage, then the visitors poured on the runs. Batsmen were still getting hit – Greg Chappell wore one on the chin from Peter Lever, whose 6–38 had Australia out before tea. Batsmen hitherto largely unsighted made up for lost time. Denness's 188 was the highest score by an England captain in Australia, while Fletcher helped himself to 146. Three 100-run partnerships dominated the middle order – two more than in the previous 10 innings. England won by an innings and four runs. Never has the importance of two bowlers – Lillee and Thomson – been better illustrated by their absence.

The game finally brought down the curtain on the outstanding career of Colin Cowdrey, who had so manfully accepted the challenge to come to the aid of his beleaguered country. He opened the innings again and the seven runs he scored took his aggregate to 165 at 18.33.

Statistically, those numbers were way, way below the standard he had set in a career to be totally admired. But Cowdrey had lost no friends through the exercise. His courage and persistence knew no bounds.

> **John Woodcock:** I know Colin was bitterly disappointed that he was unable to take up the opportunity to make a century in his final innings of the series – which turned

out to be his final appearance in Test cricket. Thomson wasn't playing and Lillee, suffering from a bruised foot, only bowled six overs. Colin was not out on five at stumps on the first day. A century was beckoning. However, on the fifth ball of the second day he fell to Max Walker for seven. Instead, Denness and Fletcher helped themselves.

Australia lost a game that was a dead rubber anyway, most judging the 4–1 outcome to have been a fair result. The home side had batted, bowled and fielded better. And it was not only Lillee, with 25 wickets at 23.84, and Thomson's 33. Max Walker toiled long and hard throughout with his naggingly accurate medium-fast deliveries, for 23 victims.

It had been a long, hard summer, not just for the players but the umpires too, who had stood in all six Tests.

> **Robin Bailhache:** By the end of that summer I hated cricket. I'd also done Sheffield Shield matches at the start of the season, Shield matches during the season and then I had to do the club finals in Adelaide. I had really, really had enough. Actually, I felt it was a bit unfair. To expect two guys to still be as good an umpire, and to be as strong and as fit by the end of that series, was asking a bit too much.

Between them, the Twins of Terror had claimed 58 wickets. Thirty-nine of those wickets were taken in the arc from wicketkeeper to gully – which tells the story in a nutshell.

Excluding the final Test (no Thomson and only a handful of Lillee overs), there was no England batsman who could look himself in the mirror and say 'I enjoyed that'.

The spirit of the game – and broken spirits

THE DEADLY pairing of Dennis Lillee and Jeff Thomson left scars on England's batting that would take a long time to heal. The visitors had no answer to the Twins of Terror, a point underlined by this comment from their captain, Mike Denness: 'As the plane left Australia for New Zealand, some of the lads said they were glad to get out alive, even if some of them didn't exactly get out all in one piece. That was difficult for me to take. They had spent three months fearing for their livelihoods and wondering if they were going to get hit on the head. I was upset I hadn't picked up on it earlier.'

None escaped without at least one bruising blow to the body. And survival at the crease meant more than simply not losing your wicket.

> **Dennis Amiss:** Of course there were no helmets or arm guards in those days. In the end we decided to put on a bit more protection, so that we could take one or two knocks and still be in the game. The mindset was 'leave as much as you can'. Get the pace and the bounce out of the ball. You're not looking to play shots against them, you're looking to survive – and to do that you had to leave as much as you could, especially early on. Not

to feel for the ball ... and try to get out of the way of the big bounce.

David Lloyd: In the second innings of the third Test at the MCG, Dennis Amiss and I put on a century opening partnership [actually 115], but then not much later we're 8-182! Looking back on the series, it was pretty much a one-way street. We had nothing to fight back with. Our bowlers had problems with injuries and our strike bowler, Bob Willis, was strapped up from top to toe. You know, he could only give you one spell.

There was precious little love lost in this battle for the Ashes. As always in these contests, this was serious business. A contest that, in a way, began with the infamous *fusarium* wicket at Leeds in 1972. Ian Chappell and his men felt robbed then and, as far as they were concerned, there would be no beg-pardons. Plus, as Chappell himself pointed out, he and his mates had been peppered and pounded by John Snow during the 1970–71 tour Down Under. In the 1974–75 series, he reasoned, he had Lillee and Thomson – they didn't have Snow – and it was payback time.

Chappell stood by his word, and his men, when he said it was up to the umpires, not him, to decide what was fair and what was not when it came to short-pitched deliveries. So, the England bats were subjected to a withering assault. They failed the test, with a notable exception. Tony Greig was worth his place in the side as a batsman alone – nobody made more runs than he over the series. Only Derek

Underwood bowled more overs and nobody took more wickets – Underwood and Bob Willis joining Greig with a series total of 17 wickets each.

And it was Greig who did the heavy lifting with the short stuff. The tall, blond South African-born all-rounder provided some much-needed sandpaper in an England tour party that was all too smooth, palpably lacking combative spirit, even character. When Chappell and his men drew the line, Greig was prepared to step over it. And thumb his nose in such a provocative manner as to more than once achieve the desired effect of putting certain Australian players off the matter of concentrating on the job at hand. His reward for his leadership was soon to come.

It was small 'w' warfare – as it should have been – no quarter asked, none given. But players on both sides agree there was never a time when relationships soured.

> **David Lloyd:** It makes my blood boil when they talk about sledging and boorish behaviour on that tour, because I think the Aussies were absolutely terrific. They played it tough, but they were bloody good company off the field. You'd get the odd comment [on the field] from Dennis, but Thommo – not a word.
>
> **Greg Chappell:** The series was played in good spirit. Absolutely. As was the tradition in those days, the two teams fraternised at the end of each day's play, had a few beers. So, off the field was fine, while on the field it was every man for himself.

> **Robin Bailhache:** There was a lot of respect for each other, among the two teams. Ian Chappell was the best skipper I came up against, the best leader of men. He led from the front, with a strict code of conduct. Sledging was light – and if there was any it was humorous.

It was also a bruising experience for two men who made up the complement of on-field personnel for the full six matches of the series: the two umpires.

> **Robin Bailhache:** If it wasn't a nightmare, umpiring all six games of the series, it was close to it. Say, it was a bad dream.

With two express bowlers in action for Australia, a heap of short-pitched deliveries and plenty of occasions when batsmen suffered injuries, Tom Brooks and Bailhache were on their toes from go to whoa. Adding another dimension was their task in adjudging the no-ball with such fast bowlers.

> **Robin Bailhache:** The good thing about Thommo was he never went near the front line in his delivery stride, while Dennis was always close but for me never over. But we had to be quick in getting our eyes up to follow the flight of the ball. Fortunately, you got to know from the back-foot plant whether you needed to take interest in the front foot.

> The problem with Thommo was that you never knew where the next ball was going ... and, if *he* [Thommo] didn't know, how could the batsman – or the umpire – know? While Dennis was at the batsman all the time, he had more control of his deliveries.

Throughout the tour, the British press corps sent stories back home complaining about the sheer brutality of Lillee and Thomson. Not always were the quotes that floated back to Australia from those press reports appreciated in the Australian camp.

> **Ian Chappell:** The reporting of the series back in England really pissed me off – and Thommo really paid for it when we went there for the return series in 1975. The English public was really down on him. They had read that all we had done was bounce the crap out of them and abuse them, which was wrong.
>   Sure, Thommo sent a lot of balls past at chin height, but they weren't bouncers – they were flying off just short of a length. And the only person he abused was himself. I mean, some of the things he said to himself after a bad delivery you wouldn't say to your worst enemy!

That impression gels with what Frank Tyson gleaned from the commentary box and recorded in the aforementioned *Test of Nerves*:

Frank Tyson: While other bowlers involve themselves in abusive verbal exchanges, Thomson remains quiet. He bowls with brimstone in his heart but lives with an olive branch in his hand. One gains the impression that he is the Happy Warrior, the fast bowler who is content doing his appointed task.

As the England party limped off to continue their Down Under tour in New Zealand, the inevitable post-mortems were held, both in private and in the public domain, as the English pondered a series of 'what ifs?' For the core of the England party as they landed in New Zealand, there was the prospect of another battle for the Ashes in a few months' time – and again coming face-to-face with the brutal battering ram of Lillee and Thomson.

Batsmen weren't the only ones bruised

RODNEY WILLIAM MARSH was the man who had the job of fielding the thunderbolts from Lillee and Thomson throughout the tempestuous summer of 1974–75. Indeed Marsh would go on to keep in every Test (and WSC Supertest) in which the two quicks combined. A few days after that Ashes series wound up, he penned a piece for *Cricketer* magazine, then edited by Eric Beecher. He revealed the same pain as the batsmen – and the same fatigue as the umpires. Let's go back in time for a totally contemporary look at the Lillee–Thomson phenomenon through the eyes of the man with the best view in the house:

Have you ever tried hammering your hands with a sledgehammer once a minute for six hours? Probably not, but if you have you'll know exactly how it feels as the man behind the stumps when Australia's two 'terror' bowlers, Jeff Thomson and Dennis Lillee, are in full force.

It's quite an experience, I can tell you. I can't remember being as relieved to be having a break from cricket as I was at the conclusion of our Ashes-winning effort. It was the first real rest I have had after 12 games of first-class cricket in a row. My hands were mighty grateful, I can assure you.

A lot has been written about my hands, and I suspect quite a few people believe I'm a softie, that I can't take a bit of fast bowling without whingeing. I must admit thoughts along those lines did occur to me, too. I wondered whether I was getting old and soft, but I don't think I am. Keeping to Thomson and Lillee, the two fastest bowlers I've ever seen, is a bruising job – literally.

Every time 'Two Up' or 'FOT' has started his run, every time I've crouched down behind the stumps in anticipation of another thunderbolt, I've wondered to myself if this will be a blow to put me out of the game. You have probably seen me grimacing as I've taken the ball on some occasions. Chiefly this is in expectation of it hurting, rather than of actual pain.

But no matter how sore my hands are, I still enjoy the challenge of keeping to these two outstanding fast bowlers. You would have to dig deep into the records to find a pair of fast bowlers to equal them in terms of sheer, unrelenting pace combined with the ability to produce one or two deadly, unplayable balls each spell.

Thommo, particularly, has the occasional ball which no batsman in the world can do much about. If you can manage to draw your bat away in the instant of a second available, you may be saved. But so often it has been a totally lethal delivery.

In that context I think the use of the bouncer by our fast bowlers has been overplayed and viewed completely out of context. The fact is, I think, that Thomson and Lillee don't get many batsmen out with the bouncer, so it is not really their dangerous delivery at all. It's the ball which kicks off a good length which is so dangerous for any batsman, and Thomson can produce it. In fact, probably the one who dreads their bouncers most of all is me – I've got to hurl myself around like an Australian Rules champion to take the ball.

Probably the question I'm most asked is to compare the pace of Dennis and Jeff. Well, I stand about a yard further back for Thomson than for Lillee, so there's my answer. I would hasten to add, however, that I thought Dennis was a yard quicker during the 1972 tour of England than he is now. Not that I think pace is everything. It's a fascinating exercise to compare these two great fast bowlers, not just as speed merchants but as effective wicket-taking bowlers in Test cricket.

Dennis, to me, is improving all the time. He may not be quite as fast as he was during his memorable 1972 tour, but he has made up for it in other ways. I feel now I know precisely what he is aiming to do with every ball. There is a decided plan to his bowling, and if he doesn't quite succeed you know he'll come back stronger.

Just watching him at the other end I can sense what he is planning to do with a particular delivery. To that extent I suppose he is predictable for me, though you must remember I keep to Dennis in almost every Sheffield Shield and Test match in which I play.

FOT and I are, of course, great mates. We talk at length about cricket tactics, about methods of getting particular batsmen out. To both of us, succeeding in taking wickets in Test cricket is the ultimate challenge. This is where I feel Dennis has matured so much since his tremendous comeback to first-class cricket this season.

In England he was a genuine great fast bowler, and he still is. But he knows he must conserve himself in certain ways, including a slightly modified action to put less strain on his back. So he has made up for it in other ways, perhaps more subtle ways. And I think he had bowled without luck up to the fourth Test in Sydney, continually chipping in with his two wickets, continually providing Jeff with the finest support any fast bowler could wish for.

I noticed during the fourth Test there was some speculation in the Press that Dennis was supposed to be jealous of Thommo's success. The author of that story, himself a former fast bowler, must have been writing to his editor's instructions. Knowing the two players – and watching them in action on the field – it's so obvious they love bowling together and are continually trying to help one another.

Watch them when one is bowling and the other is fielding at mid-on or mid-off. The fielding member of the duo will pick up the ball, perhaps give it a quick shine, walk back with the other, talking all the time about the ball coming up, about methods of attack, just trying to give the other guy that extra confidence or edge to take a wicket.

If that is the way a jealous bloke carries on, you've stumped me. And I know, too, from inside the dressing room, how Dennis and Thommo are forever discussing tactics and bowling between themselves. Sitting in a corner you'll see them talking about individual batsmen, about ways of improving their fitness or stamina, about their gear, about particular deliveries. They are a pair dedicated to each other's success as well as their own – all in the interests of Australia winning.

OK, I've talked about Dennis the bowler. What about Thommo? He has that lethal delivery he can produce, almost out of nowhere. We all know he is quick. But looking at him from a batsman's point of view (and, incidentally, I love the challenge of facing him when WA plays Queensland) I honestly believe there is no way of sorting out a fellow like Thommo. He can produce one or two wicket-taking balls every spell, and there's no batsman in the world who can do anything about it when it comes. In other words, there are some balls that no batsman alive can keep out – and 'Two-Up' has the unique, singular ability to produce such a ball consistently.

Speaking as a batsman – I batted against him in Perth in December for WA – I think you must get in early and try to get on top of him. Otherwise – forget it! In fact in that innings I played against him at the WACA I managed to hit a six off him with a Tony Greig-patented shot over slips' heads. It flew hard and high – and when I turned back to look at 'Two Up' I instantly recognised that nasty gleam in his eyes. He doesn't like to get hit around, so much so that the satisfaction of a boundary off him is often a doubtful advantage when the batsman looks back at the snarling bowler facing him – with the thought of the next ball just a few seconds away.

There are times when he gives a wicketkeeper headaches. Some of those lifting balls are impossible to take, and as the ball rockets into the fence behind me I console myself by thinking that no-one else, not even someone of Tony Greig's height, would have a chance. I'm 5 ft 8 ins and that's that. I believe I have a fairly good leap. The secret is in the timing, and it's something I've worked at perfecting over the years. But when Thommo lets fly with a wide ball, or a lifter, there's simply nothing a keeper can do except to hurl himself at it and hope he will reach.

Jeff has been marvellous for Dennis, too. You have all heard about the value of having two (or, as we have in the Test team now, three) outstanding fast bowlers who never give the batsman a chance. Well, with Dennis and Jeff, backed up by Max Walker, we are seeing it in action.

As for my own bruising time behind the stumps, I think it was largely a case of starting off with a couple of bad bruises early in the season and never having the chance to rest them after that ... I got a couple of knocks on my hands, and once you have a bruise the best thing to do is to give it rest. But of course, with the first-class cricket program drawn up as it was this season, there was no opportunity for me to rest my hands. As a result every time I received another blow on the bruises they became more deep-seated, until eventually they went right through to the bone.

Since then half-a-dozen doctors have come up to me and asked to see my hands. When I showed them, there was hardly anything to see. It's not visible, and I didn't bother about having an X-ray, because experience told me that what they needed most was rest. Each day after keeping I would massage my hands with ice, and sometimes put raw steak on them ...

The thing I most dreaded this season as Australia's wicketkeeper – taking a return from Thommo when there is a chance of a run-out. 'Two Up' has the most powerful and, at the same time, the wildest arm I've ever seen in the field. Believe me, if you ever see that scenario – Thomson returning to Marsh in a tight situation – you'll know that you've seen the first return in the game's history coming in at a million miles an hour!

FOT? Two-Up? Where did those names come from? The author was a teammate of Dennis Lillee's when he burst on the first-class scene in 1969–70 and recalls how the youngster first had a nickname pinned on him, relating to the shape and prominence of his nose. It was 'Falcon'. But it didn't stick.

As for FOT, the scene was a Sheffield Shield game at the WACA Ground in Lillee's first season for the state and at 20 years of age he was as green as the outfield grass. The opposition had a left-hand–right-hand partnership going, which meant that the young quickie at fine leg had to trek across to a new position every time a single was scored. Trouble is, he kept forgetting. Fed up, captain Tony Lock screeched down to the errant fieldsman, 'Come on Lil, you're like a fucking old tart!' Teammate John Inverarity jumped on the key initials and the nickname 'FOT' was born. This one would stick.

You have to delve into the earliest years of the fledgling British colony of Australia to find the origin of Jeff Thomson's nickname. The first mention of the game two-up was in 1798, when convicts were betting on the outcome of two pennies being thrown in the air. The game grew in popularity and was played worldwide by Australian soldiers during World War One. But the practice was illegal back home and one of the most famous of the clandestine operations, which floated around Sydney's suburbs through most of the twentieth century, was Thommo's Two-up School.

FIVE

OFF TO THE WORLD CUP

THE LAST ball of the 1974–75 Ashes series had been sent down soon after lunch on 13 February and with both Lillee and Thomson at that time hors de combat, you would have thought a long rest would be the way to go. However, there was to be a short tour to Canada on the way to England and the inaugural World Cup, followed by a four-Test Ashes series. And the Cup was scheduled to begin on 7 June. So, feet up lads? Not likely. There was more work to be done at home before all of that.

In those days great store was placed in the Sheffield Shield competition, which following the Test series had two rounds to run and both Lillee's Western Australia and Thomson's Queensland were in the hunt for victory. So, Lillee took a fortnight's rest then saddled up for his state's final game, against New South Wales in Perth, while Thomson returned to action on 7 March, to bowl his team to victory over

Victoria with a game total of nine wickets. Lillee's haul of six saw WA to a big win – and Shield triumph, by a small margin over Queensland.

Now, at last, there was time for a bit of a breather. Then a two-week stopover in Canada, where Australia managed to lose to a Canadian XI. Importantly, both speedsters comfortably proved their fitness – and readiness for the main business: the World Cup, followed by a defence of the Ashes. Australia's Cup campaign began at Leeds, with a group game against Pakistan.

The author was at Headingley and witnessed one of many occasions when Lillee imposed his will on a situation – and emerged a clear winner. Australia reached 7–278 in their allotted 60 overs, but were in danger of losing when Asif Iqbal and Wasim Raja carried the score to 5–181 with plenty of overs to spare. Ian Chappell threw the ball to Lillee, who dug deep to immediately blast through Asif's defences and bowl him. Australia went on to win the game, thanks to Lillee. His 5–34 from 12 overs would be his best return in a One-Day International.

The tournament meandered on and the Australians advanced to the final, against the West Indies at Lord's – where the Lillee–Thomson partnership took on a whole new meaning. The two almost pulled off a miracle win – with the bat.

> **Ian Chappell:** I hark back to the 1973 tour to the West Indies, when Dennis's back gave in and he was unable to bowl. It was decided that he should remain on for the rest of the tour and play occasionally as a batsman, but definitely not exert himself as a bowler

or, for that matter, in the field. He was delighted at this opportunity – and proceeded to pester me for greater opportunities with the bat.

The chance came when we were to play an unofficial one-day game against Tobago in the lead-up to the final Test. After much pestering along the way I had given in and said to him, 'Okay, you can open the batting, but only when we play Tobago'. I'd forgotten about that promise when I went out for the toss. I called correctly and gave the sign to the dressing room that we were batting. So I walk in and go to my locker and there's a batting order pinned up and there it is not Redpath, then Lillee, but Lillee, then Redpath! And there *he* is, padded up and ready to go. I might have forgotten, but Dennis hadn't! He only made nine, but he loved the opportunity to walk out first for an Australian innings.

Then, when Lillee stood out of the 1973–74 first-class season and played as a batsman in Perth club cricket, batting in a rustic sort of way, he scored the second most runs in the competition, with his highest score being 98 – tantalisingly close to what would have been his only century in serious cricket.

Ian Chappell: So he could bat. Fast forward to the World Cup final at Lord's. West Indies batted first and made 8-291 from their 60 overs. We made a real meal of the chase, a young Viv Richards involved in three costly run-outs, and when the ninth wicket fell and Thommo joined Dennis we were about done for – 58 runs in arrears.

It looked a hopeless situation, but I guess it wasn't all doom and gloom for me. Okay, we needed a miracle, but I knew a bit about Dennis's prowess with the bat and Thommo was no slouch, either. Having said that, when Max Walker was the ninth wicket to fall a few of the guys, including myself, started to pack our bags. It really was mission impossible. But all of a sudden you could hear some shouts from the balcony. They were doing more than just staying in. Next thing we're all out on the balcony, starting to think 'We can win this'. Then there was a funny incident.

Thomson lifted a ball to Roy Fredericks at extra cover and was caught. Whereupon, the huge West Indian contingent in the crowd, thinking it was all over, ran out onto the ground – in their hundreds, maybe thousands. But they weren't aware the delivery had been called a no-ball. Upon hearing the call, Fredericks had shied at the non-striker's end where Lillee was out of his ground. The throw missed and the ball was lost in the charging mob. The Australians started to run, but after completing three runs Thomson was concerned. 'No, get back you fool ... one of them could have the ball in his pocket and run us out.'

Ian Chappell: Eventually the field was cleared and Thommo asked one of the umpires, 'How many runs are you giving us?' Naturally he exploded when the answer given was 'two'. Then Dennis was asked how many had actually been run. 'You should have been counting,' he replied. 'But I make it about 17'. In the end they got four. Anyway, they put on 41 and got us to within 17 of the total before Thommo was run out by the wicketkeeper in the second-last over, trying to pinch a run.

It may have been a pleasant surprise to some, watching Dennis bat so well that evening, but there was more to come on that tour. After the Cup we went into a four-Test series against England – and in the second Test at Lord's, batting No. 10, he was unbeaten on 73 when we were dismissed 47 runs behind. He actually hooked Peter Lever for six and after that in the dressing room it was either Sir Donald Lillee – or Sir Dennis Bradman. So we found out for ourselves that he could hold a bat *and* do some damage.

Prudential World Cup – Final

Australia v West Indies
West Indies won by 17 runs
Lord's, London – 21 June 1975 (60-over match)

West Indies Innings (60 overs maximum)

RC Fredericks	hit wicket b Lillee	7
CG Greenidge	c †Marsh b Thomson	13
AI Kallicharran	c †Marsh b Gilmour	12
RB Kanhai	b Gilmour	55
CH Lloyd*	c †Marsh b Gilmour	102
IVA Richards	b Gilmour	5
KD Boyce	c GS Chappell b Thomson	34
BD Julien	not out	26
DL Murray†	c & b Gilmour	14
VA Holder	not out	6
Extras	(lb 6, nb 11)	17
Total	(8 wickets; 60 overs) (4.85 runs per over)	291

Australia Bowling

Bowling	O	M	R	W	Econ
DK Lillee	12	1	55	1	4.58
GJ Gilmour	12	2	48	5	4.00
JR Thomson	12	1	44	2	3.66
MHN Walker	12	1	71	0	5.91
GS Chappell	7	0	33	0	4.71
KD Walters	5	0	23	0	4.60

Australia Innings (target: 292 runs from 60 overs)

A Turner	run out (Richards)	40
RB McCosker	c Kallicharran b Boyce	7
IM Chappell*	run out (Richards/Lloyd)	62
GS Chappell	run out (Richards)	15
KD Walters	b Lloyd	35
RW Marsh†	b Boyce	11
R Edwards	c Fredericks b Boyce	28
GJ Gilmour	c Kanhai b Boyce	14
MHN Walker	run out (Holder)	7
JR Thomson	run out (†Murray)	21
DK Lillee	not out	16
Extras	(b 2, lb 9, nb 7)	18
Total	(all out; 58.4 overs) (4.67 runs per over)	274

West Indies Bowling

Bowling	O	M	R	W	Econ
BD Julien	12	0	58	0	4.83
AME Roberts	11	1	45	0	4.09
KD Boyce	12	0	50	4	4.16
VA Holder	11.4	1	65	0	5.57
CH Lloyd	12	1	38	1	3.16

Here we go again

AFTER THE disappointment of falling at the final hurdle in the World Cup, the focus for the two speedsters soon shifted to the defence of the Ashes. But before a ball was bowled in a Test match, between 25 June and 26 August the tourists played 11 warm-up games: one against the MCC at Lord's, the others against various County sides, a program that would never be written today. Thomson, who more than Lillee needed to learn the nuances of bowling in England, strode out in six of them. Lillee played in five.

The record shows emphatically that Lillee was suited to the conditions he met in England. For a start, being engaged with Australia's traditional foe would always raise this great competitor's fighting spirit. More, though, was his ability to adapt to the different wickets and weather. He had shown that handsomely with 31 wickets at 17.67 in five Tests on the 1972 tour.

Lillee's overall record on three tours to England says it all: 16 Tests; 96 wickets; average 20.6; strike rate, a wicket every 50.2 deliveries. Better than his full career numbers: 70 Tests; 355 wickets; average 23.9; strike rate 52.0.

> **Greg Chappell:** Dennis was a proven performer in England, but this was Thommo's first tour there – and it took him a while to get used to bowling in the vastly different conditions. He had to learn to bowl fuller, which ran against his natural approach. You were wasting your time bowling too short, mostly. You had to pitch it up and hit the seam.

Initially it was proven to be so. While Lillee and Max Walker bagged five each in the first innings of the opening Test, Thomson struggled. The Australians took charge from the get-go, but in the opinion of one prominent England batsman the outcome could – and should – have been different.

Dennis Amiss: The series began at Edgbaston, which was my home ground. The wicket had a tinge of green to it and I offered my thoughts. 'This is going to be slow and low, which won't suit their quicks, hopefully some of us can get in ... they're not going to pitch it up, they're not going to get the bounce, they're not going to get the pace off the wicket.'

I said, 'if we can get in we can get our confidence back against them'. Others agreed and we said to Mike [Denness, the captain], 'We've got to bat first on this wicket'. He agreed, but Alec Bedser, as chairman of selectors, overruled him. He said, 'It's green, you've got to bowl on it'.

They batted well on it, scored 359 and then we got caught on a rain-affected wicket and their quicks cleaned us up twice and we lost by an innings. Graham Gooch, who went on to be a very good player, made his debut and bagged a pair. It was the worst outcome for us. Had we batted first, one or two of us would have got in, then *we* would have benefited from the rain.

As it turned out, Denness's decision to send the Australia in was his last as England captain. After one over of England's first innings a thunderstorm erupted, making the pitch a difficult one. Dismissed in the first innings for 101 on the rain-affected wicket, Denness's team was asked to follow-on. Amiss was in the wars again, struck a sickening blow to the elbow by Lillee. Thomson hit his straps. Thommo found the right length, which, combined with some fearsome pace, shook England's batting to the core. Eighteen overs, 5–38 and Australia had won the opener by an innings and 85 runs with a day and a half to spare. Denness had made 3 and 8. He offered his resignation – and Alec Bedser, the man who had urged the decision to send Australia in – accepted his offer. Tony Greig was now captain.

The series then shifted to Lord's, where it was expected that the Twins of Terror would reign again. It was a wicket that traditionally offered hope for the men of pace. But while Lillee remained focused, his partner in pace was far from a happy traveller.

> **Greg Chappell:** I roomed with Thommo on that tour and he was extremely homesick, to the point he didn't really want to be there. He hated the weather and wanted to be home.
>
> One day I returned to our hotel in London, to the room he and I shared, which was just marginally bigger than a telephone box. There were two single beds which Thommo had pushed to one side of the room – and there he was, on the floor, with an electric train set and a couple of other electric games. He'd basically taken over the room.
>
> I said, 'What the bloody hell's going on here Jeffrey?'
>
> 'I've been over to Hamleys [a renowned London toy store] and I've bought these things for my boys.'
>
> At that stage he wasn't even married and didn't have any kids!

I said, 'You haven't bought them for your boys ... you've bought them for yourself'.

The train tracks went under the beds and, for the rest of the time at that hotel, there I was stepping over the train station and the racing car track in the middle, just to get to my bed and in and out of the bathroom. It was like an obstacle course.

Rod Marsh: Thommo would do extraordinary things while we were away. A lot of the time he'd have room service and not even go near the bar, where the others might have congregated. But then he'd have a breakout – and look out! Basically, though, he was a gentle soul.

One down in a four-game series, England had rung the changes. Denness had lost not only the captaincy but his place in the side. He would never play for his country again. Keith Fletcher was out too. The replacements were Barry Wood and the 33-year-old, grey-haired, bespectacled David Steele – who turned out to be a godsend for the home team.

Dennis Amiss: They brought in David Steele, a good player of quicks, and he made an immediate impact. Mind you, he wasn't scarred from the battering we'd received in Australia only a few months before.

Steele, whose determination was steely and whose hair was silvery, immediately proved a thorn in the Australians' side.

A fact that Lillee later conceded. 'Steele wasn't a great player by any means, but he was a battler. He was aware that on flat tracks all you have to do is go forward with purpose to be in command.' Steele's application of that tactic would immediately pay dividends for the England selectors and their beleaguered team.

When England batted first at Lord's, once again the deadly Lillee–Thomson pairing burst through: Wood, Edrich, Amiss and Gooch all out without reaching double figures and the score 4–49. Lillee had all four and it was all gloom and doom in the England dressing room. That was until Greig joined Steele and they put on 96. Steele was a picture of circumspection and Greig was not far behind, out of character but perhaps responding to his new role of skipper.

Lillee failed to add to his tally, while Thomson ended Steele's stay (a well-made half-century on debut) and added the wicket of Alan Knott (for an equally defiant 69). Australia ended up trailing by 47 on the first innings. Greig had fallen four runs short of a century in his fist innings as captain. Then a wonderful Edrich century in the second innings – 175 runs over nine hours at the crease – backed up by the stout Steele enabled the home side to set a massive target which was never a likelihood. The visitors comfortably played out the draw.

The Test boasted one historical first, from a seaman, Michael Angelow – who became the first streaker on the field during a Test match, hurdling the wickets at both ends. At Lord's, of all places. The mercury had nudged 94 degrees

Fahrenheit, and members had been given permission to remove their jackets in the pavilion. Angelow's mother was not impressed. 'He's in for a big ticking-off from me when he gets home', she told the *Daily Express*.

The third Test was at Leeds, and England, once more winning the toss and batting first, again established early supremacy. They led by 153 on the first innings, thanks to a fine five-wicket debut by left-arm spinner Phil Edmonds, and had Australia in all sorts of bother at 3–220 chasing 444, when fate intervened. During the night of the fourth day protestors entered the ground and vandalised the wicket. The game had to be abandoned and a draw declared.

To The Oval, with the Ashes retained by Australia and England looking to tie the series – a result that would have been fitting. It would be a six-day game. Ian Chappell won the toss for the first time in the series and Australia batted ... and batted ... finally declaring at 9–532. Lillee, Thomson and Walker then tore through and England were dismissed, way behind, for 191. Ordered to follow-on, it was England's turn to lay it on thick. Finally dismissed for 538. The tourists needed 198 runs to win but reached 2–40 before the game ended in a draw. Six days' play, but no result!

In the marathon England second innings the indefatigable Lillee racked up the amazing personal tally of 52 overs – and the remarkable figures, from such a stint, of 4–91. Over the four Tests he averaged 48 overs per game, gathering 21 wickets at the excellent cost of 21.90. Thomson bowled fewer overs, but struggled to find his best form, returning 16 wickets at 28.56. The pair had led from the front on wickets that mostly did not favour men of pace. There were better times to come.

Change at the top

AUSTRALIA had retained the Ashes, but at what cost? An exhausting six days of play at The Oval had failed to produce victory for either side. Then on the final day the Australian captain dropped a bombshell – announcing his retirement as skipper.

> **Ian Chappell:** It was a pretty easy decision. I was buggered. Maybe if we'd had six months break before we were to play the West Indies back in Australia I'd have gone one more. But I'd seen the West Indies twice in the World Cup and I thought these blokes are a pretty good side and we're going to need somebody thinking aggressively, because that would be the only way we'd beat them. That somebody wasn't me. I was worn down.

Chappell had been an innovative and aggressive leader who worked hard to forge binding relationships with his men. He'd been successful, too: from 30 Tests in the role, 15 wins, 5 losses and 10 draws. And, to put the record straight, in only 11 of those games had he been able to call on the ferocious Lillee–Thomson team. Just a few days short of his 32nd birthday, his decision to stand down came out of the blue.

Greg Chappell: I was surprised. He hadn't talked to me about it before he announced it and I remember making the comment to him, 'You could do this a lot longer'.

'No, no,' he said, 'I know that the time's right'.

That wasn't to be the end of Ian Chappell representing his country. Far from it. He would play on under his brother, then captain the Australian side in World Series Cricket before wearing the baggy green cap a final time in the last three Tests of the 1979–80 Ashes series Down Under.

Ian Chappell: The reason I decided to play on after England, 1975, was that I didn't want anybody to accuse me of not wanting to come up against the West Indies quicks the next home season. I told Greg, 'I'll be here. I'm not going to interfere, but if at any time you need some advice feel free to ask'.

Greg Chappell: True to his word he never interfered, but he must have wondered what was going on in my first Test as captain, against the West Indies in Brisbane. I won the toss and sent them in. Dennis had Gordon Greenidge lbw for nought in the first over. Then I looked around and realised I didn't have anyone in front of the wicket on the off side. I had four slips, two in the gully, a bat-pad, fine leg and mid-on but no-one in the covers ... and it did cross my mind that if ever Ian was going to interfere that was probably the time. I managed to drag someone from somewhere and put him at cover and things were right.

As it turned out the Twins of Terror in tandem would play under only two captains in Tests and World Series Cricket Supertests: the Chappell brothers. As for Ian Chappell, the responsibility of leadership seemed to have brought the best out of him with the bat. It was a stamp of the man that in those 30 Tests he scored 2550 runs, including seven centuries, at an average a tick over 50 – compared with overall Test career figures of 75 games for 5345 runs at 42 and 14 three-figure scores.

PART II
DESTROYING THE WEST INDIES

But first ...

THE WEST INDIES were on their way. It had been seven summers since they had last visited and only three players remained from that squad: Clive Lloyd, who was now captain, left-handed opener Roy Fredericks and veteran off-spinner Lance Gibbs. Viv Richards would be making his first tour of Australia, with only seven Tests and one century to his name. Michael Holding had yet to play a Test. Andy Roberts had made his international debut just the year before.

But before Lillee and Thomson had the chance to test their skills against the Caribbean cricketers, they had a little bit of work to do.

On 3 September 1975, the two pacemen had packed their bags at the end of the fourth Test at The Oval and headed home for the upcoming six-Test series, beginning in Brisbane on 28 November. But on 25 October Thomson was there for the opening game of Queensland's Sheffield Shield season, where he bowled a total of 36.2 eight-ball overs. Over the next three weeks Thomson played three more four-day games for his State – a total of 113 overs, for 26 wickets. He then had a week off before the first Test in Brisbane, but in between that game and the second Test in Perth he played again for Queensland, bowling 31.2 overs. Can you believe that? Lillee had a lesser load, but only because of Western Australia's schedule. He was only able to fit in three Sheffield Shield games – sending down a total of 86.5 overs – before the opener at the Gabba.

A healthy debate that abounds in Australian cricket these days, around the preparation of fast bowlers, goes like this: which is better – scientifically managed workloads or plain hard work on the training track? Modern thinking favours the former, with every bowler's output carefully monitored. Still, under that regime the nation's pace-bowling resources seem to be constantly depleted through injury. Old-fashioned thinking says get plenty of miles in your legs and lungs, then bowl yourself to fitness.

A good example of the success of this model was the work that Dennis Lillee did in his later role as coaching guru with Mitchell Johnson before Mitch made his very successful comeback to international cricket. When that project began, before Lillee would even *talk* technique with Johnson, he demanded a level of aerobic fitness that could only be achieved through a deep running program. Initially the subject was far from impressed with this idea. Then, like a light being switched on in his head, it dawned on him. Being strong in the lungs meant he could comfortably see out a hard day in the field. And hold up technically.

Lillee's theory is that when a fast bowler gets tired his action tends to fall apart and, with that, his effectiveness falls away sharply. Occasionally, too, this state of fatigue can leave a bowler more susceptible to injury. Lillee, himself, was renowned for his second wind; for bowling as well in the last over of the day as the first. He trained to achieve this and as a result was able to produce quality work at the end of a big workload in harness.

This was 41 years ago. There is more international cricket scheduled today, but it's extremely rare that our front-line fast bowlers step out in Sheffield Shield games, let alone have Thomson's load of four four-day games and a week's lay-up leading into a program of six Tests and a One-Day International in the space of 69 days. What would Mitchell Starc and Josh Hazlewood think about that? It would not be countenanced these days. When the Windies Tests started, Lillee and Thomson would not be lacking fitness.

Up, down, out

THE CAREER of Clive Lloyd, that tall belligerent left-handed batsman and brilliant fielder in the ring, stands up to the closest scrutiny. He was the first West Indian to make 100 Test appearances, ending his career having played 110 Tests for 7515 runs at the healthy average of 46.67, with 19 centuries.

Lloyd ascended to the throne for a tour of India in 1974–75, around the time Dennis Lillee and Jeff Thomson were putting England's bats to the sword not so far away. He would then play in the England summer of 1975, leading the West Indies to a rousing victory in the inaugural World Cup one-day competition. In between those commitments he represented Lancashire in the 1975 County competition, where he teamed up with his namesake, David Lloyd.

Of course, the England Lloyd had just had the debilitating experience of facing Lillee and Thomson Down Under. Close to the end of the County season – and nearing the time when the West Indies would head off on a similar mission to Australia – their captain for the tour cornered his Lancashire teammate in the dressing room during a break in play.

> **David Lloyd:** I remember Clive asking me about Thomson. He wanted a heads-up on the speedster with the javelin-throwing action. He said to me, 'This Thommo fellow doesn't look too special'. I couldn't help thinking to myself, 'You've got something coming, friend'. Then off they went ... and Thommo hit Clive under the chin!

Clive Lloyd headed off to Australia with his team, bearing some mixed feelings about the task that lay ahead. He knew all he needed to know about Lillee's prowess with the ball, but he still wasn't so sure about Thomson. However, one member of his team had no doubts that Thomson was definitely the danger man. Off-spinner Lance Gibbs, whose long fingers enabled him to capture Freddie Trueman's world record for wickets in Tests, was a dead-set rabbit with the bat. A true No.11.

Gibbs had seen the young Lillee when he played the 1969–70 season for South Australia. And, during that season he'd struck up a good enough relationship with Ian Chappell, also playing for South Australia, to feel able to express his concerns about Lillee's partner in pace in the coming West Indies series.

> **Ian Chappell:** Lance Gibbs probably summed up the attitude of most willow-wielders in that period. I'd known Gibbsy for a few years and at the end of the first day's play in the South Australia versus West Indies game at the start of the 1975-6 tour, he called me over.
>
> 'You've got a job to do, Ian', he said. 'I can handle Lillee, he has a wife and kids, like me. But that mad man Thomson, you've got to tell him I can't bat and he mustn't kill me.'
>
> 'But, Gibbsy,' I said, laughing, 'you're forgetting that I'm not the captain any more'.
>
> 'I don't care,' he said, wagging his finger at me. 'I'm holding you responsible for my safety.'

A month after that lead-up game in Adelaide the two sides shaped up to each other at the Gabba. The visitors chose a strong batting line-up: Roy Fredericks, Gordon Greenidge, Lawrence Rowe, Alvin Kallicharran, Viv Richards and Lloyd at six. With Andy Roberts, Michael Holding and Gibbs leading the attack, the visitors had good reason to carry confidence into the game and the series.

For Australia, emerging all-rounder Gary Gilmour, slotting in at No.7, after Rod Marsh, took the new ball with Lillee and took four wickets to Lillee's three – including Viv Richards for a duck on his Australian debut – as the

West Indies, at one stage languishing at 6–99, compiled 214. New skipper Greg Chappell then scored the first of three centuries for the series and the home side took a first-innings lead of 152.

Lillee added three to his first-innings tally, while centuries by Rowe and Kallicharran gave Australia a testing chase. This time it was Ian Chappell who posted three figures as victory was gained at a canter. It wasn't the perfect start, from both a personal and team perspective, to Greg Chappell's time as captain. All eyes shifted to the Perth wicket, where, it was thought, Lillee and Thomson – who had just one wicket for 158 in Brisbane – would relish the pace and bounce on offer as they had against the Englishmen just a year earlier.

A fighting century by Ian Chappell took Australia's first innings total to 329 – and then it was all West Indies. And most of the fun came from the flashing blade of Fredericks, a diminutive left-hander with a special brand of flourishing strokeplay. He played perhaps the innings of the series. Runs flowed like a cascading waterfall as the Australian quicks peppered him with short balls. First Thomson, then Lillee, was literally knocked out of the attack as Fredericks raced to a century off 71 balls, setting a record for the fastest hundred in Test-match cricket. The bowling is quick in Perth – which means the batting can be too. Fredericks, who also represented his country, Guyana, in squash and table tennis, finished with 169.

Clive Lloyd joined the party. There were 20 bruising boundaries in his 149. The West Indies were all out for 585,

256 runs ahead. Four Australian bowlers went for more than 100 runs and a fifth, Max Walker, had 99 next to his name. Lillee conceded 123 at about five an over; Thomson 128 at 7.5; Gilmour 103 at 7.3; and spinner Ashley Mallett 103 at 3.9.

This was a good old-fashioned mauling. But more damage was to be inflicted on the Australians. Andy Roberts, with that creeping, open-chested style of his, ripped the heart out of the home side's upper order, his figures 7–54 from 14 delicious overs of hostile pace. Left-armer Bernard Julien cleaned up the tail and, just under an hour into the fourth day, the visitors were winners by an innings and 87 runs. It was an amazing reversal from Brisbane – a point not lost on one member of the international media corps.

> **John Woodcock:** I came out to Australia, to see the series against the West Indies. I missed the first Test and saw the visitors win the second, in Perth, on the back of a marvellous innings by Roy Fredericks. On the flight out of Perth I was talking to Ian Redpath, whom I knew well, and suggested that Australia were in for a hiding in the series. He replied, 'Oh no, that won't happen again ... the way they bat that wicket suited them very well'. How right he was!

Could Greg Chappell get his men back up off the canvas in time for the Boxing Day start? He threw the gauntlet down – and it was picked up by his two new-ball heroes. Thomson hit his straps on a wicket that had a bit more grass than the usual MCG strip and bombarded the batsmen with trademark rib-ticklers, finishing with 5–62, to Lillee's 4–56. The West Indies were all out for 224.

The Aussies *were* up and about and climbed further up when Redpath and Gary Cosier posted patient centuries to help their side to a lead of 261. Apart from another enterprising century from Lloyd, the West Indies' batting lacked fibre and Australia went to win by eight wickets. This time Lillee had a match haul of seven wickets and Thomson six. Rod Marsh had a field day behind the stumps, with a total of eight dismissals – five off Lillee and three off Thomson.

1975–1976 Frank Worrell Trophy – 3rd Test – Melbourne

26th December 1975
Melbourne Cricket Ground, Melbourne
Result: Australia won by 8 wickets
Player of Match: J R Thomson

West Indies 1st Innings

R C Fredericks	c McCosker b Thomson	59
C G Greenidge	c †Marsh b Thomson	3
L G Rowe	c I M Chappell b Thomson	0
A I Kallicharran	c †Marsh b Thomson	20
I V A Richards	b Lillee	41
C H Lloyd*	c G S Chappell b Thomson	2
D L Murray†	c Walker b Lillee	24
B D Julien	c Mallett b Lillee	18
V A Holder	b Walker	24
A M E Roberts	c †Marsh b Lillee	6
L R Gibbs	not out	0
Extras	(lb 4, w 1, nb 22)	27
Total	All Out (47.0 overs @ 4.77 rpo)	224

Australia Bowling 1st Innings

Bowling	O	M	R	W	ER
D K Lillee	14	2	56	4	4.00
J R Thomson	11	1	62	5	5.64
M H N Walker	13	1	46	1	3.54
G J Cosier	4	0	15	0	3.75
A A Mallett	5	1	18	0	3.60

Australia 1st Innings

I R Redpath	b Roberts	102
A Turner	b Roberts	21
R B McCosker	c †Murray b Julien	4
I M Chappell	c Kallicharran b Gibbs	35
G S Chappell*	c †Murray b Julien	52
G J Cosier	c Kallicharran b Roberts	109
R W Marsh†	c & b Gibbs	56
M H N Walker	c †Murray b Roberts	1
D K Lillee	c Richards b Holder	25
J R Thomson	lbw b Julien	44
A A Mallett	not out	3
Extras	(b 5, lb 6, nb 22)	33
Total	All Out (118.3 overs @ 4.09 rpo)	485

West Indies Bowling 1st Innings

Bowling	O	M	R	W	ER
A M E Roberts	32	2	126	4	3.94
V A Holder	27	2	123	1	4.56
B D Julien	28.3	5	120	3	4.21
L R Gibbs	30	9	81	2	2.70
I V A Richards	1	0	2	0	2.00

West Indies 2nd Innings

R C Fredericks	b G S Chappell	26
C G Greenidge	c †Marsh b Walker	8
L G Rowe	c †Marsh b Lillee	8
A I Kallicharran	c †Marsh b Lillee	32
I V A Richards	c †Marsh b Thomson	36
C H Lloyd*	c Lillee b Mallett	102
D L Murray†	c †Marsh b Lillee	22
B D Julien	b Walker	27
V A Holder	run out	15
A M E Roberts	c Mallett b I M Chappell	5
L R Gibbs	not out	5
Extras	(b 8, lb 4, nb 14)	26
Total	All Out (69.2 overs @ 4.50 rpo)	312

Australia Bowling 2nd Innings

Bowling	O	M	R	W	ER
D K Lillee	15	1	70	3	4.67
J R Thomson	9	0	51	1	5.67
M H N Walker	19	1	74	2	3.89
A A Mallett	14	0	61	1	4.36
G S Chappell	7	1	23	1	3.29
I M Chappell	5.2	3	7	1	1.31

Australia 2nd Innings (target 52)

R B McCosker	not out	22
A Turner	b Roberts	7
I R Redpath	c sub b Julien	9
I M Chappell	not out	13
G S Chappell*		
G J Cosier		
R W Marsh†		
M H N Walker		
D K Lillee		
J R Thomson		
A A Mallett		
Extras	(lb 1, nb 3)	4
Total	2 wickets (8.7 overs @ 6.00 rpo)	55

West Indies Bowling 2nd Innings

Bowling	O	M	R	W	ER
A M E Roberts	3	0	19	1	6.33
B D Julien	3	0	13	1	4.33
C G Greenidge	1	1	0	0	0.00
L G Rowe	1	0	6	0	6.00
A I Kallicharran	0.7	0	13	0	11.14

Rod Marsh: They bowled a lot more short balls in this series, mainly because the West Indies' bats took up the challenge. And they kept on getting wickets with bumpers. So, why wouldn't you bowl them short?

A new year – and, for Clive Lloyd's men, a resolution to once again produce a reversal of form. The task was made easier by the fact that Lillee was a late withdrawal from the fourth Test, suffering from pleurisy, of all things. Thomson was back to his old tricks, breaking the thumb of opener Bernard Julien, who retired hurt, later returned and was last man standing – with an unusual way to carry the bat. In Lillee's absence Thomson put in a huge effort at the head of the attack, in the first innings sending down 25 overs and claiming three wickets. A masterly Greg Chappell century – 182 not out, having been dropped on 11 – gave his side a 50-run lead. Then, thanks to a blistering six-wicket Thomson blast, the visitors were dismissed for 128. Victory to Australia by seven wickets.

And so to Adelaide, where Lillee rejoined the fray and did his bit, with two wickets in each innings. Partner Thomson set up the ultimate victory – and series clincher – with another hostile first-innings effort: four wickets, but again going at more than six an over as the calypso batsmen went after his short stuff. In their second innings there was an ominous sign for bowlers all over the world, when a young Viv Richards stroked a fine century, before a gem from Lillee knocked back his off stump. Signs of things to come in the contest between two of the game's all-time greats.

The series had been won and, as it turned out, Ian Redpath had been right in his response to the West Indies' big win in Perth.

> **John Woodcock:** Well, Australia won the third and fourth Tests and then we went to Adelaide for the fifth. After the game, the West Indies beaten again and now totally demoralised, the Don [Sir Donald Bradman]

drove me back to my hotel. And he said to me, 'You know, there's no disgrace in being bowled out by these two. By God they're good'.

It certainly was a demoralised West Indies who arrived in Melbourne for the final stanza, a dead rubber. The best they could take out of another whopping loss was the continued form of Richards – scores of 50 and 98. From Australia's point of view, the loss in Perth aside, it was a thunderously convincing series victory against what, on paper, had seemed a more than worthy opponent. The bowlers had done their bit, but Greg Chappell's effort in compiling 702 runs at 117, with three centuries, was equally important.

In the five Tests in this series when they bowled together, the Twins of Terror bagged exactly 50 wickets. Lillee finished with 27 from his five Tests and Thomson 29 from six. Leading lights in a 5–1 series triumph.

Captain Greg Chappell said at the time, 'Dennis Lillee and Jeff Thomson were our trump cards. Even though they didn't really hit their best form until after the second Test, I thought they were the difference between us winning or losing.

'The mental side is probably the biggest factor in winning and losing a Test series. I think the West Indies came here fearing the reputations of Lillee and Thomson. I think that fear built up in their minds and I believe it played a big part in the way they approached the series. Most of the West Indians were playing English County cricket, and I'd say as well as reading a great deal about Lillee and Thomson, they also heard a lot about them from the Englishmen who had been in Australia in 1974–5.' When it came to mind games and fearing the reputation of match-winning fast bowlers, it wouldn't be long before the West Indies themselves would enjoy such an advantage.

Looking back on the 1975–76 series in later years, Greg Chappell acknowledged that, as the new skipper, he had been handed a gift on a silver platter.

> **Greg Chappell:** I was lucky to inherit a very good side. Not least of all, two great bowlers. The others – Gilmour, Walker and Mallett – were no slouches, but Lillee and Thommo were a formidable force.
>
> The good thing from my point of view was that they were very *different* bowlers. Plus, they were very *different* personalities. What motivated one didn't necessarily motivate the other.
>
> It was always a pretty tough decision: who do I throw the ball to, Dennis or Thommo? The beauty of it was that after the initial spells you could rotate them from one end and keep them reasonably fresh.
>
> I was also fortunate to have Thommo as a teammate in Queensland, which allowed me to get to know him as a mate. So I could tell by his body language where things were at ... and didn't need to ask him a lot of questions. He generally wore his heart on his sleeve.
>
> It wasn't hard to motivate him. You'd throw him the ball and he'd just want to bowl fast and get blokes out. If he couldn't get them out there'd be a few bruises along the way and that wasn't bad, either.

Clive Lloyd's troupe left the shores of Australia much as had Mike Denness's England party some twelve months before: battered, bruised and beaten. One West Indian player, not on the tour but later to make his own mark, remembers the scars borne by those who had to stand at the other end of the pitch when Lillee and Thomson were on the rampage. Colin Croft wrote, 'A few years on, I heard Clive Lloyd, Deryck Murray, Alvin Kallicharran, Bernard Julien and Roy Fredericks describe the fear of facing Dennis Lillee and Jeff Thomson during that tour to Australia. It was as if they had just finished watching a series of horror movies'.

Which, in itself, was the catalyst for a remarkable turn of events, soon to unfold, with an impact on world cricket that nobody could have imagined.

A fast reaction

THE WEST Indies captain was fed up. With the exception of the Perth Test, he and his team had been battered from pillar to post by the pace and aggression that Lillee and Thomson had turned on through that magical summer for Australian cricket. True, he had brought two speedsters with him. Andy Roberts had been around for a while, but Michael Holding was new at the business. Now, Clive Lloyd determined that, if the West Indies were to amount to much on the world stage, he would need to be in a much better position to fight fire with fire.

The batting was in good order: Fredericks, Greenidge, Rowe, Kallicharran and the nascent Viv Richards, then himself, enjoying the luxury of batting at No.6. No, he needed to find more venom at the pointy end: more fast, preferably express, bowlers to put the fear of God into opposition batting line-ups – as Lillee and Thomson had done to his team. So, before leaving Australian soil he made a commitment to scouring the Caribbean to unearth such talent.

Lloyd also sought to imbue in future West Indies teams the sort of discipline, fitness and culture that he'd witnessed in the Australian team that had just humiliated him and his minions. This was admittedly a more difficult task for a West Indies captain, given multiple nations were involved in making up the team.

But he had a plan. In a Melbourne hotel he revealed it to Rudi Webster, a West Indian–born first-class cricketer and sports psychologist, who years later wrote about it in his book, *Think Like a Champion* (Harper Collins):

> When Clive Lloyd was building his champion team, he built his leadership on three strong pillars: an agenda for change; a group of highly motivated and competent players committed to implementing his agenda; and the eradication of insularity, local prejudices, distrust and bad habits.
>
> He then told me that he would search the Caribbean for players with the 'right stuff' and would mould them into a highly motivated and disciplined unit to conquer all before them.
>
> He wanted his side to be the fittest team, physically and mentally, the best fielding team, the best bowling

team, and the best batting team. And he wanted to become the most successful West Indies captain.

He would favour players who were hardworking, enthusiastic and professional and would make self-discipline and mental toughness top priorities. Once those things were in place he would execute his plan in a forceful manner, using a quartet of aggressive fast bowlers to 'hunt in a pack' against opposing batsmen.

Clive told me: 'During the Perth Test the Australians were very uncomfortable against the pace of Holding and Roberts and I decided there and then to get two more like them to make up a quartet'.

And so began Clive Lloyd's quest. It was inspired by Australia's cricket. Lillee and Thomson were cricket's most fearsome fast-bowling combination, and they had just inspired the recipe that would reign over the game for the next two decades.

At the centre of Lloyd's quest was the hunt for 'two more' like Roberts and Holding. Immediately he was able to build on the experienced Roberts (career figures: 47 Tests for 202 wickets) and the burgeoning Holding (60 Tests, 249 wickets). Soon they were joined by the gentle giant, Joel Garner – he of the steepling bounce off a length, who would claim 259 wickets from his 58 Tests. Then came Colin Croft, with his whirling action and difficult angles, which would yield 125 wickets from 27 Tests. And Malcolm Marshall, who some rate as the very best, with his sharp pace and wonderful movement of the ball through the air (81 Tests, 376 wickets).

They were followed by the deadly accurate and indefatigable Courtney Walsh – 132 Tests for a then-record 519 wickets. Not forgetting the silent assassin, Curtly Ambrose, who was so tall he released from the stratosphere. His 405 wickets from 98 Tests earned him a knighthood.

They were the mainstays, but others came and went too: Sylvester Clarke (11 Tests, 42 wickets), Patrick Patterson (28 Tests, 93 wickets and a spell at the MCG rated by some as among the fastest ever), Ian Bishop (43 Tests, 161 wickets) and Wayne Daniel (10 Tests, 36 wickets). Then there was Franklyn Stephenson. He just couldn't get a game – yet those who saw him haven't forgotten his frightening pace. When the author was coaching Kent in the English County competition in 2003, the groundsman at The Oval showed him just how far back the wicketkeeper had to stand when Stephenson was in action. On what was generally an easy-paced wicket this fact took some digesting.

There was, as Lloyd told Webster, more to it than just finding four fast bowlers. History shows it takes a great leader to bring the West Indies together as a harmonious, disciplined group heading in the one direction. Unlike every other Test-playing states, this is a team comprised of players from multiple nations: nine Caribbean island nations – Antigua and Barbuda, Barbados, Dominica, Grenada, Jamaica, Saint Kitts and Nevis, Saint Lucia, Saint Vincent and the Grenadines, and Trinidad and Tobago; three British dependencies – Anguilla, Montserrat and the British Virgin Islands; the Dutch dependency Sint Maarten; plus Guyana, which sits on a northern tip of South America.

Lloyd would weld these disparate forces into one united fighting unit, imposing discipline to rid his team of carefree calypso cricket and leading them to the top of the tree, where they would stay for 18 years, barely losing a series.

Disaster – and triumph

PAKISTAN brought a strong side Down Under for three Tests midway through the 1976–77 season. Captained by Mushtaq Mohammad, including the great all-rounder Imran Khan, and with a batting line-up that boasted Asif Iqbal, Zaheer Abbas, Majid Khan and Javed Miandad, they set out to give Australia some hurry-up. Still, they were all mindful of the threat posed by Dennis Lillee and Jeff Thomson.

For the first time in 71 Tests Australia would field a team without Ian Chappell, who had retired (for the time being) from international cricket. The two Aussie speedsters were refreshed after a quiet winter and came into the new season bursting to follow up on the damage they'd inflicted in the previous two home series. Lillee and Thomson arrived at Adelaide, full of enthusiasm, for a game that was to begin on Christmas Eve then leapfrog Christmas Day. An odd piece of scheduling, to say the very least.

Mushtaq won the toss, it was a lovely day and the visitors chose to bat on a typical Adelaide Oval track. They planned to see out the first hour on what was known as 'the fast bowler's graveyard', then free up a bit and take charge. When Lillee and Thomson began proceedings against Majid and

Mudassar Nazar all present sat back in their seats in keen anticipation of some class action.

Ian Chappell was in the commentary box that day and witnessed one of the great tragedies in modern Australian cricket.

> **Ian Chappell:** Thommo had Zaheer Abbas missed a couple of times by Alan Turner at short mid-wicket, off skied pull shots, just before lunch. Thommo was clearly not impressed. After lunch he came out on fire, bowling like the wind. Then he dropped another one short to Zaheer, who went for and it flew up in the air forward of square leg. I reckon Thommo was thinking, 'They're not going to drop this one', so he took off after it.

Thomson confirms Chappell's summation. 'I quickly looked over and there was Alan Turner and I thought, "Shit, not you again ... I'll get it myself"'.

> **Greg Chappell:** You could see Thommo thinking, 'I'm not trusting anyone else this time'. So he spun around and raced to where it was going to land. He caught the ball, but in doing so collided with Alan Turner's head, smashing the bone in front of the right shoulder.

One of the umpires, Max O'Connell, heard the collision, which cracked Thomson's shoulderbone. 'It was like a pistol shot. I knew it was serious.'

Greg Chappell: Turner was out cold and there was Thommo slumped to the ground, grabbing his shoulder. We all took off. Nobody out there didn't realise something serious had happened. Thommo was in real trouble. We could tell from the pain on his face.

Rod Marsh: Of course he shouldn't have even gone for it, but he was so athletic that he was able to change direction and get over to where it was falling. Only trouble was, Alan Turner was camped underneath it. He just barrelled him. It was a sickening thud.

You just knew someone was going to get hurt. Turner was unconscious, but it was Thommo that everyone went to. That's when Kerry O'Keeffe came out with the famous line, 'Forget the dead, tend the wounded'.

Ian Chappell: Eventually they managed to sit Thommo up and he's holding his shoulder and looking in the general direction of the wicket when he says, 'I'll fucken kill him ... if I ever bowl again!' The boys reckon they weren't sure if he meant Zaheer – or Alan Turner!

Thomson knew as he sat there at short mid-wicket that he was in serious trouble. 'The pressure on my arm must have been great, because the collision ripped away muscle, ligaments and tissue. I wasn't in a lot of pain ... until I tried to use the arm to get up off the ground. I thought, "Shit, my arm won't move". My arm was just hanging off the shoulder.'

The injury required surgery, though Thomson fought that idea all the way to the operating theatre. He wanted to be back with his teammates at the ground and then for the team's Christmas party. He got to the party – and the surgery theatre. Next came recovery.

That was the end of the Lillee–Thomson show for the summer. For some time, in fact. Until a man called Kerry Packer decided to put his stamp on world cricket.

While Thomson gradually worked into a well-designed rehab program, Lillee soldiered on manfully – and unbelievably successfully – for the remainder of the summer. Bearing the burden of an elongated season that enabled the playing of the Centenary Test at the MCG in March, he poured out an incredible number of overs for state and country – actually, a staggering 477.4 (eight-ball) overs for Australia and Western Australia, capturing 93 wickets at the wonderful average of 18.92. Okay, how did it unfold? He played a major role in helping his state win both the Sheffield Shield and the Gillette Cup competitions. Without Thomson in the Adelaide Test he sent down a staggering 66.7 overs in Adelaide, which included a five-wicket second-innings haul and helped Australia, a key bowler short, to force a draw. Then he set out on another purple streak in the five Tests that followed, two more against Pakistan; two in New Zealand; and the Centenary Test.

Thanks to a lion-hearted 10-wicket haul, costing only 137 runs, Australia won the second Pakistan Test at the MCG by a huge margin. Pakistan drew the series with a big victory at the SCG, Lillee taking a total of five wickets. Then it was off to New Zealand and only a few days' rest before the first Test at Christchurch, where Lillee bowled a lot of overs for four wickets.

A week later, at Eden Park in Auckland, the champion tore through both the New Zealand innings for a total of 11 wickets for a mere 123 runs. Australia were winners by 10 wickets. You'd think that was enough red-blooded bowling for a while, but 12 days later the spotlight was on the MCG again, as the nobility of Australian and English cricket gathered for a replay of the very first Test, played at the ground in 1877.

Fortunately for Lillee, who was virtually running in on his knees to bowl, Australia batted first. But the rest was shortlived. Australia crashed to be 5–51 and Lillee found himself having to bat for an hour to help build something resembling a respectable total. Then he had ball in hand in the final hour on day one, trying to make amends for his team's score of just 138. He had a wicket before stumps and very smartly added five the next day for figures of 6–26 as England were trundled out for only 95.

How Lillee must have loved the MCG. It was a track not much liked by pace bowlers in those days, before the use of drop-in wickets overcame the ravages that a season of football had on the square. In the second innings Australia declared at 9–419, but then England got to 417. With victory for England within sight, Lillee found a gap in Alan Knott's defences to give his team victory by 45 runs. He had taken five wickets for the innings – meaning that for the third time in the space of five Tests against three different countries he had taken 10 or more wickets in a match. All up, 11–165 for the showcase Test. An utterly exhausted Lillee was chaired off the ground.

Some very good bowlers – Jeff Thomson included – go through a whole career without ever taking a haul of 10 wickets in a Test. Lillee had done it three times in five games. Unbelievable stuff!

However, the extraordinary workload in the back half of the season had taken its toll. Lillee badly needed a rest. On top of understandably high levels of exhaustion, his back was giving him trouble again. There was a tour to England coming up shortly, but on medical advice, which included a prognosis that if he did go to England there was a good chance he'd have a complete breakdown, he announced he would not be making the tour. Lillee said his doctor had bluntly informed him that he had the choice of touring England, and effectively winding up his cricket career, or pausing to strengthen his back so he could play for a few more summers. 'Really, I had no choice', he said.

When he put his feet up back home in Perth, Lillee had plenty of time to contemplate the next phase of his career. The cricketing world at large wasn't to know it at the time, but he had chosen to work in the future for a new master.

'It's impossible to bowl faster'

'I was 13 years old, dreaming of being a really fast bowler like Thommo ... I lived in Kalgoorlie and I asked Dad one day if there was a hotel where I could go and lift kegs

like Thommo and be strong enough to bowl as fast as him' – **A fan from Goode Beach, Western Australia.**

'*CITIUS, altius, fortius*'! Those three Latin words were chosen by the father of the modern Olympics, Baron Pierre de Coubertin, as the motto of the Olympic Games, borrowed from Father Henri Martin Dideon, the headmaster of Arcueil College in Paris, who used them to describe the achievements of athletes at his school: 'Faster, higher, stronger'. They've been an inspiration to generations of athletes from all over the world since the rebirth of the Olympic Games in Athens in 1896.

Greg Chappell has drawn a line through Jeff Thomson's extraordinary athletic ability and the time-honoured Olympic event, the decathlon – a contest over two days that includes the 100 metres sprint, long jump, shot-put, high jump, 400 metres, 110 metres hurdles, discus, pole vault, javelin and the 1500 metres. It's an unbelievably tough event.

> **Greg Chappell:** The Olympic motto says it all about Thommo: Fast, all right; high, in his action – and very strong. He had a marvellous physique – broad shoulders, narrow hips, beautifully shaped legs. A Greek-god sort of build. Graham McKenzie, another Australian fast bowler, was the only one I've seen who had a better build. Add to those assets, which Thommo possessed in spades, quite amazing levels of athleticism.
>
> He had immense strength. Few people realised that he was so strong, yet he hardly lifted a weight until late

in his career. It was from surfing, from running, jumping, climbing – doing all the things that that generation did – but a lot of it came from paddling out to the surf. He was six foot one [185 cm], but bowled more like he was six foot ten [208 cm]. He got high up on his toes and when he planted that front foot he came right up over the top of it.

He was also very flexible. Thommo was lithe, he was athletic, he could run fast, he could throw hard, he could bowl fast … and he drove fast. I remember saying at one stage, 'Forget Daley Thompson (England's decathlon champion) … if *Jeff Thomson* took to the decathlon Daley Thompson would be a distant second'. Thommo was an athlete like very few others.

We also know that Thomson would describe his bowling action in these seven words. 'I just shuffle in … and go WHANG'. But when pushed on the subject, he had a little more to say. 'Seriously, why was I able to bowl fast? I reckon it was all in the load-up … and bowling over my braced front leg … getting very tall through the crease.' For a man of dedicated action, and yet such simple self-analysis, he continued, 'The only way I can bowl is flat out. I'm not one of those guys who could slow down and use all manner of cut and swing to suit the conditions. I come in and let you know, "Hey, this is my turf … get out"'.

Ian Chappell saw enough of Thomson and the effect he had on those who had to face him. 'He made the ball climb off a good length and go past about Adam's apple height. I saw a few batsmen who faced Thommo come away with a look on their face that suggested they wished Adam and Eve had never met.'

Those who have endured the daunting task of standing and waiting for one of his deliveries – the author included – all agree on a few points. First, that on the fly he was very, very fast. Second, in suitable conditions he could make the ball take off from a length like no other. And third, his trademark load-up, with the ball at first concealed behind his buttocks then revealed in a muscular heave through the action, made him more difficult to pick up than the orthodox quick.

Thank goodness the young Thomson wasn't touched by some do-gooder coach, telling him 'You can't bowl that way – it's all wrong!' In fact, when you boil it all down his action was all *right*! The perfect side-on action. Yes, it was different. For instance, most side-on bowlers have a vigorous approach, then leap into the side-on position for the delivery stride. Not, the slow shuffle and dancer's twist into the side-on position that typified Thomson's unique style. It required great bodily strength, particularly in the upper torso, to produce such speed and lift off the wicket.

And, as the man himself says, the style was there all the time. 'The slingshot action was all natural. My old man bowled like that, so it was just hereditary. He was a good cricketer and he just got out there and bowled and that is what I did. We all sort of bowled the same, my brothers and I. And my boys bowl the same as me, but I didn't teach them.'

From Thomson's viewpoint, there was another reason why his slingshot style had a lot going for it. 'Apart from that injury in the first Test, the broken foot, I wouldn't have had an injury in a cricket match [due to my action] – no hamstrings, no backs, no nothing – the whole deal. No injuries. So what does that tell you about my action? It's got to have had something right about it. And I bowled the quickest.'

When it came to the tactical side of his business, Thommo liked to keep it simple. 'When I turned to walk back to my mark, all that was on my mind was the ball I was going to bowl next. Actually, after I bowled the previous ball, straightaway I knew what I would bowl next. You look at their feet, you look at their grip and you work them out.'

Those who saw him at close quarters will attest that Thomson was a man of very few words. 'I never said much. I was the quiet assassin. If you mouth off, you're losing the plot, you're not concentrating on what you are supposed to do.'

As Greg Chappell puts it, it was far better to have him on your side than have the prospect of him whistling the cherry around your ears as an opponent. For Chappell, then captain of Queensland, Thomson was a prime target for recruitment!

Greg Chappell: My first memory of facing Thommo was at the Sydney Cricket Ground, playing for Queensland in the last game in 1973-74. We were leading the Sheffield Shield table going into that game and first-innings points would have got us the Shield for the first time.

New South Wales had not picked Thommo at all during the season, but did choose him for this game. Before going to the ground for the first day's play I read an article in the paper where he said this was going to be his last game for the state.

I won the toss and elected to bat first, only to be confronted by this whirlwind from the Randwick end, steaming in up the hill and bowling quicker than anyone I'd ever seen. Probably as inaccurately as anyone I'd ever seen, but he frightened the bejayzus out of everyone. He finished with seven wickets and just blew us away. My attention had been captured and I couldn't wait to get down to the New South Wales dressing room after play that day ... where I knocked people out of the way to find this Thommo bloke.

I said, 'Mate, well bowled ... ... are you serious about leaving?'

'Yes I am ... I'm not going to let these so-and-sos fuck up my life.'

'Would you go to Queensland?'

'I'll go anywhere.'

'Wait there', I said and dashed out to the bar area, where I talked to some Queensland officials about getting Thommo to make the move up our way. I told them to shift heaven and earth to get him 'because I don't want to bat against him again'. I thought at the time, 'I don't care if Thommo hasn't a clue where they're going. He'll frighten these blokes out. They'll be so desperate to get to the other end they'll run themselves out!'

The Queensland hierarchy went to work and during the winter months Jeff Thomson packed up and moved north to continue his career. Meantime, Greg's brother Ian was forming his own opinion on the raw-boned speedster.

> **Ian Chappell:** I first came up against Thommo in a Sheffield Shield game in Adelaide. I missed him the first innings, but in the second one of our openers was injured so I went out to open the batting with Ashley Woodcock.
>
> Ashley took the first ball. In those days Thommo used to bowl about three leg-cutters an over and he sent down a short one to Ashley which bounced four times going through to the keeper. Seeing this, I thought to myself, 'If this bloke drops short he's got to go'.
>
> I got down the other end not long after that and then he did drop one short. Well, I got about halfway through the hook shot and *whack* it hit me on the gloves. Of course, it wasn't the leg-cutter – it was the proper short one. It was a good height for playing the pull shot, but, crikey, it wasn't the right length. I thought I might have to reassess the situation a little bit.
>
> In fact he was the only bowler that I ever considered was unhookable. The one from Thommo that you thought was short enough to hook you couldn't reach. It'd go sailing over your head – the wicketkeeper's, too. But the one that was at the right height to hook simply wasn't short enough.

One WA and Australian batsman remembers the harrowing experience of facing Thommo for the first time. It was a Sheffield Shield game in Brisbane in late 1974, just before the first Ashes Test at that ground.

Ross Edwards: We had an idea about how fast he was, and this was spelt out when we played New South Wales in Sydney the week before. They had just played Queensland and at the end of our game, while we were sitting around having a drink somebody asked Alan Turner, one of their openers, 'Thommo - how quick was he?' Turner, who is rather swarthy, went absolutely white and said, 'He's fucken quick!'

There we were, a week later in Brisbane, making our own judgement. WA batted first and as we watched Thommo our eyes were just about popping out of our heads. He *was* quick! I went in at No.4 and was at the non-striker's end, with John Inverarity waiting for Thommo. I remember thinking 'Now I'll find out how quick this bloke is'.

Usually you can hear the bowler running in, but with Thommo you couldn't because he ran in on his toes. Well, I saw Inver start to move - just as the ball hit the wicketkeeper's gloves - above his head. I thought, 'Oh jayzus, that can't be right!' Next ball Inver starts his movement earlier, this time he's three-quarters of the way up his backlift when the ball's with the keeper. I'm thinking, 'This is something outside my experience!'

Next thing I'm on strike at the beginning of a Thommo over – he bowls two no-balls and it turns out to be a 10-ball over, which is one thing you definitely don't want when you're facing him! One ball was a yorker, which flew off the inside edge of my bat and went for four before fine leg had even moved. With one ball remaining I'm thinking, 'If it's anywhere outside the stumps I'm going to let it go.' Well, it came down outside off stump, I thrust my front leg forward, it hit me on the thigh pad – and went through to hit the stumps.

Bruce Laird: I'd first seen Thommo, as a young spectator at the WACA Ground in November 1972. It was his first season, playing for New South Wales, and I watched him from side-on. I couldn't believe how far back their wicketkeeper, Brian Taber, was standing. I know everything looks quicker side-on, but from that day I knew he'd be quick.

I remember thinking at the time, 'How do you bat against that sort of pace?' Then the first time I actually faced him was in Brisbane, in a Sheffield Shield game a fortnight before the first Ashes Test of 1974–5. It was my first season for WA and the Gabba was a greentop.

While we were playing games in Adelaide, Melbourne and Sydney on the way to Brisbane we'd heard a lot about Thommo – and it was on the money: He *was* pretty terrifying.

Now we're talking blistering pace. The sort of stuff that no batsman likes to cop. No matter how good the batsman, no matter the nature of the wicket and no matter whether it's a new ball or old.

Greg Chappell: He was so quick – and so frightening – that blokes just didn't want to bat against him. There were guys literally running away. And there were guys who were normally pretty composed and solid cricketers but who were totally discombobulated when Thommo ran up and stuck the thing behind his back and let it fly.

The thing was, Thommo wasn't the best trainer in the world. His idea of a fitness program was a bit of pig shooting, a bit of fishing. Running around the oval wasn't one of his high priorities. But he was happy to bowl all day. The nets at the Gabba were so poor that he didn't bowl a single ball there in the pre-season, his only work off the long run being a few disinterested overs in club cricket.

In a trial game before his first Sheffield Shield outing he was so all over the place that Jeff Langley, who had come up from South Australia to play, was hit twice by Thommo deliveries while crouching at bat-pad. One on the leg and one on the backside. That wasn't a good look, but I was just happy to see him bowling off the long run – and to note how quick he was. I wasn't worried about the accuracy. My attitude was, he bowls so fast that we'll get 10 wickets! I satisfied myself with the thought, 'Once he gets the radar calibrated he'll be fine'.

What I found with Thommo was that his first spell of the season was generally pretty ordinary. Always frighteningly quick, but leaving a little bit to be desired, direction-wise. If I made him bowl five or six in his first spell, then his second spell would be much better and by his third spell he was fine. However, there was one time when he got to his third spell – it was with the second new ball – and he was all over the place, hardly landing the ball on the rolled-out part. We badly needed a wicket at this stage, so I ran up and asked him what was going wrong.

'Oh,' he said, 'I just can't control the swing'.

I said, 'Never mind the swing, just hold it across the seam and bowl quick, because we need a wicket'.

I was just taking off to return to the slips, confident that at least there'd be some improvement in direction, when he called me back.

'Hey, which side do you have the shiny side for the outswinger?'

I scratched my head. 'Hold the shiny side to the leg and the rough side to us in the slips – and away you go.'

'No wonder it's not going away. I've had the shiny side the wrong way.'

Another time, again the first game of a season, he was having trouble with no-balls and was all over the place. Again, I ran up from the slips and asked him what was going on.

'Mate, I've got no rhythm, I don't know what's going on ... just can't get it right.'

Feeling frustrated at this, I said, 'I don't care what you do ... short run'll do ... so long as you can make 'em play we'll get some wickets'.

I've turned to go back to my position and again he called me back. 'Hey, how many steps do I have in my run-up?'

'How the bloody hell would I know!'

'I can't remember last season, whether it was fourteen or sixteen.'

'What are you using now?'

'Sixteen'.

'Well, try fourteen and see how you go.' Sure enough it was fourteen.

Here's an example of just how quick Thommo could be. We were playing against Victoria in the poor light of a late afternoon and Mick Taylor, a handy little bat, was out there facing him. The first ball hit Mick's bat when it was still on the backswing. It gave him a helluva shock. After that he was too scared to take the bat back ... and finished up with a forward lift.

In fact, no names, but there was one player facing Thommo in a Sheffield Shield game who got one that hit the shoulder of the bat – and when it flew into the air I'm sure that from my position in the slips I heard him say 'Catch it!'

There were countless times when Dennis Lillee enjoyed teaming up with Jeff Thomson.

The dark-haired member of the Twins of Terror team remembers:

> **Dennis Lillee:** Thommo and I hardly knew each other before Brisbane, but we got on straightaway once we were in the same team. And it was just marvellous bowling down the other end to him. He was a man to put the fear of God into batsmen in any era, through pure and simple pace. It was nothing to do with guile or where the ball was going.
>
> For outright natural ability, and a bloke who didn't seem to train a lot, lived life to the full and played cricket for fun, he was amazing. He was a wonderful natural athlete, a terrifying prospect for any batsman. Off that jaunting bit of a run-up he wound up so much pace. Because he was so quick he could afford to pitch a bit fuller, but still the ball would rear up.
>
> He has always been a man of few words, almost an introvert. We often roomed together, yet we'd never talk about cricket. I used to think about these things a lot, but with Thommo it was all gut instinct. An uncomplicated guy, but, having said that, streetwise and smart. And he could turn his hand to most sports.

The man who crouched behind the wickets so many times when Thomson wound up, then unwound to release a thunderbolt, had the best seat in the house.

Rod Marsh: There were times when I thought, 'It's impossible for anyone to bowl faster'. Some say he was faster than the 160 kilometres an hour that he was measured at. I don't know, but what I *do* know is that he was faster than anyone I ever kept to.

Add to that the fact that he was able to make the ball climb from a length better than anyone I ever saw. That's what the West Indies found in 1975-6 – that a length ball could pass by their chins. That's frightening. From my point of view the worst thing about that particular series is, if you have a look at the byes: astronomical! They were going past the batsman's chin, so not a wide, then one bounce into the sightscreen. There was no hope of the keeper reaching a heap of them.

It would have been a nightmare to have to play a whole series against him. We played two state games a year against him – and that was bad enough!

There was a very high degree of respect among the batsmen who had the responsibility of taking on a rampaging Jeff Thomson, particularly on a pitch that offered a bit of bounce – and when he had a new rock in his right hand.

Viv Richards: When he found that length – basically just short of a good length – he was as good as it gets. The amount of wickets he took with balls lifting sharply off a good length was amazing. For that special delivery, no-one could match Jeff Thomson for raw, lethal pace. He was very special, you know.

Dennis Amiss: How hard was it, coping with Thommo? I wasn't around long enough! Actually, I was at a dinner, with Thommo present, some years later and was asked what it was like facing him. My answer: 'I made sure I didn't get down his end!'

John Wright: On my first trip to Australia, in 1980–81, we came up against Thommo in a warm-up game against Queensland. I opened the batting and in his first spell he was *really* quick, possibly because at the time he was pushing for a spot in the Test team. I thought to myself, 'Bloody hell ...' I'd heard all the legendary stories about him, but still it was a surprise – and I couldn't help thinking, 'How could you have faced him without a helmet?'

Of course, this was post the shoulder operation and I recall that he wasn't as quick during the rest of that game.

John Inverarity: Jeff Thomson was the fastest bowler I ever faced, so the first problem was the pace at which he was coming at you. Then there was the lift he was able to get off a length. He just got it higher than anybody else. And he was a bit harder than the orthodox bowler to pick up.

Ross Edwards: Thommo had the *fear factor*. Although no batsman's ever going to admit to being frightened, it was there. Did I ever feel for people facing him? Yes,

I did. And I remember an occasion on the 1975 tour to England when I was the only person in front of square leg when he was bowling.

Bruce Laird: The way I tried to handle his pace was to make a small back-and-across movement, not far because I liked to stay on the crease – not to commit back or forward. Probably because of my height, or lack of it, if he dropped short it was really short. To me he didn't bowl many that caught you in no-man's-land.

The thing about Thommo was that he was really quick, but he didn't move the ball like Dennis. When he pitched up you could milk him a bit. If he was short, you could flay away with the cut. If you got a bit of bat on one it was going to go.

Did I feel vulnerable when facing him without a helmet? Not really. You were perhaps more concerned about your hands, which were in the front line when you were fending one off your face. There were times at the WACA Ground, particularly if there was a bit of juice in the track, when you'd think you were behind the ball on the back foot – and it just went through you. Past your shoulders.

Geoff Howarth: We were very lucky because we faced Thommo when he was at the end of his career. Had we played him in the middle 70s we would have felt a bit more breeze coming past our nostrils. It was very easy to gain that impression from watching him on television.

But on that 1981-2 tour of New Zealand he wasn't as quick as what his reputation had indicated. What you noticed most of all was the difficulty in seeing the ball – not because of his speed, but because of his action. You only saw the ball after his bowling arm came past the perpendicular.

Thomson in his pomp was regarded by all batsmen with a rich mixture of reverence and, dare we use the word, *fear*! On the field he could be in your face, but off the field he was a different person.

Mike Brearley: Thommo came in 1981 to play at Middlesex, where I was captain, and he was a very good bloke to have with the group. He was helpful and, when he was injured, would stand in the outfield at practice and retrieve balls. A very nice fellow in an easy-going sort of way.

One of the games he did play for us was against the Australians at Lord's and he hit Graeme Wood in the ribs and was really quite upset about it. It was one thing to hit an Englishman, but another altogether to hit a fellow Aussie! When he was bowling he never said anything, just got on with the job. Though he could become quite annoyed with himself.

Bruce Laird: Thommo was pretty laconic, a great guy off the field, wouldn't hurt a flea. I never saw him get shitty with anyone. He loved kids, in fact was like a big kid himself. A practical joker, who went and bought all these tricks at a joke shop in London and would throw them around on the team bus. He used to like heavy rock – AC/DC – and would put it in the player on the bus. As far as most of us were concerned, he had shit taste in music!

He would have a few beers, but I never saw him get untidy. He was really generous and very trusting. But if he didn't like a player, he'd really get pissed off. I'm glad he and I got on so well!

Rod Marsh: Thommo wasn't a drinker. On tour he'd have a hit-out once a week – what you had to hope was that tomorrow wasn't a bowling day. It didn't matter to him. He didn't seem to care about it as much as other people would.

Ross Edwards: Thommo was a seriously good bloke, Very quiet, unassuming and not at all aggressive. In fact his bowling wasn't really aggressive ... just that he was so very fast. I'd say 'passive as a person, but dangerous as a bowler'.

Question mark

THE GREAT concern was how well – and how fast – Jeff Thomson would bowl, if and when he returned to the fold after wrecking his shoulder. Given that he had suffered such a serious, joint-shattering injury on 24 December 1976, it's a tribute to his extraordinary recuperative powers that he was even considered fit to be chosen to tour England four months later. But the man himself never gave up hope of a satisfactory recovery. 'Some people said I would never play again, but I was determined to get back to my full playing strength', he said. 'I was never going to quit.'

His advisers set Thomson a heavy workload and he threw himself into it. 'I worked really hard, even harder than I needed to work, but I made sure I did all the exercises and got myself right.' Just like Lillee, thanks to a lot of hard work Thomson made a remarkable recovery from a devastating injury, especially to his right, bowling, shoulder – a part of the body that is pivotal, literally, to a fast bowler's action. His campaign on the England tour for the 1977 Ashes series began against Kent at Canterbury in the first week of May. He had done the work and was ready to go again.

However, he was without his mate, who had stayed home to recuperate after a long, hard season. Would he still have his pace? That was the big question.

The 1977 tour of England is best forgotten by the Australians. While they were on tour news broke of a breakaway group – to be known as World Series Cricket and backed by the media mogul Kerry Packer. The cream of Australian cricket, plus a number of lesser lights, some coming out of retirement, crossed over and signed up. Complicating matters for the ill-fated England tour was the fact that many of those who had been seduced by the proposal were over there, trying to concentrate on an Ashes series. Some others of the touring party had not signed, nor been invited to sign – which did nothing for team spirit.

Of course the absence of Lillee, at that time rated the best fast bowler in the world – and an unqualified success on the wickets in England – was like a blow to the solar plexus for the tourists. Add to that all the rancour that spread like a cancer through the Australian group. Consequently, the team performed poorly.

None of that could be sheeted home to Jeff Thomson. He stood up to lead the attack like the stormtrooper that he was. He bowled a pile of overs. Four wickets in each innings in the first Test at Lord's wasn't enough to secure victory. That match was drawn, but the Australians were humbled as the next three Tests were won handsomely by the home side.

Many hours were lost through rain in the final Test at The Oval and Thomson's five wickets for the game gave him 23 for the series at 25.34. The best by an Australian on that tour. His comeback from such a shocking injury had been nothing short of stunning. But there was little to cheer the slingshot speedster as he packed his bags to head for home in Queensland. And although the slow, soft English wickets were neither to his liking, nor conducive to his bowling, there were doubts as to whether he was the bowler he had been.

> **Ian Chappell:** I sort of suspected that he might not be quite the same again – and I don't think he ever was. The big change I noticed was in the run-up. He started to actually *run* in – unlike the shuffle of previously. He still had his moments, though.

Greg Chappell: It was tragic, really. We'll never know just how good Thommo could have been. He had three and a bit series and achieved so much – while promising so much more.

Rod Marsh: The initial feelings were of great concern. We didn't realise how bad his shoulder was. It was gone. I felt then that he may never come back, and when he did it was quite sad to see that he didn't regain his full pace. I mean, he was still sharp at times.

Greg Chappell: He had to run in harder, to generate momentum. He got the velocity sometimes, but he'd lost the bounce. The ball that was pitched just short of a length and was going through chest high now was only getting up bail high. That was a huge difference. Still, there were a few really quick spells after that – one of them in that Test match in Barbados, when he got really angry.

The great divide

THE TWINS of Terror were high on the list for the World Series Cricket recruiters. Dennis Lillee was a shoe-in, even more so given his long period of rest through the time of the troubled Ashes tour in England. He most certainly would be a vitally important cog in the wheel for the WSC Australian side – which was to be led by his greatest supporter, a resurgent Ian Chappell.

Naturally, WSC wanted the dream pairing of Jeff Thomson with Lillee for the 1977–78 summer. However, Thomson was a different case. They wanted to see if the blond tearaway would recover from his serious shoulder surgery. So they waited – until he was declared fit for the Ashes tour. Then they came knocking on his door. Thomson was delighted and signed up with alacrity, a three-year deal.

Inevitably news of the breakaway group hit the newsstands in the early stages of the England tour. And with that news was the story that Thomson and his pal, Lillee, were to be in the front row when the photos were taken. While one of the 'team' had his feet up back in Perth, the other was embroiled in doing his bit to hold together a group that was in danger of disintegrating under the pressures brought about by the WSC news.

Then, late in July it emerged that one of the twins would be missing from the new order. Thomson was painted into a corner by a long-term contract with a Brisbane radio station. His payment there – worth much more than he was getting from cricket – was contingent upon playing for, or at least being available for, Australia. Reluctantly, he withdrew from WSC. The traditional cricket world breathed a heavy sigh of relief. Was the Thomson decision to pull out an indication that others might break ranks? News of the unexpected withdrawal came during the third Test at Trent Bridge and, such was the joy among the traditional crowd that Thomson, so often seen as a brigand by the English, was applauded as he walked out to bat.

These were very tough times, when animosity abounded, when former heroes quickly became villains, when teammates became enemies. But the development of WSC was a watershed for the game and, despite all the acrimony at the time, history has looked upon it kindly, seeing it as the break that modernised the game, brought it to a bigger audience – and paid players properly, thus keeping the best in the game for longer. It was hugely beneficial from that time on for those good enough to play at representative level. Rather than often actually *losing* money to play for their country, they began to enjoy their pay packets.

Spare a thought, if you will, for Thomson. For him it was a case of having mislaid a winning Lotto ticket. He had ended the shaky series in England and now traditional cricket would be his master for the foreseeable future. That meant in the coming season, a series against India – with the home side to miss 30 players from the selectors' list, including virtually all the best players. Over the next two years a raft of players would be handed a baggy green cap that in normal circumstances never would have come their way.

On the other hand, for Lillee and the other rebels it was a step into the great unknown. He would be embarking on an exciting adventure in which at long last he would be paid a salary commensurate to his value as an international superstar of his sport. Pitting his immeasurable skills against either the West Indies or a World XI, both chock-full of great players, he tore into action with a determined purpose. From a total of 14 Supertests he bagged 67 wickets at 26.94.

The pity was that there was frequently barely a crowd at the ground to witness his exploits.

Meanwhile, under the fill-in captaincy of the veteran Bob Simpson, Thomson helped Australia to victory in the first two Tests against India. The visitors won the next two and in the decider Thomson was into his fourth over – having already taken two wickets – when he strained a hamstring muscle. Despite his absence the young Australian side won the day and the series. A triumph for youth, led by experience.

Soon after it was off to the West Indies, where Simpson and his men were put to the sword by a full-strength West Indies in the first two encounters, then won the third in a thrilling finish. The fourth was lost after a disastrous fourth-innings effort, the fifth a draw. Again Thomson was the leading wicket-taker, with 22 wickets at just over 23 runs per wicket. For him, it was time now for a change. He'd had enough of playing first fiddle in a minor orchestra. But one spell of bowling in that series left indelible memories in the minds of cricket aficionados.

That one day

THE SCENE is Bridgetown, Barbados, March 1978 – the second Test of a series that started out with a horrible imbalance between the two sides. Australia fielded a team minus all of its players who had moved to World Series Cricket; the West Indies were at full strength, brimming with talent, verging on forging the dominance that would see them rule international cricket in the 1980s and beyond.

In the first Test at Port of Spain, Trinidad, Andy Roberts, Colin Croft and Joel Garner blitzed the inexperienced Australian line-up and, when the same attack threatened for the second encounter, Thomson got his dander up. Australia batted first and this time did a little better, compiling 250. Then the mighty West Indies batting line-up prepared to go to work against a largely depleted Australian attack: Thomson backed up by the medium-fast pace of Wayne Clark, medium-pacer Gary Cosier and spinners Jim Higgs and Bruce Yardley.

Desmond Haynes and Gordon Greenidge, that great opening pair, came out through the gate. There was a confident air about the seasoned campaigners as they strode towards the middle. Jeffrey Robert Thomson was standing in an aggressive pose at the top of his run-up. Teammate Clark, from his position at fine leg, sensed something special was in the wind. 'Thommo was out to make a statement. It was as though he wanted to kill someone. A contest between gladiators, no holding back on either side.' From the outset, there was a suggestion that Thomson would be seeking to readjust the balance – a full-strength side versus what was largely a third Australian XI. Things soon hotted up.

Thomson explains: 'It all started when I was bowling to Gordon Greenidge and he gloved one to gully but was given not out. Then he rubbed his shoulder. I was really pissed off and said, "Right, if that's the way you want to play, look out!" I just cranked it right up and, as it happened, on that day something within told me to just lope in as I used to and it worked perfectly. My rhythm was terrific and I bowled as quick as I had ever bowled.'

Then Thomson dismissed Greenidge – which brought Viv Richards to the crease. 'A confrontation was looming', the fired-up quickie said, looking back on a pivotal moment. 'When you're on fire and he is, too, it's something like a shootout, a question of who's going to break first.' Teammate Yardley added, 'it was clear from the outset that Viv thought the only way forward would be to go on an all-out attack. It was do or die.'

It truly was high drama at Kensington Oval. Richards was hit a painful blow on the pads first ball. A screamer whistled past the West Indian's unprotected head. Then a spilled chance at backward square leg as the batsman was hit on the gloves by another steepling flier. Two heavyweights were slugging it out: Thomson fired up and bowling at a scorching pace; Viv looking to fight fire with fire.

Another short one. This time Viv owned it, crashing it over the mid-wicket boundary. Then another point to the crazed batsman, one back over the bowler's head for four. A play-and-miss outside off stump and Thomson had had enough. 'I thought, "Fuck this, I'm going high again." I put everything I had into it, he went for it and was caught at fine leg.' A fine running, diving catch by Clark – one he knew he just *had* to take.

After that sensational spell, when Thomson claimed Greenidge, Richards and Alvin Kallicharran in the space of 41 balls, Bob Simpson, captain of the Australian team, said, 'Thommo clearly showed today who is the fastest bowler in the Caribbean – and that means the fastest in the world. Just looking at the way the ball was hitting the wicketkeeper's gloves, it was so much quicker than anything else. What Thommo also showed us was that the West Indian batsmen aren't too keen on the really quick stuff, either.'

John Benaud, brother of Richie, himself a three-time Australian Test cricketer who then became a national selector, was looking on in awe from his seat on the safe side of the boundary, immortalising proceedings as a journalist. He wrote, 'My favourite Thommo moment was in the Barbados Test of 1977–78, when I saw him tear into Greenidge, Haynes, Richards, Kallicharran and Lloyd. If those elite batsmen were not intimidated by his pace and aggression, then body language is a flawed yardstick. Thommo took 6–77 off 13 overs in that one innings. Think about it – a wicket every two overs!'

If nothing else, Jeff Thomson possesses a very wry sense of humour. At the end of play that day he said, 'That was gutsy, the way Gordon rubbed his shoulder, because his broken hand must have been hurting like hell'.

What speeds did the slingshot superstar rack up that day? Those who were there – the cricket-hardened Kensington Oval crowd included – were in awe. From his position in the gully, Australian batsman Craig Serjeant said Thomson's second ball to Richards was the quickest he'd ever seen. The evidence strongly suggests he had peaked that magical day at a speed well over the 160 kilometres an hour mark. Just ask the West Indies captain, Clive Lloyd. He said afterwards that this was the fastest new-ball bowling he'd ever seen. And the legend lived on.

Ian Chappell: When World Series Cricket was in Barbados in 1979, the locals who'd been there for years and years – and had seen them all – were on hand. You'd go up and ask them 'Who's the fastest bowler you've ever seen?' and they'd say, 'Ooh, that Jeffrey Robert Thomson, man, he got pace like fire'. They'd seen the fabled spell he bowled at the ground to Gordon Greenidge and Viv Richards when the Australian Test team had been there under Bob Simpson.

The quickest

WE DO KNOW when and where the 'Rawalpindi Express' – Pakistan's Shoaib Akhtar – bowled what is officially considered to be the fastest ball sent down in a game of cricket. It was 22 February at the picturesque Newlands ground at Cape Town in South Africa, during the 2003 World Cup. Akhtar sent down a lightning bolt to England's Nick Knight and became the first to record a delivery at more than the magical 100 miles an hour (160 kilometres an hour) in an official ICC match. The speed was 161.3 km/h.

What we don't know is when, where and how fast was Jeff Thomson's quickest. They just didn't have the recording facilities when Thomson was in full flight. But we do know that he was recorded at 160.6 km/h by what was considered then to have been a reliable method in December 1975. This occurred at the WACA Ground in Perth, in match conditions, during the second Test against the West Indies.

But might he have, as was suggested in the previous chapter, actually been out beyond that mark on other occasions? There are those who think – and would bet – that, at his fastest, he could well have been in the 170s. For a start, there's Thomson himself; the batsmen who faced him, including Viv Richards, Dennis Amiss and Greg Chappell; the keepers who kept to him – Rod Marsh and John Maclean; and the bowlers vying for the title, notably Michael Holding.

Mirror, mirror on the wall, who was the fastest of them all? Unfortunately (or is it happily, for it leaves room for constant conjecture?), we will never know, simply because the method of measuring a bowler's velocity was developed only quite recently, in terms of cricket's long history – long after the likes of Harold Larwood and Frank Tyson set tongues wagging with their frightening exploits. Add to that the fact that there has even been much conjecture about the validity of the measuring method, which involves the use of radar-gun technology. Also questions are raised about the measurement of a fuller-pitched delivery, compared with a short one. It often seems that the full-pitched delivery registers greater speed. Plus, there's the matter of where in its flight the ball is picked up by the radar. It seems that the latter question may have an answer – thanks to a chance discussion at a social gathering in Adelaide.

> **Greg Chappell:** Some years ago now I was at this function and the subject of Brett Lee being timed at more than 160 was raised. When asked for my opinion, I said I was convinced that Brett wasn't as fast as that. As

it turned out, there were some policemen in the group and one of them said, 'Well, has there been anyone quicker?'

I said, 'I'm here to tell you that Thommo was clocked at 160, but there was a big difference between his 160 and Brett Lee's 160!'

Then one of the policemen piped up and said, 'Oh, different technology'.

'What do you mean?'

He said, 'In the old days the technology was picking the speed up at the end of the ball's travel, whereas now they pick it up as it leaves the bowler's hand. If Thommo was timed at 160 by the old measurement, he'd be 170 today!'

I have to say he *was* faster than 160. I mean I faced him in the nets and even when he wasn't flat out he was still quicker than anyone else.

A Channel Nine WSC special from the late 1970s backs this up. Measuring the bowlers in a competition to see who was fastest, Thomson was. He was registering just above 140, his fastest 147.9. That's the speed Glenn McGrath got to at his quickest – and no-one thinks McGrath was in Thomson's league for pace. Funny thing is, Thommo had been having a beer before he was asked to join in the competition. This was during the time he was playing for neither the Test team nor WSC. And it was almost 100 degrees in the old measure.

This talk questioning the method of recording speed is music to Jeff Thomson's ears. He has long contended that the method of measuring speed when he bowled is not the same as the method today – meaning we are not comparing apples with apples. 'When they timed me around the 161 mark, that was done at the batting end. These guys today are timed at the bowler's end. Who's standing two metres in front of a bowler facing the ball? Nobody. They're trying to make them look as quick as us. We were timed further down the pitch, where it slows down. If they had timed me out of the hand, it would have been close to 180.'

Despite that, Thomson still rates among the quickest ever measured. The record books have it thus:

Shoaib Akhtar (Pakistan 2003)	161.3
Brett Lee (Australia 2005)	161.3
Shaun Tait (Australia 2010)	161.3
Jeff Thomson (Australia 1975)	160.6
Andy Roberts (West Indies 1975)	159.5

It is interesting to note that the top three in the current fastest ladder were measured in the current millennium. Thomson and Roberts were recorded long before that. In the minds of those who played with and against Thomson, he *was* bloody quick. Former Australian captain Kim Hughes said, 'He was as far ahead in terms of speed as Bradman was ahead of the rest as a batsman. At his fastest he would have been around 170. One day in the mid–70s at the WACA Ground, John Maclean (the Queensland wicketkeeper) was standing so far back you'd have been excused for thinking he was in another game!'

Maclean would know as well as anyone just how fast Thomson was. 'I recall two times for Queensland when he really let rip. In Brisbane against Victoria, late in the afternoon he was so fast that for them it was seriously protection of your life. Another day in Sydney, they were five for 160-odd. Something got him fired up – and I'm going back about a metre every ball. Then he started tailing them in and he cleaned them up for less than 200. He had talked about "blood on the pitch". Well it was lucky there was none that day.'

Viv Richards, soon to become one of the world's premier batsmen, emerged more than a little bruised from that tough baptism against Thomson in the 1975–76 series. 'Lillee and Thomson were very quick, very quick. For that very special delivery nobody could match Thommo for raw, lethal pace. Once when I was batting with Lawrence Rowe he was hit on the head and when I went up to him he said he didn't see it.'

> **Rod Marsh:** Some say he was faster than the 160 he was measured at. I don't know, but what I *do* know is that he was faster than anyone I ever kept to.
>
> **Ian Chappell:** Thommo remains the quickest I've ever seen – not that much faster than Michael Holding, but far and away the most lethal because of that ability, particularly in Australia, to get the ball throat-high from just short of a length. Think of this, you had about 0.47 of a second to react once he delivered. It didn't allow you time to change your shot. If your first choice was wrong, you had to hope your luck was in.

Greg Chappell: Who was the quickest? I'm asked the question often and I repeat what I heard Michael Holding say, 'We were all quick on our day, but then there was Thommo – he was in a class of his own'.

Dennis Amiss: The fastest? Obviously Thommo – and for those two-and-a-half years, the most frightening. Yes, with Michael Holding, who was dynamite in 1976. Plus, Malcolm Marshall, who could be very slippery when he wanted to be. Thommo hit the wicket harder than any bowler I faced.

John Wright: The two guys who stood out to me in terms of pace were Jeff Thomson and Michael Holding. No question. To me they were a yard above everyone else – and there were some quick people around in those days.

Thomson ... Holding ... the fastest? With that catapult action, Thommo hid the ball till the last moment, whereas with Michael you saw the ball right through the action. You had to take that into account.

In an article Phil Derriman wrote for the Fairfax newspapers he quoted the England player Mike Selvey on the first ball he saw Jeff Thomson bowl. 'It was very fast and pitched just short of a length before taking off like a missile, searing past Tony Greig's nose and Rod Marsh's despairing leap before splintering into the sightscreen. My flesh went cold.'

As for the man himself, well it was simple: 'The only way I can bowl is flat out.' He also had no doubt who was the fastest. 'The boys will tell you I bowled a lot faster [than 160]. I'm not just an old guy reminiscing, but I bowled miles quicker than that. I know what I did. I know the results. I know what I hit, the bones I broke and the guys who were too scared to play shots.'

Together again

GOING INTO the 1978–79 season, WSC was showing signs of thriving while the Australian Cricket Board was praying for a successful series against England to save its position. But Jeff Thomson was far from committed to the cause of the traditional game. He wanted to be reunited with his pal Lillee – sooner, rather than later. He played just one game for Queensland at the start of the season, a one-day affair against South Australia, and took 6–18, bowling as fast as ever. But then he stepped away. He became embroiled in court cases, all the time making it clear that he wanted out of his ACB contract and into the one he had signed to play for WSC.

Meanwhile, Dennis Lillee was leading the WSC attack in four Supertests, two each against the World XI and the West Indies. Despite the mountain he had to climb, bowling day in, day out to the likes of Barry Richards, Viv Richards, Zaheer Abbas, Gordon Greenidge, Clive Lloyd and Javed Miandad, once again the champion stood up to be counted. He ended the season with 23 wickets at 16.60.

Soon, things were happening behind the scenes that would result in Thomson's wishes coming true, rather earlier than he might have hoped. He had steadfastly remained out of action for Australia and Queensland after that first one-dayer at the start of the season. Late in the season, the second Australian summer of WSC, the word 'compromise' started floating about in the ether. In a move that surprised most observers, the ACB announced a decision to release Thomson from his contract. He was free to do what he had signed a contract to do a couple of years before: head the WSC attack with Dennis Lillee.

As luck would have it, the WSC troupe was due to fly out to the Caribbean, for a five-Supertest series against the mighty West Indies. The burly New South Wales quick Len Pascoe, who happened to be Thomson's best mate from their days together at Punchbowl Boys High and then at District club Bankstown, would provide support to what was arguably Australia's greatest-ever new-ball pairing.

Lillee was thrilled to be back in harness with Thomson. 'It was great working with him again,' he said, 'even though he was under-prepared for all the bowling that was asked of him. I must say that his presence was heaven-sent for me – and the side, of course'. Being there was all Thomson had expected it would be. 'Boy did I enjoy this series', he said, 'I was with a good committed team. Dennis, Lennie (Pascoe), Mick (Malone) and myself would give it to the Windies. It was all-out war and we wanted to beat them on their home soil.'

So it was that the familiar pairing – Lillee and Thomson – who opened fire in the first Supertest, at Kingston, Jamaica.

Lillee took eight wickets and Thomson three, but the Australians were skittled. Clive Lloyd had put his plan into action – the Windies boasted a formidable four-man pace attack of Andy Roberts, Michael Holding, Colin Croft and Wayne Daniel. The second Test was abandoned as a draw after a riot broke out, Thomson running into form with three wickets in the first innings, the same as Lillee. It was one that got away from Australia, who had more than a sniff of victory when the game was called off.

At Trinidad for the third Supertest, Thomson played a strong hand in a narrow victory by Australia. In the West Indies first innings he bagged Roy Fredericks, Lawrence Rowe, Viv Richards and Clive Lloyd on his way to figures of 5–78, which would turn out to be his best return in a Supertest.

The fourth Supertest, at Guyana, was abandoned without a ball being bowled, thanks to a riot in the stands, and declared a draw. In the rescheduled three-day game Thomson was again among the wickets, taking four including Fredericks, Rowe and Richards. The fifth, at Antigua, was also drawn, this time Lillee claiming four in the West Indies' only innings.

Five games, two of them curtailed by crowd behaviour. The series was tied one-all. Lillee led the way with 23 wickets at 28.39; Thomson second with 16 at 29.75. Lillee looked back with mixed feelings. 'The riots, the tight schedule and the fact that it came hard on the heels of a really tough summer back home certainly coloured my time in the Caribbean.' Thomson loved it. 'This was the toughest cricket of my career. Talk about war on the cricket field.'

The rebel Australians returned home in mid-April and throughout the rest of the month and into May speculation about a peace pact between the two warring factions – the Australian Cricket Board and Kerry Packer's World Series Cricket – bubbled away. The murmurings turned into something more than that when the cricket media were summoned mid-afternoon on 30 May 1979 to the Victorian Cricket Association's boardroom. The gathered throng suspected they knew what was coming – and were not disappointed. This was the day cricket called a truce.

ACB chairman Bob Parish and Lynton Taylor, representing WSC, were there to announce the end of hostilities. Compromise. Parish read a prepared statement setting out the terms, which included the pot of gold at the end of the rainbow, as far as Kerry Packer was concerned: the right to telecast cricket on the Channel Nine Network, a right that continues nearly four decades later – more than ten years after Packer went to meet his maker. There were other concessions from both sides and Parish ended his dissertation with the words: 'The Board is unanimously of the opinion that its decision to accept the proposal from PBL (Publishing and Broadcasting Limited, on behalf of the Nine Network) is in the best interests of Australian and international cricket'.

As far as Lillee and Thomson were concerned, and for that matter all the Australians who had played for WSC, it was peace but with a price. The team for the second World

Cup one-day series, again to be played in England, had been chosen and would not be changed to include 'rebel' players. Without them the Australian World Cup campaign would be a fizzer.

PART III
BREAKING THE PARTNERSHIP

Ups and downs

WHEN AUSTRALIAN cricket settled back into a routine following the great compromise, Greg Chappell returned to the captaincy of the Test team, with Kim Hughes, who had taken over as leader in the latter stages of his absence, as deputy. Many, the author included, felt that Rod Marsh deserved that position. It was a period of distillation as those from the WSC list were thrown in the melting pot with those who had enjoyed the ride with the traditional side.

Going into the 1979–80 season, with a split tour of three Tests each against the West Indies and England, speedster Rod Hogg and left-armer Geoff Dymock, along with Lillee, Thomson and Len Pascoe from WSC, were putting their hands up for a game. It turned out the crowded board would make things difficult for Thomson. However, he was chosen to join Lillee and Hogg for the first Test, against the West Indies at the Gabba. Lillee and Thomson took four wickets each as the game was drawn. Thomson, whose wickets were Haynes, Greenidge, Kallicharran and keeper Deryck Murray, bowled first change in Brisbane in both innings – and was not selected for the next two Tests, which the Windies won comprehensively.

Hogg lost his spot to injury, and Dymock opened the bowling with Lillee against England in Perth – but Thomson was back in the team. Strangely, in both innings of this encounter Thomson was used at *second* change, after Lillee, Dymock and *Greg Chappell*. A total of 33 overs produced three Thomson wickets to Lillee's six for the game. Dymock was the hero of a win for Australia, with nine wickets.

This Test was to become known as the 'aluminium bat game'. Lillee took to the crease carrying an aluminium bat, which he was marketing with a Perth friend. He had faced four balls with the bat when England captain Mike Brearley asked the umpire to order Lillee to replace it with a wooden bat, because, he said, this one was damaging the ball. After more than ten minutes' haggling over the issue, Lillee threw the bat away in disgust, took a wooden blade and the game continued. There would be repercussions.

> **Mike Brearley:** When Dennis came out to bowl after that, he got Geoff Boycott out for a duck – and Geoff complained to me that we had stirred Dennis up and made him bowl faster!

Clearly the selectors had Thomson in the sights of their guns. The Perth game was his last at the top level in 1979–80. Lillee played all six Tests that summer. He worked hard for 12 wickets in the three games against the talent-laden West Indies, but dominated against England. In the third Test against the English he bowled Australia to victory –

and a 3–0 series whitewash – with an 11-wicket haul at, you guessed it, the MCG.

This gave the gathering veteran a staggering total of 35 scalps from the six Tests. And when he bowled John Lever in the first innings at the MCG he became the second-fastest Australian, behind leg-spinning whiz Clarrie Grimmett, to capture 200 Test wickets. Lillee reached the milestone in his 38th Test, Grimmett in his 36th.

Plus, the 11 wickets for the game drew out this incredible Lillee statistic for the MCG: in nine Tests, to that stage, he had captured 58 wickets at an average of 6.44 per Test, five wickets in an innings six times and ten wickets in a match three times. Remember, in those days, before the introduction of drop-in wickets at the famous venue, the MCG track was rarely helpful to the quicks – the pounding of football sprigs through to the end of September meaning the absence of grass cover that tends to make a fast bowler smile. All of which makes Lillee's returns on the ground even more spectacular.

Thomson played out the season with Queensland, gathering 33 wickets at 19.21 from six outings. Those numbers would seem good enough to gain him a place in the touring party for the Centenary Test at Lord's, at the end of August – but the selectors did not see it that way. It was Pascoe, not Thomson, who would join Lillee with the new ball. Pascoe felt Thomson should have been chosen and, such was the bond of friendship between the two, that Len told his pal he was withdrawing with a 'pulled hamstring'. Thomson was having none of that. 'You do that, Lennie,' he said, 'and I've pulled a hamstring as well.'

Sadly, for all the heraldry and drum-beating, it was the fickle English weather that won the day at Lord's. In England's first innings Lillee claimed four wickets, Pascoe five. The two had one each in the second as the home side played out the draw.

And so to the 1980–81 season. Thomson was again unable to impress the national selectors – despite his 36 wickets for Queensland at 25.38. But the gathering years were doing Dennis Lillee no harm. Going into the 1980–81 season he was 31 years old and into the *veteran* classification, but it turned out to be another vintage summer. As Thomson toiled away for Queensland, Australia played three Tests each against New Zealand and India and the home side used Lillee with Hogg and Pascoe. Operating off a shortened run and bowling mainly within himself, Lillee mostly called the shots through the summer. He claimed a total of 35 wickets in the six games – and in the final game of the season, at the MCG, he broke Richie Benaud's Australian record of 248 Test wickets.

As good as all of that was, there was more to come soon after for the ageing champion, during the 1981 tour to England, which had its ups and downs for the Australians. There were six Tests, and Lillee played them all under the duress of a long-running bout of viral pneumonia. He shunned practice games and work in the nets, preserving himself for the big stuff, when he bowled off an even shorter run-up and regularly took a bag of wickets using an armoury of exquisite skills. Lillee finished with the wonderful total of 39 wickets, bowling in tandem with WA teammate Terry Alderman, who took 42.

Despite those joint heroics, England won the series. Largely thanks to Ian Botham, who scored more runs and took more wickets than any other teammate. Botham was a true matchwinner, a bull of a man who took the game by the scruff of the neck. He was true to his methods in the third Test at Leeds. At the crease when England, having followed on, were 7–135 and still needing 93 runs to avoid an innings defeat, Botham let loose, smashing the Australians all over the park to set up an amazing victory. Needing only 130 to win, Australia were dismissed for 111.

Controversy dogs the story of that game. Lillee and Marsh had taken up the extraordinarily generous odds of 500–1 on England winning the game, set by bookmakers on the fourth day when the home side's chances were, indeed, a shade the other side of nil. As Greg Chappell must live with his 'underarm ball' decision, the two West Australians have to live with the fact that they had a wager on the opposition – a combined 15 pounds – and won.

That aside, the series was also fraught with personality conflicts, involving Lillee, Marsh and Kim Hughes, who was captain in the absence of the non-touring Greg Chappell. None of this would have happened had Marsh been appointed Australia's captain – ahead of Hughes, who was his junior in the WA side that Marsh had led brilliantly before the game was turned upside-down by the advent of World Series Cricket.

The Twins of Terror were reunited for all three Tests of the home series against Pakistan at the start of the 1981–82 season. But while Lillee thrived, with a total of 15 wickets, Thomson claimed only six. A blot on the series was Lillee's stoush with Javed Miandad during the Perth Test. It was a case of two confrontational personalities clashing, and resulted in an unseemly sight as umpire Tony Crafter came between them, Lillee shaping up in a boxer's stance while Miandad raised his bat above his head with 'attack' written all over it. As both Lillee and his captain, Greg Chappell, would later reveal, the Pakistani had jabbed Lillee with his bat when running past – an act that the recipient couldn't abide.

It is worthy of note that in the third Test – at the MCG – Lillee went wicketless. So, too, did Thomson. It would be the only time in a completed Test that the Twins of Terror failed to produce a wicket between them.

For a totally different story, in the case of Lillee, fast forward a fortnight. Same venue – the MCG – different team, the West Indies, beginning a three-Test series. This time without Thomson alongside him, Lillee set the ground ablaze. On day one, Australia struggled against the fire of the Holding, Roberts, Croft and Garner onslaught. Without a breathtaking Kim Hughes century – as fine an innings as you'll ever see – Australia, all out for 198, would have been out of the game. Hughes had relinquished the head role to Greg Chappell, in the captaincy merry-go-round that marred the team.

Enter Dennis Keith Lillee. Alderman opened the bowling with him and took the first wicket (Faoud Bacchus), then Lillee stormed in shortly before stumps with a match-defining burst. He had Desmond Haynes caught and nightwatchman Croft lbw, bringing the man Croft was sent out to protect to the crease. Snorting like a wounded bull, Lillee produced one of the best deliveries of his decorated career – to crash through Viv Richards' defences and bowl him. Stumps, West Indies 4–10.

On the second day the tourists put up stubborn resistance. Clive Lloyd went, to the spin of Bruce Yardley, bringing wicketkeeper Jeff Dujon to the firing line. He and Larry Gomes had put on 72 when history beckoned for Lillee. He had Dujon caught in the deep to equal Lance Gibbs's world record of 309 Test wickets. Then Gomes edged one to Greg Chappell in the cordon – and, just like that, the record changed hands. Lillee had seven wickets in the first innings, three in the second and Australia won a game against the odds, thanks largely to one of his greatest individual performances.

Lillee was then joined by Thomson for the remaining two Tests against the West Indies. At the SCG Lillee took a total of six wickets (from 59 overs all up), Thomson three in the first innings. It was as though Lillee's body was calling for a breather in the third Test, at the Adelaide Oval. He ran foul of groin problems, bowled only 8.5 overs for the game, and failed to claim a wicket. Thomson meanwhile took six, and the three-match series was split, one Test each.

'A captain's dream, a batsman's nightmare'

Lillee was purposeful, aggressive, abrasive, confident and destructive, the one fast bowler who was respected but also mostly hated by all. And that was probably what drew me to him. He was the bowler I wanted to be. – **Colin Croft, 27 Tests for the West Indies.**

THE WORD that best summarises Dennis Keith Lillee is the word 'dedication'. For he is an athlete who wrung every drop out of the gift of his body, his ability – and the opportunities they afforded him. He was dedicated in the first instance to bowling as fast as he could. This was before his back injury. After that he was dedicated to his year-long recovery; dedicated to his craft, modifying his action more than once; and dedicated to his team and teammates.

The author played a lot of cricket with him for Western Australia and offers this ultimate tribute: he set out, without fail, to make his first ball of the day his best of the day, to be equalled only by his last ball of the day. And when you run in a long way and shake the very bones of your body with the crashing effort after effort of bowling fast on a hot summer's day ... that takes some doing. Never mind the nature of the wicket, the quality of the batting, the number of near misses and dropped catches or the state of the game.

He was perennially a man on a mission. Take that back to when he was a *boy* on a mission. Years before he made his first splash in the Test arena, in the Adelaide Test of the

1970–71 Ashes series, this fellow was making his mark. In Perth cricket circles you heard about 'this kid Lillee' long before you set eyes on him. His work ethic as an under-age player was such that when the others were going home after practice sessions, he'd be out running laps.

Ian Chappell: Certainly I'd heard a bit about Dennis before I actually saw him. We were in India and South Africa in 1969-70 when he broke into first-class cricket. He got a pile of wickets against [my team] South Australia – including 7-36 in the Perth game. I remember seeing Les Favell before the next season began and him going on and on about how quick this Lillee was. And Les was no slouch against something fast, so that gave me a bit of an inkling.

I remember vividly his Test debut, in Adelaide, January 1971. He made a real impression on me for his pace but probably the most important thing was his ability to swing the ball away from the right-handers. He took 5-84 in the first innings and really troubled the English batsmen.

Rod Marsh: When he came on the scene he was a tearaway and none of the other Australian bowlers at the time were with him in terms of pace. At that stage in his career he was wild. By that I mean his action wasn't refined, his arms and legs were all over the place, but he was a *proper* fast bowler. Just ran in and bowled as fast as he could. In England in 1972 he was rapid. At Lord's, when Bob Massie took eight wickets in each innings he got the other four and he bowled very fast.

John Inverarity: I remember him arriving on the scene for Western Australia. Standing in the slips and making inevitable comparisons with Graham McKenzie, for whom I had the highest regard. I thought he was better than Garth, which was high praise indeed.

Ross Edwards: I first played against him in one of his first grade games. It was at the Perth club's home ground, Lathlain Park, on the flattest deck you've ever seen ... and I made a hundred. That day he was quick, but erratic. A young, wild kid – that was all. He had natural speed, but because he was all over the place he wasn't at all dangerous.

The second time was in a state trial game, when he kept pitching up half-volleys to me – almost as though he was wanting to get me in the state side. The third time was when I played for New South Wales after World Series Cricket. This was in Sydney and I knew what he was trying to do – working away to get me caught in slips or gully. Eventually he got me out.

Bruce Laird: I faced him in a Perth first-grade game when he was 18. He ran in for miles and just bowled as quick as he could. And even at that age he was bloody scary. There were no helmets and he got them through all right. As he matured as a bowler, he gave very few chances for a batsman to get on the front foot with purpose – and he was able to swing it.

John Wright: Dennis actually bowled to me as a 15-year-old! It happened when he came over with the Australia B side in 1970. When they played in Christchurch my uncle, Sir Alan Wright, who had a farm nearby and was a member of the New Zealand Cricket Council, hosted the Aussies for a day out. My father and I went up for the occasion.

There were other kids there and we were playing a bit of knock-up cricket on the lawn with a tennis ball, when Dennis came across and bowled a few balls at me. The next time he bowled at me was on our 1980–81 tour to Australia. He was in the twilight of his career, but he was still nippy and able to get a bit of bounce.

Dennis was a helluva bloke to play against. He was aggressive on the field, but I got on really well with him. I mean, we were a mob of youngsters and learnt a lot by mixing with the Australians, particularly during the one-day series after the Tests.

Through it all he was a very generous competitor, probably a bit mellow towards the end of his career, and he and I became good mates. I remember asking him on one occasion what he looked for in an opening batsman. The response: knowing where your off stump is; good body language; looking confident (we were young and perhaps a little overawed); and strong off the back foot. That was really interesting.

Not surprisingly, up there in the Dennis Lillee fan club was Jeff Thomson. He singled out his partner's *will* – a common theme among those who've ever been close enough to make real judgement. 'He never thought anything was impossible. Always wanted to win. On the contrary I'd be a bit of sleeping tiger. If Dennis sensed that, he used to wind me up. His determination would stand out and he was aggressive, always full-on. Without him it would've made my work twice as hard.'

Ian Chappell: I never once recall hearing Dennis ask for a fieldsman to be moved into a defensive position after runs had been taken from his bowling. He was more likely to ask for the bat-pad to be moved a yard closer or an extra slip to be added. Dennis was only interested in taking wickets and he was never interested in their cost.

John Inverarity: It was a pleasure to captain him [at Western Australia]. I don't think there was ever a time when he was other than wanting to bowl – and after he'd bowled a lot in the day and the new ball was due at half-past five, you looked in his direction and he was nodding and already warming up. I can't imagine a better player to captain.

And, like all of his many teammates down the years, I was just happy to be on the same side as Dennis. At one stage I was living in England and due to return home to Perth. Dennis contacted me and asked if I'd like to play club cricket with him at Melville when I got home.

I thought, 'Well, I'd rather be on the same side than against him ...' So the answer was yes.

Bruce Laird: Dennis was a great competitor. Mind you, he's like that with everything he does. He's like a dog with a bone. He won't let go! If he says he's going to do something for you, he'll do it. No matter what it takes. That was reflected in his bowling. He had such drive. Determination. As well as being skilful and quick.

Ross Edwards: He had a fantastic cricket brain. A lot of that was due to his natural inclination to learn – and the main teacher was Ian Chappell. You wouldn't see Ian run up from the slips to talk to FOT, but before the match, at lunchtime and at tea time you'd find him sitting down talking to him. Getting him – and the other bowlers – to *think*.

He was never *really* quick – though he could get one out every now and then – but he learnt to bowl as quick as he wanted to in the given circumstances. And he bowled with great intelligence. When things weren't going well, he'd cut his speed down and be more of a stock bowler. He would try things out, sometimes ridiculous things. But if he got a wicket, the change was monumental: all of a sudden he'd go into *rage* mode. And he was quick when that happened.

Ian Chappell: I've always described Dennis as a captain's dream and a batsman's nightmare. There were a few times when I was accused of over-bowling him and I've replied, 'Have you ever tried to take a bone off a Doberman?'

I remember in the last World Series Cricket series, in the Caribbean, we were playing in Trinidad, where the grass on the track was pretty sparse and the weather was up there with Brisbane in terms of humidity. Dust was coming up when you ran in. I had bowled Dennis for a long spell, longer than I had realised, and when I went up to him I found he couldn't talk. I thought, 'Heck, I've overdone it!'

He was the best bowler I ever saw. He was fast, fiery and fearsome. He also had all the tools, which he kept finely tuned by training extremely hard – *and* he was a fast learner. On top of that, he was the most determined cricketer I've come across. If any batsman ever mastered Dennis's bowling (which was rare), he still had to overcome his iron will.

Lillee is universally respected and admired throughout the game, by teammates and opponents. From the very top of the list of his opponents, Viv Richards: 'I have always respected Dennis as one of the best fast bowlers I have ever faced. He was a fierce competitor and had a tremendous will to win. The quality of his bowling at the end of a day's play, even at times when he had been toiling, was the same as when he started.

'Regardless of how much you might have thought you were "in", you knew he would always think he could get you out. He was always pretty accurate with his line and if you missed the bouncer you were hit. What is more, he never bowled a short ball without a reason.'

Richards' captain, the tall, belligerent-hitting left-hander Clive Lloyd, agrees. 'You could never risk a moment's carelessness, or say that you dominated him. He was always working out ways to get your wicket. He won games on his own on quite a few occasions. He put fast bowling at the top, really. His action was perfect.'

West Indian Michael Holding is renowned for his classical beauty: the run-up, the delivery action, the follow-through. He says, 'I remember admiring his rhythm and run-up, particularly the slow build-up of pace'.

Fellow Windies quick Colin Croft hunted in that team's pace packs of the late 70s and early 80s. He said, 'since the age of 12, when I saw my first Test match at the Bourda in Georgetown, I have seen many great fast bowlers. Based on longevity, destructive ability and menace, Lillee, with his tigerish instincts, gets my vote for the best of all time. He came back from a grave injury, reinvented himself and transformed into a more cunning and productive bowler. What a cricketer. What an inspiration. DK [DK Lillee]: the fast bowler I hated, the fast bowler I loved. And the one I admired the most. There are great ruthless, destructive fast bowlers. Then there is Dennis Lillee.'

Rudi Webster was the man who saved Dennis Lillee's career. It was he who, while working as a radiologist during the

Australians' 1973 tour to the West Indies, discovered the tiny fractures of the lumbar vertebrae that were causing him so much trouble. Coincidentally, when Greg Chappell suffered an uncharacteristic slump in 1981–82, he turned to Webster, by then a sports psychologist, for advice. A fast-medium bowler himself, boasting 272 wickets in 70 first-class games for Warwickshire and Otago, he's a man close to Lillee's heart. Let's hear from Lillee, in an interview Webster included in his book, *Think Like a Champion*:

> There are three areas I would discuss – training and physical fitness, skills training and mental training.
>
> Physical fitness is very important. I always set myself goals at training – so many laps, so many push-ups, etc. Every time I went to training I tried to go past these goals. I would say to myself, 'One more, five more, ten yards more, twenty yards more'. In theory what you are doing is pushing your body, which is controlled by the mind, through the barriers. You are training your mind and body to go to their limits.
>
> It is amazing how much more you can get out of your body when you push yourself mentally. Your body often has reserves that you don't realise are there. Your mind gives in before your body does, when you stop trying. If you push your mind through the barriers at training you will be able to push it through them during the game.
>
> There have been times when my feet were sore, my legs and back were aching, when I have had difficulty

breathing and felt faint, but I was able to continue because I had pushed myself at training. If you are rooted physically, the mind can get you going again.

The second area is technical skills. I think you should practise the basic skills over and over until you get them right and then keep on practising to maintain them. You must practise them under the same conditions you will encounter in the game.

Preparation and practice are very important. At practice you only have about two or three hours, so make the best of them. Don't waste your time. A lot of people fail to develop their skills because of poor preparation, planning and organisation at training, a poor attitude or because they spend insufficient time practising them.

Your mind controls both your fitness and technical skills. As far as fitness is concerned, it is the mind that gives up first, not your body. And as far as the basic technical skills are concerned, if you don't use your mind to concentrate and practise properly you won't improve your skills.

In the game if you don't use your mind to think clearly and positively, to concentrate well, to maintain self-confidence and to handle the pressures of the game, you won't use those skills properly. Your performance would then be substandard. So you see they are all tied up.

The newspapers and television have created a myth about me and have built up my ability and reputation much higher than they really are. I use this to my advantage. I don't try to change it, although I believe that it is wrong to be built up like that.

Sometimes, I say to myself, 'That's not right – but if the batsmen think that I am better than I really am, that's good for me'. Why not let them continue to think that way? If they believe it, that is one more thing in the back of their minds that they have to worry about.

Once the seed is planted in their minds it is very difficult for them to stop it from growing. All it requires to make them uneasy is a good ball or a simple remark like, 'I enjoy bowling to you ... it's just a matter of time'. Sometimes you play little games and put on an air of superiority that tells them, 'I'm in charge ... I will get you soon ... I am better than you'.

ON THE RETURN from his back injury, Dennis Lillee went from being a racing car to a saloon car. From Formula One to Rolls-Royce. He worked off a shorter and more controlled run-up, in the main bowling within himself a yard or two slower than had been the case with the earlier model, yet occasionally firing out a real bullet. And refining all the skills necessary to still be a threat to the world's best batsmen: control of line and length and movement of the ball through the air and off the wicket. Good judges say the Rolls-Royce model presented a different, but even greater, threat to the batsman. As you will read later, statistical analysis proves this to be true.

Rod Marsh: In the early days there was a lot of pace and a lot of willpower. As happens with most fast bowlers, they get an injury and have to refine their actions. I think as a result of that process Dennis became the great bowler that he finished up being.

He was capable of assessing situations and bowling according to them. So, after the back trouble, when there was a bit of juice in the pitch he'd run in and bowl around the 135 km/h mark, which is fast enough. But he had one up his sleeve: at 145! He'd bowl line and length basically, looking to swing the ball and work it off the wicket.

But if the pitch didn't have any grass on it and was very flat, he'd start bowling cutters. If you have a look at his record, his performances at the MCG were unbelievable. No other fast bowler did well at 'the G', but he found a way to get wickets there.

John Inverarity: I don't think he ever bowled better than he did in the series against England (1974-75) and the West Indies (1975-76). Maybe he was a yard quicker before the back injury, but he still had pace and now had a stronger body, better rhythm and better control. He was more consistent.

Mike Brearley: I thought Lillee was the best bowler I ever faced. First of all he was aggressive, second he never ever gave up – *and* he was just as combative and good at six o'clock as he was at eleven. Add to that the fact that he bowled such a good line and swung the ball away. He could bowl to a seven-two off-side field and you never got anything to score off on the leg side. And there were very few balls you could leave *easily*.

He was what I'd call an *honest* bowler. He'd keep coming at you, but wouldn't do something completely unusual. You'd get a full mixture of deliveries from him and, despite what he's quoted as having said, I don't think he tried to hit a batsman. I think he bowled to get him out. He was more *overtly* aggressive than Thomson, more directly expressive, possibly because he was more accurate and, when I played them both, he was quicker.

Geoff Howarth: As a team, Dennis and Thommo were very aggressive, but I don't recall them having too much to say. Okay, you'd get the odd expletive from Dennis if you played and missed too much – but there was never any verbal warfare. Mind you, he and I did cross swords during the first innings of the first Test at Brisbane in 1980–81. Dennis was bowling and I was at the non-striker's end when I noticed he was bowling these no-balls. I'm not talking half a millimetre or so, they were ten to fifteen millimetres over. Which were going unnoticed by the umpire. After a while I pointed this out to the umpire and said, 'It's bad enough facing Dennis Lillee without him being allowed to go over the line and not be called'. To back up what I was saying,

I later heard that Richie Benaud had made mention of this overstepping during the Channel Nine coverage.

Shortly after this Dennis did get a wicket – and I had noted that his front foot was over by a long way. I made mention of this to the umpire and Dennis, on his way back past me next time, turned and said, 'You just concentrate on what you have to do!' My response was, 'Hey, it's very easy to bowl and keep your rhythm when the umpire's not calling it when you bowl a no-ball'.

Those who knew Dennis Lillee well appreciated that he possessed quite a sense of humour. He could tell a good joke, and laugh heartily at a good one being told. He was a practical joker by nature and often would keep the dressing room or the team bus amused. In fact, there was rarely too much tension in the dressing room during a period when his team's control of the situation lay in the balance and the next man in would be tightening up a little inside. It was time for a Lillee trick and suddenly the breathing patterns would settle down. Nobody was immune.

> **John Inverarity:** Late in the season when he stood out of bowling because of his back injury I went to the WACA Ground to have a net with him. It was a hard wicket and he was trundling them down at not much more than medium pace. I was feeling as comfortable as you can when facing Dennis. Then, all of sudden he let one go. I ducked and it flew over my head and right out

of the nets, over the road and crashed on the full into the fence around the Gloucester Park trotting track.

I tried to gather myself and looked back at him. He had something of a smile on his face ... and he said, 'Oh, you know, just wanted to see if I still had something there'. That was in March and he came back to full action six months later.

Playing with Lillee for Western Australia, on many occasions the author saw the result of this strident never-say-die attitude, of his sheer *will*. There was a Sheffield Shield game in Sydney in the 1972–73 season, before his injury, when the author was acting captain. A declaration set New South Wales a target of 325 to win.

At 4–97 the home side was in trouble. Then Doug Walters stepped in, his magnificent 159 taking the game away. As a partnership between Kerry O'Keeffe and Brian Taber was icing the outcome, the author tried to convince Lillee that to bowl on was pointless. 'Nup, we're still a chance, only need one of these ...' You couldn't wrench the ball out of the champ's hands – and, like the captain on the bridge, he (and the author!) eventually went down with the sinking ship.

In that innings he bowled 29.2 eight-ball overs. It was later that season in a Test against Pakistan, that the back injury first appeared. Fast bowlers can pay a price ... if their will knows no bounds!

THE BEST bowlers bring a lot of skills to the table – and one of the more important ones is memory. Recalling the strengths and weaknesses of an opposing batsman allows a planned attack to be mounted from the get-go. Out there in the middle there's little time, really, for a wait-and-see strategy. With that sort of approach, by the time a bowler has made his discoveries, too often the horse has bolted: the batsman has hit his straps and is no longer vulnerable.

Dennis Lillee wouldn't deny that early in his career his first intention was to run in hard and just blast away. Full of hope that he'd be able to produce the jaffer, the one that not even the best batsman, in form and settled, could deny. But when the penny dropped for Lillee, when he began to add mind-power to his game, there was no greater quickie-with-a-plan. And he had a sharp memory to add to all the other skills and instincts that go into the making of a great fast bowler.

In that 1972–73 series against Pakistan, he often bowled to Majid Khan, as pretty a batsman as you'd ever see. While those of lesser ability *hit* the ball, Majid *caressed* it. Perfect poise, balance, timing and placement. Let Lillee tell the story:

'He used to wear a big-rimmed, white canvas hat, which was unusual. We had gone from peaked caps to floppies and I had never seen one of these. He wore it out to bat. A couple of times I went close to knocking it off his head with a few sharp deliveries. We got on very well and at the end of the tour he promised me that if I ever did knock it off, it was mine to keep.

'I remembered and the next time we played them, four years later, I actually did knock it off. I had followed through, as I was inclined to do, and he was so composed. He just bent down, picked it up and walked the couple of paces and gave it to me, saying, "as promised". It was a great memento.'

Lillee took the hat home. His wife, Helen, noticed how sweat-stained and dirty it was, and put it in the washing machine. It came out shrunk and shredded. Lillee kept it anyway. 'It is a relic I treasure because of what happened and the fact that he remembered what had been said years before.'

Things went well with Majid Khan, but woe betide the player who dared to get on the wrong side of the champion. That player could expect retribution. We have already noted Lillee's reaction to being bombarded by Tony Greig in the opening Test of the 1974–75 Ashes series. Not only Greig, who could handle himself, but other, less capable England batsmen were on the receiving end of Lillee's response for the remainder of the series.

It wasn't the only time. Playing for Western Australia, Lillee had a lasting contretemps with Victorian quickie Alan Hurst. It all began one blustery day at the WACA Ground, in a Sheffield Shield game. The Victorian, who was sharp enough to keep even the best on their toes, was bowling from the southern end on a typically bouncy track with an unusual breeze for the Perth ground – strong and right at his back. With this for support, Hurst launched a barrage of short stuff at the WA tail. Lillee was not impressed.

In those days of bonus batting and bowling points it was not at all unusual for a captain to declare at eight or nine down, thus denying the opposition a point. Victoria did this on two occasions in the following years, meaning that Lillee was denied the chance to bowl at Hurst. Eventually the time came, in a one-day game at the MCG, where of course there would be no declaration. Dennis wasn't going to miss his opportunity. He sent one after another whistling past Hurst's nose and even ignored a suggestion by the mid-off fieldsman that, surely, enough was enough.

When the innings ended and we were walking from the field, the look on Hurst's pallid face said it all. Like, we're square now ... eh? Lillee waited and as the Victorian passed close by at the boundary gate, he spat out, 'And there's plenty more where they came from ...' Like the elephant, Dennis Lillee didn't forget.

A study in contrasts

HISTORY SHOWS that Test teams that boast a battering ram of quality fast bowlers are the teams most likely to dominate just about anywhere in the world. Since the curtain came down on the 'Lillian Thomson show' – as it was inevitably known – there has been no better example of this than the way the West Indies established and maintained dominance through the 80s and 90s. Inspired by the Lillee–Thomson combination, Clive Lloyd led the charge with the team whose creation he had masterminded, with four quicks pawing the ground at the top of their marks. Viv Richards inherited the team, and continued the dominance. Facing pace all day from both ends – it was relentless. Trained well to execute their bombardment, a battery of pace bowlers presents a storm front that offers little or no respite.

The point-four-something of a second that elapses between the ball being released and it reaching the batsman should leave the receiver in absolutely no position to do anything but simply hope for the best. Yet the really good ones sometimes can find a way. Those who witnessed Thomson's inspired spell in Barbados in the West Indies in 1979, arguably the fastest bowling of all time, say that Viv Richards could only have been guessing where Thomson would pitch the ball. He was ready and waiting for one searing Thomson flier and took it over the forward square leg boundary with such force that observers say it seemed to shake the stand. He essayed a similar shot to another short one, but the delivery got big on him and the best he could do was belt it back over the bowler's head with a cross-bat swipe.

When facing pace bowling, most batsmen use what are called 'trigger movements', like taking the bat up and moving their feet into what they consider to be the ideal position to deal with the oncoming missile. These movements usually begin as the bowler goes into his delivery stride. But this is a dangerous ploy when facing someone of genuine pace. You can be caught still making your moves when the ball is upon you. In these situations of rare pace, the author (and many others, too) would begin his move (usually well back and across) at an earlier stage. With somebody as fast as Thomson that would mean early enough to be set and still when the ball was released. Such a plan offers a half-chance of survival, but not necessarily of exercising a scoring shot – particularly one in front of the wicket.

Quicks in combination make the best teams – but is the individual express bowler at the top of the food chain in Test cricket? Consider: the top three wicket-takers in Test history are spin bowlers. Sri Lanka's Muttiah Muralitharan stands supreme with 800 wickets, followed by Australia's Shane Warne on 708 wickets and the Indian leggie Anil Kumble with 619. They are followed, well back, by three fast-mediums: Glenn McGrath, 563, Courtney Walsh, 519, and England's James Anderson.

Way back on the list are the genuine speedsters. First Dale Steyn in the low 400s, then Dennis Lillee with 355, then Allan Donald on 330, Brett Lee on 310 and Michael Holding with 249. Where's Jeff Thomson? The big difference between the quicks and the spinners is that the former played far fewer Tests. Why? Because bowling at great speed exacts a far greater toll on the body. They just can't last as long as a tweaker. To give you an idea, had Lillee bowled at his career success rate in as many Tests as Warne, he would have taken 735 wickets, to Warne's 708. Muralitharan played 133 Tests; Lillee 72, Thomson 51.

But who would you rather face – Muralitharan or Lillee (each on a wicket helping their style of bowling)? The author saw the former at close hand when he worked magic for Kent in the English County competition in 2003. He was perfecting the doosra – the one that looks like an off-spinner, but actually bites back the other way – and was all but unplayable. He could make them turn bowling on glass! Survive? With huge difficulty, with as many as five men hovering in close. Score? Well, the only player to get a real piece of Murali during that brief period was Middlesex wicketkeeper David Nash, who succeeded by fiercely playing the sweep shot to a close leg-side boundary.

The author also saw plenty of Dennis Lillee, both as a teammate and a broadcaster and writer, and both the earlier crash-and-bash model and the refined, well-oiled machine of the second phase of his career. He also faced Lillee in club games, trial games and in the nets. It was the stuff of which nightmares are made. The pace, the control, the movement of the ball through the air and off the wicket – and the diabolical aggression, that in-your-face stuff that could make a batsmen shiver and wish he was at another ground. Who would you rather face? To stay in and score runs, Lillee, by a whisker; to stay alive, Murali, by a country mile.

Cricket is a supremely individual sport – at any one time only one person is active, be it bowling, batting or fielding. And yet combinations, in both batting and bowling, are vital – and there has never been a combination like Lillee and Thommo. Their differences complemented each other.

To look at Lillee first. The mob in the outer put fuel on the fire when he was in action. Their chants of 'Lil-lee ... Lil-lee ... Lil-lee ...' and 'Kill ... Kill ... Kill ...' were enough to send shivers down the spine of anybody within cooee of the ground, let alone the poor batsman waiting for crowd-stimulated aggression to explode before his very eyes. And don't for one minute try to say that those cries didn't put some extra pep in the champ's step. It certainly helped in the sweltering Colesseum that is the MCG, where his greatest feats were achieved. That extra step often carried him through to a domineering position close to the batsman in an exaggerated follow-through – accompanied by the Lillee glare. Plus, a trademark flick of perspiration from the fevered brow.

The whole Lillee package was enough to put the wind up even the most resolute of contenders with bat in hand. Add to that his pace – not far short of express – plus his ability to put the ball where he wanted, often whistling by his foe's nose. And, of course the batsman had no protective headwear in the early years.

As the author can attest, it could even be intimidating to those whose job it was to stand in the cordon waiting for an edge. You were standing so far back that there was time for the copyrighted Lillee cry of 'ca-a-a-tch ...' to register before the ball reached your hands. You simply daren't fumble a chance. Though there was a game, Western Australia versus New South Wales in Sydney, when the author and, standing next to him, John Inverarity, contrived to turf four slips chances between them off his bowling. A highly agitated Lillee romp mid-wicket after the fourth offering hit the turf resulted in him being reported by the umpire.

Thomson was different. Oh yes, he was *different*! A terrifying prospect for the poor batsman for three reasons: one, he was simply so very fast; two, because before his shoulder injury he could make the ball fly off a length; and, three, for the very reason that he didn't always know where the ball was going as it left his hand. Think of this: If the bowler didn't know, then how could the batsman possibly have a clue? Equally disconcerting was that all this fury came from the most unpretentious, shambling run-up.

And if that approach to the delivery point didn't suck the batsman in, then there was another dimension to the man. While Dennis Lillee represented outright firebrand aggression, accompanied by a bit of verbal directed at the batsman, Thomson was fast bowling's quiet man. Not a sound, unless he was chastising himself. Not a change of facial expression. Nothing. Nothing but stealth and deadly purpose.

Ian Chappell wrote after the 1975–76 home series against the West Indies that 'on the field they are alike yet in many ways very different. They are both intensely competitive and believe firmly in the old adage that fast bowlers should hate the opposing batsman.

'Lillee and Thomson have been headliners since they became a partnership and have certainly carried all before them. They have also brought with them enormous crowds, plus a spate of good fast bowlers around Australia.

'Dennis concedes every run begrudgingly – in the mould of Freddie Trueman – where he considers any addition to the batsman's total is rather fortunate and is occasionally prompted to explain this reasoning to the batsman himself.

'Jeff Thomson is different. In fact, generally when you talk to him on the field when he is bowling, all you hear is a stream of abuse aimed directly at himself for his terrible bowling. I have never known a bloke who bowls so consistently badly in his own eyes, yet goes on getting bundles of wickets.'

Greg Chappell: They were a nice mix of styles. Once Thommo got his radar calibrated he knew where they were going. And he had a really good yorker, which was shown in the second innings at Brisbane in 1974–75.

Dennis Amiss: They were so different in their method that they were the perfect foil for each other. Dennis just had that great control of line and length – you know, 'Caught Marsh, bowled Lillee' or 'Caught Chappell, bowled Lillee' – just coming at you on that line outside off stump.

Dennis also varied his pace a lot – and he just kept running in. I don't what he was on, but it was working! I mean he would bowl a mountain of overs, then come in off his short run and bowl some more.

Robin Bailhache: They complemented each other, because they were so different. Dennis was able to move the ball through the air, but with all due respect to Thommo, he was too quick for that. He was pure pace. Who did I think the better bowler in that 1974–75 series? Well, Dennis was better in the sense that he could do what he wanted with the ball, whereas Thommo was better because he had frightening pace.

Dennis was very aggressive … to anybody. But Thommo hardly said a word and the only time he spoke was when he talked to himself. He'd be very critical of himself if he didn't bowl one where he wanted to. Then he'd mutter and mutter and carry on. Having said that, he never sledged.

John Wright: I grew up listening to these blokes play on the radio and then you end up playing against them, which took a bit of an adjustment. Dennis was more your standard type. He'd get in pretty close to the stumps, but I found that in some way you could set yourself up defensively. Thommo was the opposite – you just didn't know where it was coming. They were a great pair, because they complemented each other so well.

Mike Brearley: Lillee was everything classical, really. As with Michael Holding. You could pick up the ball more easily with him, because everything was, as it were, straight. Plus, with him he knew where it was going! Thommo was different. His hand going back to his right ankle, then the sling. I thought this made it more difficult to pick up the ball. Plus, I don't think he quite knew where it was going.

Geoff Howarth: I used to say to myself, 'Hey, you must be playing with the big boys now. It's not backyard cricket, you'd best be on top of your form to cope with them'.

Rod Marsh: Keeping to Dennis was great. I felt as though I knew what he was going to bowl, because I had watched him that carefully and spent that much time with him, travelling together, rooming together, playing together, for the state and in the Test team. It was a joy keeping to him, because I felt I was always in the game.

On the other hand, keeping to Thommo was exciting. You never knew where he was going to go. He tested my skills, sometimes to the limit.

In terms of me, as the wicketkeeper, being involved with them, I could talk to Dennis but there was no point in trying to talk to Thommo. He was just a natural and more or less did what he felt was right at the time.

Dennis was always in the batsman's face. More so than Thommo. If Thommo bowled a good one he'd smile, because he was happy with himself. If he bowled a bad one he'd abuse himself.

Bruce Laird: If conditions suited Thommo he was bloody dangerous, but funnily enough, I'd rather face him than FOT. Dennis could bowl anywhere and look like taking a wicket with every ball. No question Thommo would be having a go, but he'd be pretty straight up and down. And his length ... to me, often he was either short or full and because he didn't swing it you felt you were never going to nick him.

Ross Edwards: Did Thommo have an *aura*? If you were the batsman he did! Whereas Dennis had an aura because of his personality, which he exhibited both on and off the field. Thommo's aura came from his devastating capacity to bowl.

The same was evident to those observing the game from the other side of the fence. Writing in the London *Telegraph*, TV personality and dyed-in-the-wool cricket fan Michael Parkinson summed it up succinctly. 'What made them formidable was their different approach to the same job. Lillee's run to the crease was long and dramatic in its acceleration and gathering menace. In the delivery stride the left arm was cocked, the head still and aimed down the wicket with the left shoulder as the sight. Thomson by comparison ambled to the crease but in the delivery stride the casual was transformed into the dramatic.'

The difference between the two was visible. Thomson's cruisy run-up that transforms through an explosion at the crease into unbelievable pace, versus Lillee's longer and more energetic approach that morphs into greater control and guile; Lillee's fitness-derived ability to sustain effort for long periods, even in sweltering heat, compared with Thomson's short-burst rampages; and Thomson's almost-apologetic outward display against Lillee's naked aggression.

In technical terms both were side-on bowlers, though Thomson was really beyond side-on. In the delivery stride Lillee's back foot would land in a position just forward of square to the batsman, whereas Thomson's would face backwards, almost to point at the man standing at mid-on. However, to get into his release position each bowler adopted a different technique.

In Thomson's case, at the end of a tippy-toe creep in from a relatively short approach, he crossed his feet over in the load-up – a move described as balletic. A virtual pirouette. It was yet another aspect of him that was unique. For Lillee to achieve his side-on position he needed a run-up that allowed the build-up of sufficient pace to enable a significant leap during which he was able to make the change from being chest-on to the batsman.

The secret to Thomson's pace was his method of taking the ball back behind his buttocks and then hauling it through with a supremely muscular heave. To make this work as well as it did when he was in his prime, Thomson required significant development of his upper torso – reputedly done by hauling wool bales and beer kegs on the Sydney wharves, augmented by regularly heaving a surfboard through the seas along the city's coastline.

Lillee, too, had good upper-body development. However, his was a more meaningful run to the delivery position, once described as 'a steam train taking off, slowly building up speed' to reach a maximum a few strides before the leap into the delivery position. With both men there was a purposeful presentation of the front arm, designed to drive the action through its full arc. There were times in Lillee's early days when that follow-through part of the action was so strong that he would occasionally scrape the fingers of his bowling hand along the ground on the follow-through.

There is another follow-through. That is when the bowler moves down the wicket in the process of slowing down after release to a stop. The lack of speed in Thomson's approach meant this was a relatively short distance from sending the projectile on its way. For Lillee, who thundered through the crease, it was considerably longer. In fact, often more by design than necessity, he would end up right down in the batsman's face. Offering a wry grin – or some advice like, 'I've been waiting for you to come in!'

In full flight in his early days, Lillee was an awesome sight. He oozed macho persona. That mane of black hair, the drooping moustache and the shirt unbuttoned low, revealing a thatch of dark hair and a gold necklace from which dangled a tiny golden cricket bat. There was aggression written all over his every act. Then there was the man's pleading, begging appeal, a great piece of cricketing theatre: legs spread, knees bent, hands in the air and both index fingers pointing to the heavens. How could an umpire say no?

There was less of all of this with Thomson. As he put it, he just went 'WHANG'. In his case, actions spoke louder than any words. He possessed the unique ability to bowl bloody quick – lightning fast. And that's a commodity very few could boast. It's an odd fact, isn't it, that the fastest bowler had the shortest run-up?

Many a lesser bowler, the author included, will happily attest to the fact that life is a great deal easier when bowling at the other end to a champion speedster. As Ian Chappell noted earlier, Dennis Lillee's bowling helped Bob Massie take 16 wickets at Lord's.

When a fast bowler is paired with another at the other end, it's different. Frank Tyson wrote:

Not only does success wait upon the fast bowlers who possess extreme pace and hunt in convenient double harness, but also the crowds fawn upon them. The mob have a primeval desire to see the ball bounce at stellar velocity and the batsmen ducking and weaving in their equally primitive wish for survival ... There is no doubt that Lillee contributed much to the 33 wicket success of Thomson in the (1974-75) series. His foreseeable length and line acted as an excellent foil for Thomson's unpredictability.

Thomson could bowl the perfect inswinging yorker, such as the one which hit the base of Tony Greig's stumps in Brisbane, yet the very next ball would be so wide down leg side that even the agile 'keeper Marsh could not make enough ground to prevent it from smashing against the fine-leg hoardings.

But the Queenslander surprised me in the first Test by the degree of accuracy which he attained, and the amount of outswing which he produced. A dual strange facet about Thomson's surprising bowling was the way in which he seemed to bowl faster into the wind than Lillee did with it, and the manner in which he appeared to bowl better and faster with the old ball than he did with the new.

The author can testify that there was suddenly a stark difference in the batsmen's attitude when the bowler at the other end was Dennis Lillee. There was often a little game within a game, as the batsmen tried to get off strike to Lillee.

Perhaps more importantly, when facing the lesser bowler patience tended to fly out the window. They now approached him with a more aggressive attitude. Like, 'I'm going to be in survival mode against Lillee, so if I want to score runs I'd better get after the other bloke'. That was a whole new scene. Risks not normally taken made for opportunities not normally enjoyed by the lesser bowler. A much greater chance of success for him.

Lillee and Thomson were well aware of the advantages of bowling in tandem.

First, here is Thomson on bowling with his mate: 'He had that special belief – always thought he was going to do something special – and that's what made him the bowler he was. He was the enforcer, the guy getting in the face of the batsmen. I loved the way he got up the batsman's nose. He was a ratbag.

'He'd be bowling off-cutters and that sort of thing, and I'd just try to bowl really quick and scare the shit out of the batsmen. It was a great attack, because we'd go hard for the opening spell, get a couple of wickets each. And then we'd come back to finish them off. His determination would stand out and he was aggressive, always full-on. He would never laugh off anything.'

Now Lillee, on the benefit of having Thommo at the other end: 'I always felt that if I wasn't getting wickets, he would. He says he felt the same about me. There were days when he bowled like the wind, when I'd be inclined to think my role might be to just keep it tight and let's do the attacking from his end. My job then was more to play a support role.

'I used to love standing close in when Thommo was bowling. You could see the fear in their eyes. The psychology of fear is an important ingredient in fast bowling. The reason I loved bowling with him so much was because we fired each other up. I know I got quite a few of my wickets because batsmen were glad to get away from Thommo.'

The fear, the laughter

THERE HAVE been few, if any, new-ball combinations to make as devastating an imprint on opposition batsmen as did Dennis Lillee and Jeff Thomson during their reign of terror. The naked aggression, high skills levels and iron will of Lillee combined with the withering, mind-bending pace of Thomson to produce a partnership the likes of which cricket had not seen before – nor has seen since.

For those who faced them in full flight, particularly before Thomson's career-changing injury in December 1976, there was one mental consideration: the fear factor. Not that there was much respite at the other end.

> **Mike Brearley:** Mentally with both of them, as was the case with all fast bowlers, you had to overcome the apprehension of being hit. That's one thing. Then, when playing in Australia, you had a crowd calling 'kill ... kill ... kill ...' as Lillee ran in.
>
> Add to all of that something that Dennis had in common with, say, Viv Richards and Shane Warne: they walked with a strut, a type of arrogance ... that it

was their stage, that they owned the place. You had to make sure you didn't get intimidated by that. Not necessarily frightened, rather a feeling of not having the right to be there.

David Lloyd: You didn't actually feel fear, but you did feel a sort of hopelessness at times, a sense that you couldn't cope.

Geoff Howarth: If you made the mistake of thinking about them in awe of their ability – how great they were and their reputation – then you would struggle. You wouldn't be sufficiently concerned about your own game. You were in danger of losing your confidence, or your ability to play them.

As West Indies skipper Clive Lloyd said, after his team had been battered during the 1975–76 tour of Australia, while the ball was new and hard and the pitch fresh and bouncy it was a particularly testing time for the batsman. 'You knew you were taking your life in your hands, because we didn't wear helmets in those days and they were that quick.'

Lloyd's West Indies teammate – and batting champion – Viv Richards adds to the story. 'He (Lillee) was a Trojan. No matter what the circumstances – the wicket or the weather – he would always get something out of it. He was the best fast bowler I ever encountered … for aggression, for never-say-die attitude, for being the most troublesome individual to me. After each bouncer would come the famous glare, and maybe some choice words to let you know there was another one coming and it would be even faster than the last.'

> **Mike Brearley:** For the Australians' tour to England in 1977, when Thomson played but Lillee did not, I wore a little skull cap for head protection. I thought they would mock me for this, but actually at the end of the series Rod Marsh said to me, 'You are entirely right, but it's not big enough'.
>
> I wore it in the Trent Bridge Test of that series and in playing a shot it fell off ... whereupon a wag in the crowd called out, 'Why don't you pin it on with a six-inch nail, Brearley?'

The Brearley design, basically a skull cap, was immediately picked up by the author's West Australian teammates John Inverarity and Ric Charlesworth, then India's Sunil Gavaskar, before bigger and better models were developed soon after.

The author was fortunate enough to play *with* Lillee, but understood via experience the raw challenge of waiting for Thomson to unleash one of his thunderbolts. He happily took the advice of colleague John Inverarity: begin a distinct back-and-across movement immediately the bowler locked into his pre-delivery position, with the ball concealed behind his buttocks. To move any later in the delivery action would have been too late. Others had their own methods.

> **Mike Brearley:** With Lillee I would try to stay upright (and not fall over to the off) and be prepared to let the

ball go on the swing and the bounce – especially on a pitch like Perth. With Dennis, in particular, I would try to leave as often as possible early on. Later in the innings – and the game – when he was less able to bowl the out-swinger and there was less carry to the slips he would tend to bowl a little straighter. Then you were more vulnerable to being bowled or lbw, rather than caught in the cordon.

With Thommo, it was more a matter of picking up the ball early enough. Making sure that you looked at his hand, rather than the whirl of his arm.

David Lloyd: The team attitude in 1974–5 was, 'We've got to wear them down …' We had Dennis coming back from injury, and Thommo a bit of an unknown, though as the series unfolded we really did get to know him! The plan was to get through their opening salvo and into some calmer waters against Max Walker and Ashley Mallett.

For me, though, the basic plan was, 'I'm not going to hook and just take what's on offer'. By the same token, the cut shot was important. Not only for me; in that series Greigy and Knotty used it to great effect.

John Wright: To me, batting against them was more than making runs. I just wanted to gain their respect. The last thing you wanted was to be known as someone who backed away.

Dennis Lillee could be at once the most fierce – and fearsome – competitor imaginable and yet enjoy some fun out in the middle. For example, his on-field exchanges with colourful English umpire Dickie Bird ... taking an apple off the lunch table in a County game and sending it down. On another occasion in a County game sending down a tennis ball that had strayed onto the ground. Take the mask off and you might find a wry sense of humour.

> **Mike Brearley:** I remember an occasion when I was facing him in a Test match and played a defensive shot back down the pitch, which was about all I was capable of! As it rolled towards him, he pretended that the force of my shot had stung his hand. He had a little grin about it ... and I thought it was quite nice, actually.
>
> In more recent years I've grown to know Dennis better and better. When he comes to London we catch up and we have dinner together when I'm in Perth. I enjoy his company very much.

The author had his experiences with the Lillian Thomson duet. In hindsight the great joy, indeed relief, at being in the same side as Dennis Lillee. It was hard enough facing him in the nets off a half-pace run-up with an old ball, merely going through the paces, let alone the agony of trying to survive – and score a few runs – while facing an angry tiger.

With regard to Jeff Thomson, the author had the very good fortune to be a middle-order batsman for WA – at the back end of a very capable and resolute top-order – and consequently very rarely faced him when he was in full flight with a new cherry in his hands. But there was one day when the wrath of Thomson made itself known.

It was the Gillette Cup final in Brisbane, 1975–76. At the time, one-dayers still tended to be a bit of a wild, uncultured slog-athon. The record books show two consecutive sixes. What they don't show is that one was a top-edged hook that flew over fine leg, the next a swipe at one in the slot that sailed over long-on. Hmmm, sixes off successive Thommo deliveries, what might be coming next? The next one whistled past my head – without hitting the pitch.

Thomson himself had no doubt about what was going through the batsmen's heads. When asked years later if the batsmen were afraid, he was characteristically blunt: 'Yes, definitely. Not just the Poms, a whole heap of batsmen. I really mean that. I knew they were. They were shitting themselves. I could see it, I could smell it.'

The numbers

IN THE YEARS between 29 December 1972 and 18 June 1983, Dennis Lillee and Jeff Thomson paired up in 26 Test matches, five World Series Cricket Supertests and 31 One-Day Internationals. There was cause for celebration, indeed genuine relief, for batsmen the world over when for a long time only one of the Twins of Terror was in the Australian line-up. From the time of Thomson's devastating shoulder injury, Christmas Eve 1976, to 23 February 1979, it was either one or the other, but never both, out there for Australia.

Lillee was unavailable for the 1977 tour to England, being otherwise engaged with World Series Cricket. Their reunion eventually came during the final activity of WSC, a tour to the West Indies.

Lillee played 70 Tests, 14 WSC Supertests and 63 ODIs; Thomson 51 Tests, five Supertests and 50 ODIs. So many opportunities missed for the devastating pair, particularly those years in the earlier stages of their combination, when they were sweeping all before them.

After Thomson's injury-spoilt debut, they started with a bang in their explosive destruction of England in 1974–75, claiming 57 wickets between them. The next summer their systematic demolition of the West Indies yielded 58 wickets. At the other end of the spectrum, the nadir of their time together was the third Test against Pakistan at the MCG in December 1981, the only completed Test match in which neither man took a wicket.

In the 11 Tests Lillee played before he was laid low with the back injury he took 51 wickets at a strike rate of 58.0, while in the 59 Tests that followed his comeback he took 304 wickets, with a much better strike rate of 51.0. Barely believable, but statistically, at least, the remodelled Lillee was more of a handful than the original.

Contrast that with what happened to Thomson in the years beyond his catastrophic shoulder injury. In the 17 Tests before Adelaide he had 80 wickets at the outstanding strike rate of 48.5. Post that sad, tragic date, he played 34 Tests and took 120 wickets at the far inferior strike rate of 55.4. There was a wide gap, in terms of performance, between Thomson before and after the injury. Seventeen Tests before the injury returned 4.70 wickets a game; after his comeback 39 Tests and Supertests produced 3.48 per game.

Lillee's overall strike rate of a wicket every 52 balls is bettered only among Australia's pace bowlers: Glenn McGrath (51.9) and Mitchell Johnson (51.1). Thomson comes next, claiming a wicket every 52.6 deliveries.

Coincidentally, the man dismissed most frequently by Lillee and Thomson was the same man: England wicketkeeper Alan Knott, the doughty contestant who put up sterling resistance in 1974–75. Lillee got him 12 times, Thomson nine. If Supertests are included – which Ian Chappell has long advocated – Lillee had the great Viv Richards 16 times, Knott and Gordon Greenidge 13 times each. For Thomson it was Knott nine times and Richards eight.

What about their favourite venues? Lillee *loved* the MCG. Fourteen Tests, 82 wickets – an astonishing 5.85 wickets per game, with seven five-wicket innings and four 10-wicket matches. In England his best ground was The Oval: 27 wickets from just three Tests. Thomson fared best at his two 'home' grounds: the SCG – five Tests, 29 wickets; and the Gabba – six Tests, 29 victims.

Of Lillee's combined 422 wickets in Tests and Supertests, more than a quarter – 108 – were openers. Openers accounted for just less than a quarter of Thomson's wickets – 51 of 216 wickets in Tests and Supertests.

For Lillee there was no better personal period than early 1977, when, in the space of six weeks he put together a 10-wicket match in three Tests against three different countries. In that golden hat-trick of Tests, Lillee took 32 wickets for 423 runs.

Lillee finished his career with 167 wickets from 29 Tests against England, a mark surpassed only by Shane Warne's 195 from 36 matches. Lillee's love of playing in England is underlined by this statistic: 16 Tests, 96 wickets – exactly six per game.

He became Australia's greatest Test wicket-taker in the final Test of the 1980–81 season, at the MCG. First he trapped India's Sunil Gavaskar lbw, to equal Richie Benaud's mark of 248 ... then he had Chethan Chauhan caught to claim the record – and saluted Benaud way up in the Channel Nine commentary box.

Lillee's 355 wickets place him third on the list of Australian wicket-takers, behind Shane Warne (708) and Glenn McGrath (563). While he was a player, he became Australia's leading wicket-taker when he surpassed Richie Benaud. He was the greatest wicket-taker of all when he took his 309th wicket, Larry Gomes, caught by Greg Chappell at the MCG in December 1981. And, of course, Lillee ended his storied career as the world record-holder in Tests, with 355 wickets.

Lillee and Thomson could not have done it without Rod Marsh, the stocky, pugnacious man who stood way back behind the stumps for every ball they fired down in those combined Tests and Supertests. In those games he completed a dismissal on 45 occasions for Lillee and 26 times for Thomson. Indeed, when it comes to wicketkeeper-bowler combinations in Test matches, the Lillee–Marsh team still holds the world record at 95.

Lillee and Thomson played 26 Tests together, their team averaging a win every 1.85 Tests. Lillee without Thomson, every 2.58 Tests; Thomson without Lillee, every 3.57 Tests.

The final dance

TEN DAYS after the Adelaide Test against the West Indies, that ended on 3 February 1982, when groin problems brought him to a halt, Lillee joined Thomson for one last dance: a three-Test tour to New Zealand. It had been a toss-up as to whether or not Lillee was fit to travel. The groin problems were causing both pain *and* the need to modify his action. The doctors gave him a cautious all-clear. Then, bowling in the first Test at Wellington the groin troubles were followed by a slipped disc in his spine. It was going to be a tough time for the champion.

It was also a controversial time for cricket relations across The Ditch. It was the first time Australia had been in New Zealand since the infamous underarm incident, which had occurred a year earlier when Trevor Chappell bowled a delivery underarm to conclude a One-Day International final at the MCG, denying tailender Brian McKechnie the chance to hit the six needed for victory. Geoff Howarth captained the Black Caps in that game and was now going to lead them again on his home soil.

> **Geoff Howarth:** We were to play three One-Day Internationals prior to the first Test. The first of these was in Auckland. There was a huge crowd, a sellout. People were baying for Australian blood because of

the underarm business. Well, they really enjoyed the outcome, with New Zealand winners by 46 runs despite a fine Greg Chappell century. Then, thanks to some terrific bowling by Dennis Lillee and Terry Alderman, Australia won the second and the third [one-dayers].

The end of that little hit-out brought the three Test matches into focus. And feelings were still running deep among the New Zealand supporters.

Geoff Howarth: There was the washed-out first Test at Wellington, then we went to Auckland for the second Test. You could tell there was still plenty of anger in the crowd. They really got behind Richard Hadlee, obviously a great bowler and leader of our attack. He took two wickets in the first innings and five in the second and we won by five wickets, New Zealand's second-ever Test victory over Australia.

The Twins of Terror, though in the twilight of their wonderful careers, were an ever-present danger for New Zealand's top-order batsmen. Thomson was still renowned for his ability to achieve great pace.

John Wright: There were two or three times on that tour when he was very, very quick. The Australians played a warm-up game against Northern Districts at Hamilton – and Thommo played. Well, this umpire kept no-balling him and, naturally, the more he did it the more angry Thommo got – and the quicker he bowled!

In terms of the Tests on that tour, I particularly remember the first innings in the third at Christchurch. Thommo went right through us [4-51 off 21 overs]. That's what I imagined he was like at his best, because that day he was *lightning*. There was one ball in the second innings that just exploded off a length. I remember fending it off the helmet area with my gloves.

We followed on and in the second innings I got a few [141]. There were spells in that innings where he didn't have the bite that I imagine he would have had when he was on top. But with Thommo you didn't want to be at the right end when he was in the wrong mood.

1981–1982 New Zealand v Australia – 3rd Test – Christchurch

19th March 1982 – AMI Stadium, Christchurch
Result: Australia won by 8 wickets
Player of Match: G S Chappell

Australia 1st Innings

B M Laird	c †Smith b Troup	12
G M Wood	c Hadlee b Snedden	64
J Dyson	c Crowe b Hadlee	1
G S Chappell*	c †Smith b Coney	176
K J Hughes	b Hadlee	12
A R Border	b Snedden	6
R W Marsh†	c Cairns b Hadlee	23
B Yardley	c Cairns b Hadlee	8
J R Thomson	b Hadlee	25
D K Lillee	c & b Hadlee	7
T M Alderman	not out	1
Extras	(b 2, lb 8, nb 8)	18
Total	All Out (89.5 overs @ 3.93 rpo)	353

New Zealand Bowling 1st Innings

Bowling	O	M	R	W	ER
R J Hadlee	28.5	5	100	6	3.47
G B Troup	11	1	53	1	4.82
M C Snedden	18	2	89	2	4.94
B L Cairns	21	3	74	0	3.52
J V Coney	8	2	15	1	1.88
J F M Morrison	3	0	4	0	1.33

New Zealand 1st Innings

B A Edgar	c Dyson b Alderman	22
J G Wright	c †Marsh b Lillee	13
J F M Morrison	lbw b Thomson	8
G P Howarth*	c Alderman b Thomson	9
J V Coney	b Lillee	0
M D Crowe	c †Marsh b Lillee	0
R J Hadlee	c †Marsh b Thomson	40
I D S Smith†	b Thomson	0
B L Cairns	run out	3
M C Snedden	b Alderman	32
G B Troup	not out	0
Extras	(b 8, lb 2, w 1, nb 11)	22
Total	All Out (52.2 overs @ 2.85 rpo)	149

Australia Bowling 1st Innings

Bowling	O	M	R	W	ER
J R Thomson	21	5	51	4	2.43
T M Alderman	19.2	3	63	2	3.26
D K Lillee	12	6	13	3	1.08

New Zealand 2nd Innings

B A Edgar	c †Marsh b Alderman	11
J G Wright	b Alderman	141
J F M Morrison	lbw b Chappell	4
G P Howarth*	c Wood b Border	41
J V Coney	b Border	0
M D Crowe	b Yardley	9
R J Hadlee	c Alderman b Yardley	0
I D S Smith†	c Wood b Yardley	0
B L Cairns	lbw b Yardley	16
M C Snedden	b Border	20
G B Troup	not out	8
Extras	(b 4, lb 7, w 2, nb 9)	22
Total	All Out (97.3 overs @ 2.79 rpo)	272

Australia Bowling 2nd Innings

Bowling	O	M	R	W	ER
J R Thomson	19	5	54	0	2.84
T M Alderman	23	5	66	2	2.87
G S Chappell	18	5	30	1	1.67
B Yardley	27	7	80	4	2.96
A R Border	10.3	4	20	3	1.90

Australia 2nd Innings (target 69)

B M Laird	c †Edgar b Snedden	31
G M Wood	c Coney b Hadlee	15
J Dyson	not out	14
G S Chappell*	not out	3
K J Hughes		
A R Border		
R W Marsh†		
B Yardley		
J R Thomson		
D K Lillee		
T M Alderman		
Extras	(b 2, lb 2, nb 2)	6
Total	2 wickets (25.3 overs @ 2.71 rpo)	69

New Zealand Bowling 2nd Innings

Bowling	O	M	R	W	ER
R J Hadlee	8	2	10	1	1.25
M C Snedden	4	0	15	1	3.75
B L Cairns	9	1	28	0	3.11
J V Coney	1	0	2	0	2.00
J F M Morrison	2	1	6	0	3.00
J G Wright	1	0	2	0	2.00
M D Crowe	0.3	0	0	0	0.00

For the New Zealand batsmen there was a sense of respite in that second innings. Lillee bowled 12 overs in the first innings, badly damaging his right knee in the process, and didn't bowl at all in the second. So, the last hurrah in Tests for the Twins of Terror had been the first innings at Christchurch, nine years and two months after they had first joined forces in a Test match. Lillee 3–13; Thomson 4–51. With some help from Terry Alderman (2–63) they had fired

New Zealand out for 149 in the first innings and set up an eight-wicket victory for their side.

From there the pair would go it alone in Tests. But it would not be for too long. Retirement – and a long, long rest – was not far around the corner.

Partnership broken

THE YEARS were taking their toll. Thomson would tour Pakistan in the spring of 1982, playing all three Tests, taking only three wickets. It sounds bad – when you realise that Pakistan won all three Tests, two of them by nine wickets, the other by an innings and three runs, it's even worse – only 25 Pakistani wickets fell in the series. Both Tests and one-day matches were marred by crowd disturbances that resulted in the ill-starred Kim Hughes leading his men from the field more than once. Not a happy tour at all.

Come the 1982–83 domestic season, Lillee played the first Test against England, taking four wickets, then bowed out with knee troubles for the remainder of the international summer. His absence from the Ashes series opened the door for Thomson to return for the remaining four Tests, he stood up very well with 22 wickets at the ripe average of 18.68.

It was in the Boxing Day Test of that Ashes series that Thomson had his second flirtation with batting immortality for Australia, almost eight years after he and Lillee went so close to snatching victory in the final of the inaugural World Cup. Approaching stumps on the fourth day, Australia was looking down the barrel at 9–218 – way off the victory target of 292. There was little but forlorn hope in the home team dressing room after the ninth wicket fell – and Jeff Thomson nonchalantly walked out to join his captain, Allan Border. Thomson a real tailender, Border palpably out of form and the MCG track playing its usual late-in-the-game tricks, its variable bounce making it very difficult for a class batsman and a real nightmare for a tailender.

Border was a picture of composure as he and Thomson picked up runs whenever they were on offer. Thomson remembers, 'We decided to take all the runs, singles included, every time, not just at the end of an over to give AB the strike. The victory target was a long, long way off, so we had to take every run and that meant my being exposed to the danger end a fair bit'.

The pair pushed on to stumps, 37 runs away from an improbable triumph. Free entry was advertised for the final morning, and, as it turned out, an estimated 18,000 turned up in the hope of witnessing one of cricket's miracles. There was a roar from the crowd when Border and Thomson strode out to face destiny. The no-nonsense Thomson turned to his partner and said, 'If it's good enough for these people to turn up in support of us, let's give 'em their money's worth, let's go down fighting'.

The odd couple went on to put up a helluva show. Seventeen overs negotiated, four runs to win. If ever England had produced a match-winner, it was Ian Botham. In their moment of need they turned to the brilliant all-rounder. Botham sent a short one down to Thomson, who went after it – edging to a regulation catch to slip. But Chris Tavare couldn't hold on. The ball spilled free. Thankfully for him, the ball flew up, not down, and Geoff Miller next to him caught the ball on the rebound.

For Australia it was a case of so near, yet so far. For Thomson it was one of the worst moments of his cricketing life. It was years before he could even bring himself to talk about it. For Mr Magic Botham, the wicket of Thomson took him to the wonderful statistic of 1000 runs and 100 wickets in Tests against Australia.

The caravan rolled on to the Sydney Test. Australia had to win or draw to regain the Ashes lost to Botham and England away in 1981. Thomson, bowling first change while Hogg and Geoff Lawson opened the bowling, got his revenge. He took five wickets in the first innings and two in the second. The match was drawn, the Ashes regained. And he got Botham both times. 'Beefy never got any runs against me', he said years later, with some satisfaction.

Limited overs, limited joy

AFTER LILLEE returned to Test-match action for a one-off clash against the burgeoning Sri Lanka, in Kandy, adding three wickets to his career total, it was off to 1983's World Cup, again in England.

The Twins of Terror bowled together in two of Australia's six qualifying games in what was another failed campaign. The first game was against Zimbabwe – Lillee bowled first change, Thomson second change, claiming just the one wicket between them, as Australia fell to ignominious defeat. In the fifth game, against the West Indies at Lord's, neither was able to take a wicket – the only occasion this happened in the 31 times they combined for Australia in an ODI. When they trudged off the ground in defeat, it was the last time they would walk off a ground together. Lillee 0–52; Thomson 0–64.

The international one-day game was in its infancy when these two began their careers. One-Day Internationals began when Australia and England shaped up for one at the MCG in January 1971, a random fixture to make up for the third Test, which had been abandoned without a ball being bowled because of rain. By the end of their careers, it was dominating the Australian cricket calendar thanks to the introduction of day-night cricket that WSC pioneered, and every four years, the World Cup bringing together all of cricket's far-flung nations.

Indeed, it was Australia's first game of that memorable 1975 Cup campaign, versus Pakistan at Headingley on 7 June, when the Twins of Terror first teamed up in an ODI. It was also the game in which Lillee returned his best ODI figures: 5–34 from 12 six-ball overs. Thomson, having slogged 20 from 14 balls including two fours and a six to get Australia to a competitive 278, took 1–25 from eight overs.

It is fair to say that in those early years of the short form, Lillee was more suited to the game than was Thomson. Control of line and length mattered most, attributes that Lillee possessed in spades, while Thomson did not. Lillee also was imbued with a degree of animal cunning, an innate ability to size up a situation and bowl accordingly, be it the format of the game, the condition of wicket or the nature of the opposition batting. For his part, Thomson was most adept at simply tearing in and firing red-hot missiles at the batsman.

As a result, Lillee's numbers over a career spanning 63 ODI games are more than respectable by anyone's measurement: 103 wickets at an average of 20.82 and a cost of 3.58 runs per over. Against that Thomson's career numbers: from 50 games, 55 wickets at 35.30, with an economy rate of 4.32. Lillee's career figures compare favourably with the return of a more recent Australian ODI champ, Glenn McGrath: from 250 games, 381 wickets at 22.02, with an economy rate of 3.88.

Lillee and Thomson lined up together for Australia in 31 ODIs. Lillee's superior ability in this form shows up in the fact that in those games he took 52 wickets, while Thomson had 27. Shuffling up and going *whang* was not enough. One-day cricket was not made for express bowlers. An edge too easily goes for four and Thomson's best work was done with a packed slips cordon, an unaffordable luxury in one-day cricket.

Lillee perhaps put it best when answering the author, who was one of several who interviewed him, Rod Marsh and Greg Chappell for *Cricket Year 1982*, edited by Ken Piesse. Asked if there was too much one-day cricket, Lillee said, 'It promotes too much negative bowling and this can reflect on performances in Test matches and Shield games'.

One last time

GIVEN THOMSON'S excellent form in the Tests against England in 1982–83, it was strange that he would be overlooked throughout the five-Test 1983–84 contest against Pakistan, even if he had fared poorly against them in their previous two series. As for Lillee, after a slow start, by his stellar standards, he finished the series with a rush – taking 19 wickets in the final three Tests. The fifth, at the SCG 2–6 January 1984, will long be remembered as the swansong of three great Australian players: Lillee, his great mate Rod Marsh and Greg Chappell.

At 34 years of age, Lillee had had enough. But he went out with all guns blazing: 4–65 in the first innings, 4–88 in the second. Fittingly, he took a wicket with his final delivery on the big stage, that of tall Pakistan bowler Sarfraz Nawaz. That was his 355th, at the time the world record for Tests. He could put his feet up while watching the Australian openers knock off 35 runs to win the series 2–0. Marsh finished on a high note, too, with five dismissals in Pakistan's second innings to also end his career with a world record 355 dismissals – a freakish coincidence happily synchronising these players who were so integral to each other's success. With even greater symmetry, Chappell went out with a century, pairing with the one he made on debut against England in Perth's inaugural Test in 1970.

Thomson was not done yet, despite having been overlooked through the 1983–84 season, then again in 1984–85 when the West Indies toured for five Tests. He was picked to tour England with Allan Border's team in 1985, Captain Grumpy having taken over when Kim Hughes resigned in tears during the West Indies tour. It was an Ashes tour best forgotten for the Australians – the series lost 3–1. It was no better for Thomson. He played in the first Test at Headingley, took only two wickets and then waited until the fifth at Birmingham for what would be his final Test match appearance. He turned 35 during the game and took 1–101 in England's only innings. There were echoes there too of his first Test, long ago, when he returned 0–100 in Pakistan's first innings at the MCG in the dying days of 1972.

Opener Graham Gooch was his only wicket, a consolation prize of sorts for Thomson being the fact that this was his 200th wicket in Tests. Not that Thomson took much joy from the milestone. 'It wasn't satisfying for me', he said. 'I struggled through that Test through the sheer fact that AB had picked me and I wanted to do the job for the boys. So it didn't mean anything to get the 200th wicket – it was just another wicket'.

Two bright flames – when as one, a blinding light – finally doused.

STATISTICAL ANALYSIS

Compiled by Lawrie Colliver

DENNIS KEITH LILLEE

Born 18 July 1949

First Test 29 January 1971

Last Test 2 January 1984

First ODI 24 August 1972

Last ODI 18 June 1983

First Class 1969–70 – 1988

Career figures

	M	Balls	Runs	Wkts	Avge	Best	5WI	10WM
Tests	70	18,467	8493	355	23.92	7–83	23	7
Supertests	14	3441	1800	67	26.87	7–23	4	0
ODIs	63	3593	21,445	103	20.82	5–34	1	0
First Class	198	44,806	20,695	882	23.46	8–29	50	13
List A	102	5678	3259	165	19.75	5–34	1	0

Combined Tests and Supertests

	M	Balls	Runs	Wkts	Avge	Best	5WI	10WM
Tests	70	18,467	8493	355	23.92	7–83	23	7
Supertests	14	3441	1800	67	26.87	7–23	4	0
Total	84	21,908	8673	422	20.6	7–23	27	7

Batsmen dismissed most in Tests

APE Knott (Eng)	12
IVA Richards (WI)	9
DI Gower (Eng)	9
JH Edrich (Eng)	8
GA Gooch (Eng)	8
DL Amiss (Eng)	8
G Boycott (Eng)	7
IT Botham (Eng)	7
KWR Fletcher (Eng)	7
JM Brearley (Eng)	7
RW Taylor (Eng)	7

Batsmen dismissed most in Supertests

CG Greenidge	8
IVA Richards	7
CH Lloyd	5
RA Austin	5
CL King	4
RC Fredericks	3
AW Greig	3
JC Allen	3
DL Murray	3
DL Haynes	3

Batsmen dismissed most in Tests and Supertests

	Tests	ST	Total
IVA Richards	9	7	16
APE Knott	12	1	13
CG Greenidge	5	8	13
DI Gower	9	0	9
DL Murray	6	3	9
AW Greig	6	3	9
JH Edrich	8	0	8
GA Gooch	8	0	8
DL Amiss	8	0	8
CH Lloyd	3	5	8
G Boycott	7	0	7
IT Botham	7	0	7
KWR Fletcher	7	0	7
JM Brearley	7	0	7
RW Taylor	7	0	7

STATISTICAL ANALYSIS

Wickets taken by place in batting order in Tests and Supertests

	Tests	ST	Total
Openers	87	21	108
No 3	41	5	46
No 4	38	5	43
No 5	28	8	36
No 6	31	8	39
No 7	33	6	39
No 8	36	5	41
No 9	24	1	25
No 10	25	5	30
No 11	12	3	15
Total	355	67	422

Ten or more wickets in a Test match

v England, Oval, 1972	10	181
v Pakistan, MCG, 1976–7	10	135
v New Zealand, Auckland, 1976–7	11	123
v England, MCG, 1977 Cent Test	11	165
v England, MCG, 1979–80	11	138
v England, Oval, 1981	11	159
v West Indies, MCG, 1981–2	10	127

Tests before and after 1973 injury

	Tests	Balls	Runs	Wkts	Avge	Best	5WI	10WM	SR
Before	11	2959	1232	51	24.16	6–66	4	1	58.0
After	59	15,508	7261	304	23.88	7–83	19	6	51.0
Overall	70	18,467	8493	355	23.9	7–83	23	7	52.0

200+ wickets in Tests and Supertests for Australia to Sept 2017

	Games	Balls	Runs	Wkts	Avge	Best	5WI	10WM
SK Warne	145	40,704	17995	708	25.42	8–71	37	10
GD McGrath	124	29,248	12186	563	21.64	8–24	29	3
DK Lillee	84	21,908	8673	422	20.55	7–23	27	7
MG Johnson	73	16,001	8891	313	28.41	8–61	12	3
B Lee	76	16,531	9554	310	30.82	5–30	10	0
CJ McDermott	71	16,586	8332	291	28.63	8–97	14	2
NM Lyon	69	16,368	8564	269	31.83	8–50	12	2
JN Gillespie	71	14,234	6770	259	26.14	7–37	8	0
R Benaud	63	19,108	6704	248	27.03	7–72	16	1
GD McKenzie	60	17,681	7328	246	29.79	8–71	16	3
RR Lindwall	61	13,650	5251	228	23.03	7–38	12	0
JR Thomson	56	11,333	6077	216	28.13	6–46	9	0

Top strike rates for bowlers with 300+ Test wickets to Sept 2017

	Tests	Balls	Runs	Wkts	Avge	Best	5WI	10WM	SR
DW Steyn (SA)	85	17,286	9303	417	22.31	7–51	26	5	41.4
Waqar Younis (Pak)	87	16,224	8788	373	23.56	7–76	22	5	43.5
MD Marshall (WI)	81	17,584	7876	376	20.95	7–22	22	4	46.7
AA Donald (SA)	72	15,519	7344	330	22.25	8–71	20	3	47.0
FS Trueman (Eng)	67	15,178	6625	307	21.58	8–31	17	3	49.4
RJ Hadlee (NZ)	86	21,918	9612	431	22.30	9–52	36	9	50.8
MG Johnson (Aust)	73	16,001	8891	313	28.41	8–61	12	3	51.1
GD McGrath (Aust)	124	29,248	12,186	563	21.64	8–24	29	3	51.9
DK Lillee (Aust)	70	18,467	8493	355	23.92	7–83	23	7	52.0
B Lee (Aust)	76	16,531	9554	310	30.82	5–30	10	0	53.3

Wickets by Test venue

	Tests	Balls	Runs	Wkts	Avge	Best	5WI	10WM
Adelaide	9	2479	1206	45	26.80	6–171	4	
Auckland	2	578	261	15	17.40	6–72	2	1
Birmingham	2	474	172	11	15.64	5–15	1	
Brisbane	6	1175	625	31	20.16	6–53	2	
Christchurch	2	466	202	7	28.86	3–13		
Faisalabad	1	126	91	0				
Kandy	1	180	107	3	35.67	2–67		
Karachi	1	234	98	0				
Kingston	1	192	132	0				
Lahore	1	252	114	3	38.00	3–114		
Leeds	3	738	290	13	22.31	4–49		
Lord's	4	1190	584	17	34.35	4–43		
Manchester	2	775	298	14	21.29	6–66	1	
MCG	14	3833	1798	82	21.93	7–83	7	4
Nottingham	2	502	155	14	11.07	5–46	1	
Perth	7	1856	817	30	27.23	5–18	2	
SCG	8	2191	1036	43	24.09	4–40		
The Oval	3	1136	475	27	17.59	7–89	3	2
Wellington	1	90	32	0				
Overall	70	18,467	8493	355	23.9	7–83	23	7

STATISTICAL ANALYSIS

Best single-innings performances at the MCG

	Overs	Mdns	Runs	Wkts
v WI 1981–2	26.3	3	83	7
v Eng 1977	13.3	2	26	6
v Eng 1979–80	33.1	9	60	6
v Pak 1976–7	23	4	82	6
v WI 1975–6	11.3	0	63	5
v Eng 1979–80	33	6	78	5
v Eng 1977	34.4	7	139	5
v Pak 1976–7	14	1	53	4
v WI 1975–6	14	2	56	4
v India 1980–1	25	6	65	4

Tests in England

	Tests	Balls	Runs	Wkts	Avge	Best	5WI	10WM	SR
1972 Ashes	5	1499	548	31	17.68	6–66	3	1	48.3
1975 Ashes	4	1242	460	21	21.90	5–15	1	0	59.1
1980 Cent. Test	1	204	96	5	19.20	4–49	0	0	40.8
1981 Ashes	6	1870	870	39	22.31	7–89	2	1	47.9
Overall	16	4815	1974	96	20.60	7–89	6	2	50.2

Wickets in Ashes Tests

	Tests	Balls	Runs	Wkts	Avge	Best	5WI	10WM	SR
1970–1 (Aust)	2	499	199	8	24.88	5–84	1	0	62.3
1972 (Eng)	5	1499	548	31	17.68	6–66	3	1	48.3
1974–5 (Aust)	6	1462	596	25	23.84	4–49	0	0	58.4
1975 (Eng)	4	1242	460	21	21.90	5–15	1	0	59.1
1981 (Eng)	6	1870	870	39	22.31	7–89	2	1	47.9
1982–3 (Aust)	1	426	185	4	46.25	3–96	0	0	106.5
Overall	24	6998	2858	128	22.30	7–89	7	2	54.7

Lillee in England Tests that were not for Ashes

	Tests	Balls	Runs	Wkts	Avge	Best	5WI	10WM	SR
1976–7 (Aust)	1	383	165	11	15.00	6–26	2	1	34.8
1979–80 (Aust)	3	931	388	23	16.87	6–60	2	1	41.7
1980 (Eng)	1	204	96	5	19.20	4–49	0	0	40.8
Overall	5	1518	649	39	16.60	6–26	4	2	38.9

JEFFREY ROBERT THOMSON

Born 16 August 1950
First Test 29 December 1972
Last Test 15 August 1985
First ODI 1 June 1975
Last ODI 3 June 1985
First Class 1972–73 – 1985–86

Career figures

	M	Balls	Runs	Wkts	Avge	Best	5WI	10WM
Tests	51	10,535	5601	200	28.00	6–46	8	0
Supertests	5	798	476	16	29.75	5–78	1	0
ODIs	50	2696	1942	55	35.30	4–67	0	0
First Class	187	33,318	17864	675	26.46	7–27	28	3
List A	88	4529	3103	107	29.00	7–22	1	0

Combined Tests and Supertests

	M	Balls	Runs	Wkts	Avge	Best	5WI	10WM
Tests	51	10,535	5601	200	28.00	6–46	8	0
Supertests	5	798	476	16	29.75	5–78	1	0
Total	56	11,333	6077	216	28.13	6–46	9	0

Batsmen dismissed most in Tests

APE Knott (Eng)	9
RGD Willis (Eng)	7
AI Kallicharran (WI)	7
IT Botham (Eng)	7
IVA Richards (WI)	5
CH Lloyd (WI)	5
CG Greenidge (WI)	5
AW Greig (Eng)	5
DL Amiss (Eng)	5
MH Denness (Eng)	5
MC Cowdrey (Eng)	5

STATISTICAL ANALYSIS

Batsmen dismissed most in Supertests

IVA Richards	3
MA Holding	2
CH Lloyd	2
RC Fredericks	2
LG Rowe	2
CG Greenidge	1
AME Roberts	1
DL Murray	1
J Garner	1
DL Haynes	1

Batsmen dismissed most in Tests and Supertests

	Tests	ST	Total
APE Knott (Eng)	9	0	9
IVA Richards (WI)	5	3	8
RGD Willis (Eng)	7	0	7
AI Kallicharran (WI)	7	0	7
IT Botham (Eng)	7	0	7
CH Lloyd (WI)	5	2	7
CG Greenidge (WI)	5	1	6
AW Greig (Eng)	5	0	5
DL Amiss (Eng)	5	0	5
MH Denness (Eng)	5	0	5
MC Cowdrey (Eng)	5	0	5

Wickets taken by place in batting order

	Tests	ST	Total
Openers	48	4	52
No 3	26	2	28
No 4	19	2	21
No 5	20	1	21
No 6	19	2	21
No 7	25	1	26
No 8	10	1	11
No 9	10	2	12
No 10	13	1	14
No 11	10	0	10
Total	200	16	216

Wickets by Test venue

	Tests	Balls	Runs	Wkts	Avge	Best	5WI	10WM
Adelaide	6	864	504	24	21.00	4–68		
Auckland	1	138	52	0				
Birmingham	2	282	160	6	26.67	5–38	1	
Bridgetown	1	114	99	6	16.50	6–77	1	
Brisbane	6	1396	697	29	24.03	6–46	2	
Christchurch	1	240	105	4	26.25	4–51		
Faisalabad	1	138	79	0				
Georgetown	1	218	140	5	28.00	4–57		
Karachi	1	192	119	2	59.50	1–16		
Kingston	1	222	114	3	38.00	2–61		
Lahore	1	144	97	1	97.00	1–73		
Leeds	3	678	407	9	45.22	4–113		
Lord's	2	591	292	11	26.55	4–41		
Manchester	1	276	97	3	32.33	3–73		
MCG	7	1427	830	26	31.92	5–62	1	
Nottingham	1	282	137	3	45.67	3–103		
Perth	5	1097	571	21	27.19	5–93	1	
Port-of-Spain	2	354	224	6	37.33	3–64		
SCG	5	1243	621	29	21.41	6–50	2	
The Oval	2	483	222	10	22.20	4–50		
Wellington	1	156	35	2	17.50	2–35		
	51	10,535	5602	200	28.01	6–46	8	

Tests before and after 1976 injury

	Tests	Balls	Runs	Wkts	Avge	Best	5WI	10WM	SR
Before	17	3878	2024	80	25.30	6–46	5	0	48.5
After	34	6657	3578	120	29.82	6–77	3	0	55.4
	51	10,535	5602	200	28.01	6–46	8	0	52.6

LILLEE-THOMSON COMBINED

Lillee career

	M	Balls	Runs	Wkts	Avge	Best	5WI	10WM
Tests	70	18,467	8493	355	23.92	7–83	23	7
Supertests	14	3441	1800	67	26.87	7–23	4	0
Combined	84	21,908	8673	422	24.39	7–23	27	7

Lillee with Thomson

	M	Balls	Runs	Wkts	Avge	Best	5WI	10WM
In Tests	26	6449	3126	119	26.26	5–15	5	0
In Supertests	5	1084	653	23	28.39	7–23	1	0
Total	31	7533	3779	142	26.61	7–23	6	0

Lillee without Thomson

	M	Balls	Runs	Wkts	Avge	Best	5WI	10WM
In Tests	44	12,018	5367	236	22.74	7–83	18	7
In Supertests	9	2357	1147	44	26.07	7–23	3	0
Total	53	14,375	6514	280	23.26	7–23	21	7

Thomson career

	M	Balls	Runs	Wkts	Avge	Best	5WI	10WM
Tests	51	10,535	5601	200	28.00	6–46	8	0
Supertests	5	798	476	16	29.75	5–78	1	0
Combined	56	11,333	6077	216	28.13	6–46	9	0

Thomson with Lillee

	M	Balls	Runs	Wkts	Avge	Best	5WI	10WM
In Tests	26	5359	2778	98	28.34	6–46	4	0
In Supertests	5	798	476	16	29.75	5–78	1	0
Combined	31	6157	3254	114	28.54	6–46	5	0

Thomson didn't play any Supertests without Lillee

Together in ODIs

	M	Balls	Runs	Wkts	Avge	Best	5WI
Lillee	31	1845	1161	52	22.32	5–34	1
Thomson	31	1679	1164	27	43.11	2–36	0

Results in Tests played

	P	W	L	D
Lillee overall	70	32	15	23
Lillee with Thomson	26	14	4	8
Lillee without Thomson	44	18	11	15
Thomson overall	51	21	18	12
Thomson with Lillee	26	14	4	8
Thomson without Lillee	25	7	14	4

Tests before and after Thomson shoulder injury, 1976

	M	Balls	Runs	Wkts	Avge	Best	5WI	10WM	SR
Lillee before injury	27	7233	3267	130	25.13	6–66	7	1	55.6
Lillee after injury	43	11,234	5226	225	23.23	2–36	16	6	49.9
Thomson before injury	17	3878	2024	80	25.30	6–46	5	0	48.4
Thomson after injury	34	6657	3578	120	29.82	6–77	3	0	55.4

Dismissals with Rod Marsh as wicketkeeper when Lillee and Thomson combined

	M	Ct
Lillee in Tests	26	37
Lillee in Supertests	5	8
Total	31	45
Thomson in Tests	26	25
Thomson in Supertests	5	1
Total	31	26

Bowler/wicketkeeper combinations in Tests

DK Lillee/RW Marsh	95
GD McGrath/AC Gilchrist	90
M Ntini/MV Boucher	84
B Lee/AC Gilchrist	81
SM Pollock/MV Boucher	79
MD Marshall/PJL Dujon	71
MG Johnson/BJ Haddin	71
JH Kallis/MV Boucher	69
JM Anderson/MJ Prior	68
IT Botham/RW Taylor	60
SK Warne/AC Gilchrist	59

ACKNOWLEDGEMENTS

In making a journey such as this, through a maze of events across the cricketing world, I have been extremely fortunate to have been able to add my own close observations of this magical period in Australia's rich cricket tapestry, as a player, broadcaster, journalist and writer of cricket books. To have played with Dennis Lillee (for Western Australia) and against Jeff Thomson (for Queensland) and have sat in a commentary box and tried to find the words to describe the way they worked so successfully together. These experiences offered me a rare insight into the crippling effect that not one, but two, great fast bowlers can impose on batsmen. Even the best in the business were compromised. Unashamedly so.

Beyond my personal reflections – and those of the list of my interviewees – I have used these books for research purposes:

Dennis Lillee, *Dennis Lillee: An Illustrated Autobiography*.
 South Melbourne, Victoria, Affirm Press, 2016.
Dennis Lillee and Bob Harris, *Lillee: An Autobiography*.
 London, Headline Book Publishing, 2003.
Ashley Mallett, *Thommo Speaks Out: The Authorised Biography
 of Jeff Thomson*. Crows Nest, NSW, Allen & Unwin, 2009.
Sir Vivian Richards and Bob Harris, *Sir Vivian: The Definitive
 Biography*. London, Michael Joseph, 2000.

My most sincere thanks to the authors of all of the above, and to the countless other writers of newspaper and magazine articles, whose work I have been able to reference.

Plus, I wish to thank Pam Brewster, Publisher at Hardie Grant Books, for having set me the task and for her continued support through the project. My thanks, too, to Michael Epis, for his untiring efforts in knocking the manuscript into shape. And, to Lawrie Colliver, for the invaluable Statistical Analysis.

Importantly, thanks to my wife Joan – for putting up with my lengthy absences at the keyboard and for always being a valued sounding board. For one who knew virtually nothing about cricket before meeting me, she has been an unstinting supporter of my writings on the great summer game.

Finally, thanks to Dennis Lillee and Jeff Thomson ... both absolute inspirations then, and now!

> *'Ashes to ashes ... dust to dust ...*
> *if Thommo don't get ya ... Lillee must ...'*
>
> (Paul Rigby, cartoonist)

THE ART and MAKING OF HOGWARTS LEGACY

WRITTEN BY
Jody Revenson & Michael Owen

BLOOMSBURY
CHILDREN'S BOOKS
LONDON OXFORD NEW YORK NEW DELHI SYDNEY

An Insight Editions Book

CONTENTS

CHAPTER 1:
The First Mission 9

Ancient Magic 20
A Wizard's Field Guide 22

CHAPTER 2:
Where Our Story Starts 29

The Player's Choices 80
Cinematics: Bringing the Story to Life 82

CHAPTER 3:
Establishing the Locations 85

The Room of Requirement 128
Traversing the Highlands 182
Extracurricular Activities 184

CHAPTER 4:
The Beasts of Hogwarts Legacy 189

Animating the Beasts 212

CHAPTER 5:
Golden Paths and Dark Mysteries 217

Playing Your Way 224
Casting a Spell 226

Continue Play 248

Acknowledgements 250

FOREWORD

Just one year before *Harry Potter and the Philosopher's Stone,* the first book in the Harry Potter series, was published, a group of friends started a small game development studio named Avalanche Software. Over the next 25 years, as more Harry Potter books and films were being released and embraced around the globe, the team at Avalanche honed their craft, working on dozens of games based on the biggest franchises in the world. Even if one practised Divination, one might never have foreseen all that would eventually happen. Avalanche was ultimately invited to join Warner Bros. Games and given access to Warner Bros.' vast library of amazing stories and characters. There was never a question: the Wizarding World was Avalanche's destiny.

J.K. Rowling, author of the Harry Potter books, brilliantly imagined a world parallel to our own, where magic is real. So real that even schools are dedicated to the study and practice of all things magic. The wizarding world – and the most famous of those schools, Hogwarts School of Witchcraft and Wizardry – are tantalisingly close, just beyond seemingly impenetrable brick walls behind a small London tavern and at King's Cross Station. The books invited us behind these enchanted, academic walls to follow the story of a young boy's discovery that he is a wizard and his eventual realisation of his magical potential. We all loved it, and wondered if we, too, had hidden magical potential.

That fan fantasy, to attend Hogwarts ourselves, to hone that hidden magical potential was our North Star from the very beginning. But this target came with inherent challenges. We would be walking a thin tightrope to bring this magical world to life in an interactive experience. Reading the books and watching the films have given fans vivid pictures in their heads as to what the wizarding world might look like. However, this would not be Harry's story. In fact, the player would not be a mere visitor to the world, or a tourist visiting a Harry Potter film set. The player is a witch or wizard, exploring Hogwarts, Hogsmeade, the Forbidden Forest and the surrounding area for their very first time – discovering for themselves the various surprises, charm, secrets and mysteries around every corner. We knew that what we were creating had to be authentic to what the books and films have introduced combined with our shared collective imagination, but also feel fresh and new.

'Authentic'. No word was repeated more throughout the development of this game. The architecture, fashion, furnishing, terrain and weather had to be authentic to the Scottish Highlands of the late 1800s, and, more importantly, the story, characters, humour, charm and magic had to be authentic to the wizarding world. Topics of creative conversations varied, from the profound, such as choosing what is right over what is easy, to the surreal and frankly odd, like the proper presentation of Dugbog dung. Regardless, each creative conversation was approached with the same earnest desire to get the wizarding world of the late 19th century right.

So many passionate and incomparably talented people put their heart and soul into *Hogwarts Legacy*. When players find themselves exploring behind those enchanted brick walls, I am confident they will recognise an authentic world that has been created from years of scrupulous research and dedicated hard work, and feel the shared love and respect for that world.

This book is a tribute to that work and passion. It is our honour to share the behind-the-scenes efforts of bringing the wizarding world to life in *Hogwarts Legacy*.

Page 2: The Three Broomsticks by Sébastien Gallego
Page 4: The Sorting Hat by Nasan Hardcastle
opposite: Castle Ruins and Gringotts (in-game renders) by the Environment Team; Intro Void by Ben Simonsen

CHAPTER 1
The First Mission

Would you have ever imagined that maybe, just possibly, we might be living side by side with a parallel, unseen magical society? J.K. Rowling imagined it, and in June 1997, upon publication in the United Kingdom of her first book, *Harry Potter and the Philosopher's Stone*, the world discovered that in this realm brooms are used not just for sweeping but also for flying, and students learn to cast spells and charms, brew potions and care for magical beasts at Hogwarts School of Witchcraft and Wizardry.

Since the publication of the first book, the wizarding world of Harry Potter has been realised in film adaptations and theme parks, as well as video games where gameplay was set in the eras familiar from Harry Potter's attendance at Hogwarts (the 1990s) and Newt Scamander's adventures in the Fantastic Beasts films (the 1920s). Fans of the wizarding world have dreamed of attending Hogwarts ever since the books introduced us to the story of the Boy Who Lived.

In November 2017, Warner Bros. Interactive Entertainment established Portkey Games, dedicated to creating wizarding world mobile game and video game experiences inspired by Rowling's original stories. (Because these games launch the players into their own wizarding world adventures, the division was named after the magical item from the lore that transports wizards and witches from place to place.) While the content for *Hogwarts Legacy* has not been written by J.K. Rowling, the creative team at Avalanche Software has been entrusted with the privilege and responsibility, as part of the Portkey Games label, of charting new territory anchored in wizarding world lore and inspired by her original writing.

The game-development team, embracing what was already known about the wizarding world, challenged themselves to expand on it for not only a return to Hogwarts but also an immersion in an as-yet-unseen era – the late 1800s. 'We asked ourselves how we could draw from the rich library of characters, creatures and themes,' says **Adrian Ropp, Head of Story** for the game, 'and imagine how those details would influence the school more than a century before Harry Potter's arrival. Who was the headmaster? What challenges did students face? What influenced their society before Tom Riddle, before Newt Scamander?'

Being Harry Potter fans themselves, the team deliberated on what a player would want if they had the opportunity to attend Hogwarts. Of course, they'd want to become a powerful witch or wizard, and have the opportunity to make friends, an experience so central to the Harry Potter saga in general.

To fulfil this mission, the team settled on three pillars to guide them: authenticity, heroism and magic.

PAGES 8-9: Bog by Mike McCarthy
OPPOSITE: Architect Statue (in-game render) by the Environment Team
BELOW: Hogwarts Exterior by Joshua H Black

AUTHENTICITY

Everything in the game must be authentic to the world fans love. 'Maintaining the authenticity of that world not only engages players, it keeps them engaged,' says **Narrative Lead, Moira Squier**. 'While we have expanded the wizarding world to allow for a wonderfully immersive game, we are well aware that if we stray too far from the rules of the world with which fans are familiar, we will lose their confidence in us, and the magic will be lost. We want fans to know that we hold the lore as dear as they do.'

Head of Story, Adrian Ropp was quite aware of the surreal nature of the story meetings they held to address this pillar. '"How long do house-elves live?" "Are Graphorns omnivores?" These are the types of questions that drove us towards authenticity and the types of questions you only think to ask when you have steeped yourself in the lore.'

OPPOSITE LEFT: Abandoned Hamlet by Vanessa Palmer
OPPOSITE RIGHT: Intro Locket Vial by Danny Russon
TOP: Hogsmeade Entrance Bridge by Danny Russon
LEFT: Around Hogwarts (in-game render) by the Environment Team

Intro Sea Stack by Mike McCarthy and Vanessa Palmer

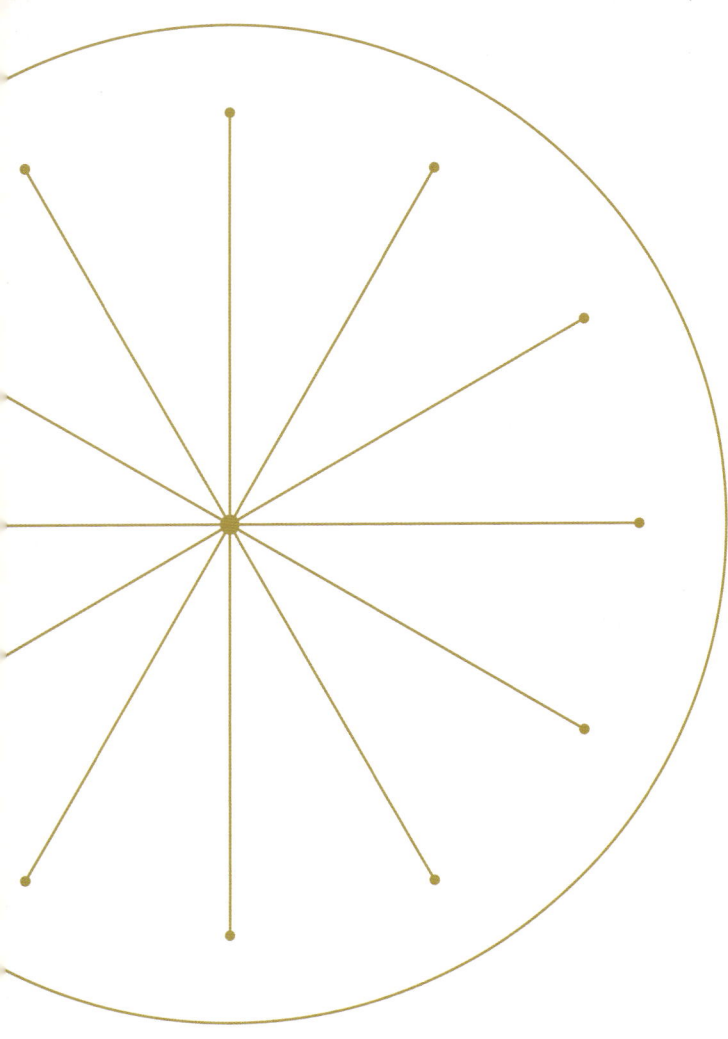

HEROISM

'This game doesn't retell the story of Harry Potter,' says **Art Director, Jeff Bunker**. 'This is the player's journey. It was important to us that the player didn't feel like a tourist visiting a Harry Potter film set or theme park where all the charm, mystery and magic had already been revealed. We want the player to feel just like Harry, experiencing Hogwarts and Hogsmeade and the Forbidden Forest for the first time, not knowing what to expect.'

As Harry Potter was the hero of his own undertaking to defeat Voldemort, so is the player the hero of their own mission to save the wizarding world from a Dark use of ancient magic in *Hogwarts Legacy*. 'The avatar is the only one who can see traces of this magic, so they alone can follow a path set by witches and wizards hundreds of years ago – it cannot be done by anyone else,' says **Narrative Lead, Moira Squier**.

One of the most important aspects of a hero is how they decide to achieve the quest set before them. 'Harry Potter knew that the choices he made mattered,' says Squier. 'Our game not only allows the player to create an avatar that reflects their physical identity, it also – via the choices they make – allows them to express their personalities and particular points of view and affect the world around them.'

At the start of the player's path they know very little magic, but as the story unfolds, they become highly skilled and can defeat the villains who want the ancient magic power. Then, by the end of the game, the player decides either to use the power they have gained for themselves, share it with the world or keep it hidden – thus being affected by their journey in one of at least three ways.

OPPOSITE: Troll Fight (in-game render) by the Environment Team; Graphorn Gate by Mike McCarthy; Troll Den by Vanessa Palmer

MAGIC

Every part of the world must be filled with magic. The wizarding world is *literally* filled with magic. Magic is what separates it from our 'real' everyday world. 'I've always said that one of the reasons the wizarding world is so appealing is that it's just a step away from our world,' says Squier. 'It *could* be real. The characters and bits of everyday life are familiar, but with a magical edge.'

In the game, magic is celebrated in every way, from spectacular challenges to the most mundane of interactions, and the Avalanche team honed in on any and every opportunity to include magic, so that the player continuously knows that they are in a world unlike their own. Whether at Hogwarts, in Hogsmeade or traversing the Highlands, the player is surrounded by witches and wizards, fantastic beasts and dangerous, Dark enemies. 'Even the simplest moments are magical – levitating something out of their way, summoning a book from a shelf or lighting their way with a wand – reminding the player that they are in a world that's just beyond our own,' says Squier. 'And, of course, the spectacle of magic is a beautiful thing to portray visually in the game.'

As magic is central to any experience within the wizarding world generally, and at Hogwarts in particular, the team knew they had to get it right. 'In the wizarding world, magic isn't mystical or otherworldly,' says **Art Director, Jeff Bunker**. 'Like Snape describing "the subtle science and exact art of potion-making", magic is something real! This is, after all, Hogwarts School of Witchcraft and Wizardry, where students come to study magic the way we Muggles study physics and chemistry. This very physical nature of magic in the wizarding world allows us as developers to find ways to allow the player new, visceral ways to touch the world magically and have the world magically act and react. It opened up a whole new world of possibilities for our artists – literally.'

Players live in the wizarding world, where they attend classes at Hogwarts, visit the Three Broomsticks in Hogsmeade and explore the Forbidden Forest. They can freely cast magic as an actual witch or wizard. 'The three pillars were designed to ensure that we created an experience that would make lifelong fans and players who aren't as familiar with the wizarding world feel like they have travelled to an extraordinary place and time,' says Squier. 'These pillars kept us focused on what makes the wizarding world so special and provided clear guideposts for everyone at every stage, from story to design to implementation to marketing, to follow as we expand the wizarding world into something grander and more immersive than ever before.'

TOP: Hallowe'en in the Great Hall by Joshua H Black

LEFT: Mirror Arch by Vanessa Palmer

ANCIENT MAGIC

Ancient magic is a powerful form of magic, said to be woven into some of the greatest moments of wizardry and witchcraft. It is at the front and centre of the *Hogwarts Legacy* storyline, starting with the player's admittance to Hogwarts School of Witchcraft and Wizardry as a fifth-year student. It provides a brand-new story for the wizarding world, but the concept of ancient magic is not new.

'The idea of ancient magic is actually seeded in the Harry Potter books,' says Squier. As Albus Dumbledore explains in *Harry Potter and the Half-Blood Prince*, 'The castle is a stronghold of ancient magic … there are still mysteries to unravel, stores of magic to tap.'

'We didn't want every mystery in the castle to be able to be buttoned up and explained,' adds **Hogwarts Art Lead, Boston Madsen**. 'The castle's personality and mystery should be bigger than just the story we are telling in this game. Dumbledore was at Hogwarts far longer than most, and even he said he didn't know everything about the castle that there was to be known.'

Ancient magic is also the reason Dumbledore sends Harry to live with his Aunt Petunia Dursley after the death of his parents. Voldemort was aware of ancient magic, but despised it, and underestimated the power of the loving sacrifice Lily Potter made to protect her child. 'She gave you a lingering protection he never expected,' says Dumbledore in *Harry Potter and the Order of the Phoenix*, 'a protection that flows in your veins to this day. I put my trust, therefore, in your mother's blood. I delivered you to her sister, her only remaining relative.'

The notion that traces of ancient magic exist in the world is found in the books, Squier points out, recalling another quote from Dumbledore in *The Half-Blood Prince*: 'Magic always leaves traces … sometimes very distinctive traces.' Squier notes that Voldemort, too, was well aware of ancient magic and its traces – and was frustrated by how it had protected Harry. 'His mother left upon [Harry] the traces of her sacrifice,' Voldemort acknowledged in *The Goblet of Fire*, 'this is old magic. I should have remembered it, I was foolish to overlook it … ' 'And, of course,' Squier adds, remembering *Harry Potter and the Deathly Hallows*, the trace is 'the charm that detects magical activity around under-seventeens.'

'The books only touch on that type of magic,' she continues. 'And it fascinated us that there may be more to it. If it's "ancient", when did it start? What happened to it? Could one actually wield such magic? We saw Grindelwald do some amazing things in the Fantastic Beasts films. Was his ability to control others drawing on ancient magic? All of these things informed our decision to go down that path in the game.'

While travelling to Hogwarts with Professor Eleazar Fig, it doesn't take long for the protagonist to discover their rare ability to detect and wield this ancient magic.

TOP: Ancient Magic Repository by Danny Russon

RIGHT: Ancient Magic Artefact and Ranrok Ancient Magic by Danny Russon

A WIZARD'S FIELD GUIDE

The Hogwarts professors and the Ministry of Magic provide the player with a *Wizard's Field Guide* to help them catch up with their fellow fifth-years. Presented by Professor Matilda Weasley on the player's first day, the guide is initially mostly empty. As locations, activities, collectables and quests are discovered, however, the guide fills, serving as a to-do list, reference and goal tracker.

Development of this comprehensive field guide began with the standards the team had set. 'It was important to the team that the concept of progress at Hogwarts was linked to progress in the game everywhere,' explains **Game Director, Alan Tew**, 'that it allowed for a strong sense of player freedom within the world, and that it represented the effort an actual Hogwarts faculty would put into helping a student in such circumstances to catch up.' Tew reminds us of a similar situation from the third book/film adaptation when, 'Hermione was loaned a Time-Turner to stay on top of her extracurricular ambitions!'

The primary goal for the field guide's design was to make sure it felt like it belonged in the wizarding world. 'That it had a charm and character,' says Tew, 'with a mind of its own, as it sought to fill itself with information from your surroundings onto different-sized pages it would gather and compile for you.'

Avalanche went through numerous iterations until they landed on the final look of the *Wizard's Field Guide*. The idea of a field guide, which could be integrated throughout the game, answered the team's search for a user interface that felt magical but not overbearing to the player. The final implementation is easy to navigate and fits into the overall design.

For the player, the *Wizard's Field Guide* incorporates everything needed to progress through *Hogwarts Legacy*. Maps offer navigation through the complex corridors of Hogwarts, the bustling streets of Hogsmeade and the vast Highlands area surrounding the castle and grounds. Active quests and challenges provide a kind of to-do list of level-up activities. Player progression can be tracked as talents and gear upgrades become available. Collections of knowledge are revealed as the player continues to explore and learn. Incorporating all of this and more into the field guide proved to be a challenge.

The game's concept of earning XP strictly through challenges shares similarities with other RPG systems. This provides a comfort of familiarity 'that we assume understanding,' says Tew, 'and just different enough that assuming causes problems. It's a major priority and effort to ensure that players understand challenges and can use the guide to navigate the world around them easily.'

'The field guide, in many ways, is our interface,' the Game Director explains, 'and its pages are used to represent everything in the game the player might want to do. And there are a lot of things to represent. From maps, to gear, to challenges, to rewards, owl post, mission information, collections of everything

OPPOSITE TOP LEFT: Field Guide Opening by Danny Russon

OPPOSITE TOP RIGHT: Field Guide Book by Vanessa Palmer

OPPOSITE BOTTOM: Field Guide (in-game cinematic) by the Environment Team you've discovered, information about everything you're missing, potion recipes, spell notes, potting requirements, beast compendiums, enemy logs, random notes and more. All of it tries to come together under one wrapper, and that's no easy feat.'

Tew closes with his hope that everyone enjoys the final product that they have developed, 'Pay attention to what's in your challenges and collections, and your legacy should be richer for it!'

24

IT IS YOUR CHOICES

As Albus Dumbledore says to Harry in the film *Harry Potter and the Chamber of Secrets*, 'It is not our abilities that show what we truly are. It is our choices.' It would not be surprising to know that the biggest creative choices during the creation of *Hogwarts Legacy* were what would be put in the game, and what wouldn't make the cut. 'The wizarding world spans such a long period of time across numerous books and films,' explains **Creative Director, Marcus Fisher**, 'and as such, there is so much more material throughout its life span than we could possibly fit into a single game experience. Not for lack of trying!' If there weren't times where the words 'Sorry, no' had to be used for some of the myriad ideas offered, development of the game might have gone on for as long as Hogwarts has been around.

'Just speaking to magic alone,' continues Fisher, 'between all the books, films and reference there are so many spells, jinxes and curses even some of our most ardent superfans had no idea existed until we really started digging deep. And though the team was excited about them all, we were forced to discipline ourselves and narrow down to a core set that we thought would best serve the wizarding world gameplay experience.' The same philosophy needed to be applied to any element the team felt must be included to remain true to the property. 'For example, we knew we wouldn't be doing right by the fans if we didn't incorporate mounts and broom flight. We knew full well that including these, on top of everything else, would be a considerable effort, to say the least, but we also knew that for the fans who want to fly a Hippogriff over the lake, like Harry did, we couldn't say no to taking on the challenge.'

OPPOSITE TOP: House Points Hall (in-game render) by the Environment Team

OPPOSITE BOTTOM LEFT: Owl Post Field Guide Drawing by Vanessa Palmer

OPPOSITE BOTTOM RIGHT: Broom Bright Spark Field Guide Drawing by Nasan Hardcastle

LEFT: Horklump Juice Field Guide Drawing and Chest Inventory Field Guide Drawing by Vanessa Palmer

TURN OF THE CENTURY

Hogwarts Legacy is set in the wizarding world of the late 1800s, allowing for new locations, new professors and new enemies. 'The late 1800s was distant enough that it wouldn't touch on any of the characters in the wizarding world familiar to fans from the Harry Potter and Fantastic Beasts books and films – except for, of course, ghosts at Hogwarts, like Professor Binns,' explains Squier, 'but close enough that players will feel as though the characters they interact with in this game are connected to, and in some cases are precursors for, the characters we know from more recent times.'

The team considered the possibility of placing the game during the present but knew they would have had to account for what happened to all the characters already known and loved from the books and films. 'Our challenge had less to do with time, and more to do with taking the fans to places that hadn't been explored visually in the films or even beyond what was written about in the books,' says Jeff Bunker. 'The wizarding world is more timeless than the Muggle world. So, it was really as simple as just excluding anything obviously modern or anachronistic and having fun with all of the possibilities of anything older.'

For Hogwarts, an institution that has been around for at least nine hundred years by the era of *Hogwarts Legacy*, there would certainly be elements that existed through the centuries. Nearly Headless Nick would be floating around, loyal and cheerful as ever, and the Forbidden Forest would be forbidden, as well as home to centaurs not keen on human interaction. The village of Hogsmeade would be there, with the added advantage of a wand shop maintained by an Ollivander, whose family had been making wands since 382 BCE. But unquestionably, things would also be different at the school and its surroundings. The goblins in this time certainly don't all work at Gringotts, for example.

The nineteenth-century period is different enough from today's world that the characters, locations and costumes would be entirely new for the wizarding world. However, the setting of 1890s Britain still needed to allow the dialogue, story content and characters to mesh with more modern sensibilities so that today's player can understand and relate to the game's world. And as each era has its own slang and euphemisms, creating the wizarding jargon added another enchanting layer. 'One of the most fun challenges was trying to create insults that made sense in the 1890s wizarding world that could sound remotely shocking today,' says Squier. 'Calling someone a cape-flapper still makes me laugh.'

TOP: London by Vanessa Palmer

OPPOSITE TOP AND BOTTOM: Salon (in-game render) and London by the Environment Team

ADVANCED IN YEARS

In addition to placing *Hogwarts Legacy* in a new original wizarding era, the next crucial decision the team debated was, what year at Hogwarts should the player enter? Most wizards begin their training at the age of eleven, but unusual circumstances have the player arriving late, at the age of fifteen – and for good reason. 'If the player had arrived at Hogwarts as a first-year, they would be much too young for the story we wanted to tell and the responsibility they were going to shoulder,' Squier explains. 'Also, we wanted to ensure that the player wasn't starting so late that their story would be ending at Hogwarts before it really began and that their new friendships would have time to develop.'

Over the course of the game, the player learns their role in a world-threatening plot by goblins and Dark wizards working to unleash a dangerous, ancient power. Before the player can save the wizarding world and master their own special power however, they must first be sorted and learn the basics of magic.

Starting the game outside the school underlined the fact that this world of *Hogwarts Legacy* is significantly bigger than the building and its grounds. 'This is a wizarding world no one has seen before,' says Squier. 'We wanted the player to be able to experience a diverse and wide-ranging wizarding world *and* have the Hogwarts student experience that fans have been awaiting for decades.' While the adventure begins outside the castle, to complete the challenges ahead the player must not neglect their schoolwork. 'They need to strike a balance between both to succeed,' adds Squier.

CHAPTER 2

Where Our Story Starts

As the game begins, the player is encouraged to create an avatar that best represents the look of their character. A character-creation tool allows them to customise their avatar, modifying major features with an extensive set of options that grant players thousands of combinations built on top of the original presets.

'Hogwarts Legacy is all about you, the player, getting your welcome letter to Hogwarts,' says Jeff Bunker. 'This is your story and these are your choices. Visually, there is nothing that can reflect that idea more than choosing how your avatar looks.

This will be obvious to the player, as the very first thing you encounter as you start the game is the character creator,' he adds. 'There, you will find limitless combinations of heads, hairstyles, eyebrows, eye colour, skin colour, complexions, scars or blemishes, glasses and voices to choose from to reflect the witch or wizard you want to be.'

Of all the characters in Hogwarts Legacy that the developers needed to create (and there are hundreds), the most challenging might have been the player's avatar. 'Although the avatar is one character from the player's perspective, the avatar is like a thousand characters to us – or a million, if you think of all the possible combinations,' says **Characters Art Lead, Tyler Lybbert**. 'This is not just in facial features, eye colour and hairstyle, but also in the clothing that is acquired by the player throughout the game. There are so many outfits, school uniforms, robes, coats and, of course, scarves and hats,' Lybbert explains. 'And one of the most difficult things was getting all those layers of clothes to work well together, fit together, move and flow together. That was a monumental challenge.'

Player character development is very different from NPC development. 'We wanted to give the player a chance to build their own character,' Lybbert adds. 'So the number of options was of utmost importance. It took a team of talented artists to construct those options so that they work well together, no matter what combination the player chose.'

PAGES **28-29**:
Hogwarts Exterior (in-game render) by the Environment Team

OPPOSITE: Merlin Robe by Danny Russon

TOP: Avatar Clothing by Vanessa Palmer

Hogsmeade by KARAKTER Design Studio

WELCOME TO HOGWARTS

Unforgettable characters and stories developed in the books and films inspired new characters for *Hogwarts Legacy*, although there is an inherent resonance in all witches and wizards that embeds in the wizarding world. 'We drew on a little bit of Dumbledore, Snape, McGonagall, Trelawney, Umbridge and Hagrid when fleshing out the detailed backstories and characteristics of certain professors,' says Moira Squier. 'And there are certainly timeless bits of Harry, Ron, Hermione, Luna, Draco, Neville, Ginny, Percy and Seamus – to name a few – to be found in the students at Hogwarts in the late 1800s.'

It was important to ensure that every character – from the most prominent professors and students to the less frequently-encountered hamlet shopkeepers – had fully formed, engaging personalities that fit within and flesh out the intricate wizarding world of the late 1800s, while including a diverse spectrum of characters with different life experiences and points of view.

Many wizarding families go back for generations, and so the presence of some of their members as students or professors at Hogwarts in the period in which the game is set should not be surprising. And digging deep into the lore that has already been established allowed the appearances of wizards who would be appropriate to the late 1800s or known to those fans who are steeped in the wizarding world.

OPPOSITE LEFT: Headmaster Black by Ryan Wood

OPPOSITE RIGHT: Hog's Head Vendor (in-game render) by the Environment Team

TOP: Hogwarts Valley (in-game render) by the Environment Team

LEFT: Hog's Head by Ryan Wood

RIGHT: Levioso Statue (3D render) by the Character Team

In this way, the player's experience in the game is tied to the wizarding world with which fans are so familiar without seeming to clone the Hogwarts of the books and films. There couldn't be an Ollivanders wand shop without an Ollivander, and so Gerbold Ollivander, the grandfather of Garrick Ollivander, maintains the branch in Hogsmeade. 'Amongst the family names we knew would have existed during this time frame, we chose to focus on a few that would be significant to fans,' explains Moira Squier. 'We know that a family like the Weasleys has been around for hundreds of years, so it made sense that there would be a Weasley or two at Hogwarts. In fact, we couldn't figure out a world in which there wasn't at least one.'

'We definitely wanted a connection to the present-day Weasleys,' says Tyler Lybbert, 'although we didn't want to be too precise about it. It had to make sense and add a bit of delight.' Matilda Weasley, the Transfiguration professor and Deputy Headmistress, is immediately recognisable as belonging to the family we all know and love. Her no-nonsense attitude, red hair and the twinkle in her eye are typical of the Weasley women we know. 'Garreth Weasley, the fifth-year student with red, bushy hair and enough freckles to fill a face, screams "Weasley!"' adds Lybbert, 'but with his own flair.'

On the Darker side, there is Ominis Gaunt, a descendant of Salazar Slytherin himself and a relative of Tom Riddle, and Victor Rookwood – a predecessor of the Death Eater Augustus Rookwood.

'Other names will be familiar to those who really know their lore,' says Squier. 'For example, Sacharissa Tugwood, who we know from lore became a famous potioneer known for her beauty products, but would have been a student at Hogwarts during our time. So we thought it would be a nice nod to wizarding history to get the player to help her find ingredients for some of her early experiments.'

OPPOSITE: Peeves by Ryan Wood

BOTTOM: Gerbold Ollivander (3D render) and Ollivander Process by the Character Team

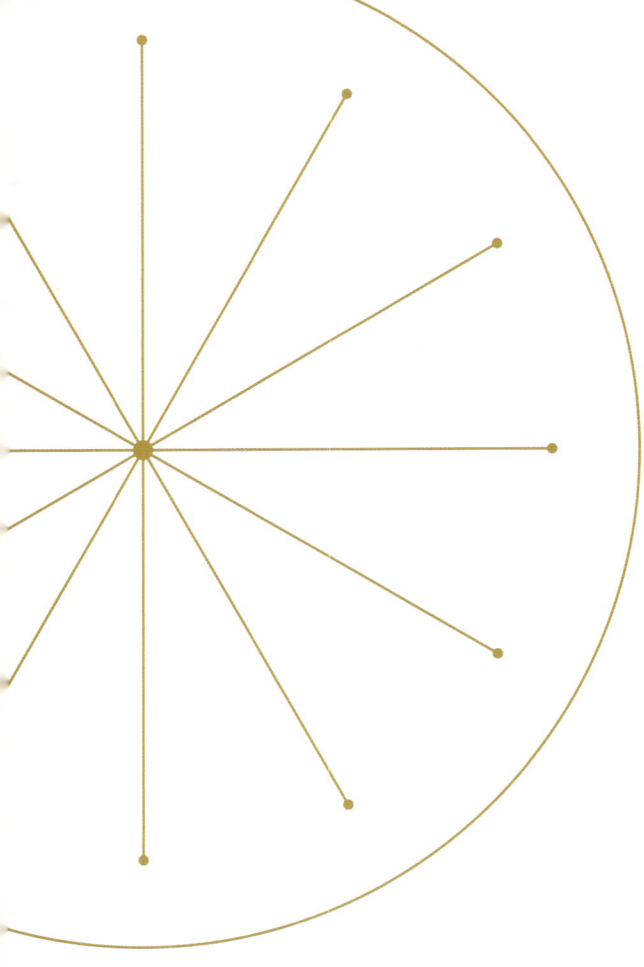

With two exceptions (Phineas Nigellus Black and Professor Binns), there are new professors and students at Hogwarts the artists were tasked with bringing to life. 'It all starts with the story and the personality, and we go from there,' says Lybbert. 'What does the story need from this character? What are those quirks, interests, faults and virtues that make this person unique? Then visually, what does all that inspire? How do we support all that visually? Hopefully when you first see one of these new characters you instantly get a sense for who they are and what they might be like. Then, as you watch them move, emote and talk, who they are really blossoms from there. So, we start with the story needs and then try to "plus" that character with every step through concept to the finished, fully animating, fully alive character. It's an extremely fun and satisfying, although difficult, process.'

Biographies were created for each character – some extremely detailed, including not only where they lived and what they did but also histories that explain the psychological makeup of their personalities. 'Our Story Team did an exceptional job of developing our characters,' says Lybbert. 'They were thorough in their quest for authenticity and it came through in their writing of the backstories and bios: how old, where from, likes, dislikes, virtues and foibles.' Along with assignment of idiosyncrasies and motivations, each character was sorted into one of the four Hogwarts houses. 'This kind of depth made it easy to feel inspired about the visuals and animations of the characters,' he adds. The artists referred back to these biographies frequently as they developed a character.

Inspiration for the physical look for the characters in Hogwarts, Hogsmeade and the Highlands came from various sources, including the Hogwarts personnel painted in the portraits created for the films, some of whom would have been around during the late-nineteenth-century timeline, and illustrative artwork created for the printed versions of the novels. 'How could we not?' asks Lybbert. 'There is so much in these stories, films and illustrations! Although we are attempting to create our own cohesive style in and of itself, we are surely inspired by all of these works of art.' The same inspirations influenced the concept art not only for the characters but also for all they would use or encounter, although inspiration is just that – suggestions, options and promptings. 'It's always great to gather all that has been done before you on a reference page and study it before you even put pencil to paper,' says **Sébastien Gallego**. 'But again, we never took anything as is. We wanted to put our own twist on the wizarding world. From the Sorting Hat to the house crest patches on the student cloaks, we redesigned everything!'

OPPOSITE: Fastidio the Poltergeist by Sébastien Gallego; Fat Friar Ghost, Gringott Guard and Beatrice Green by Vanessa Palmer

Dark Swamp by Vanessa Palmer

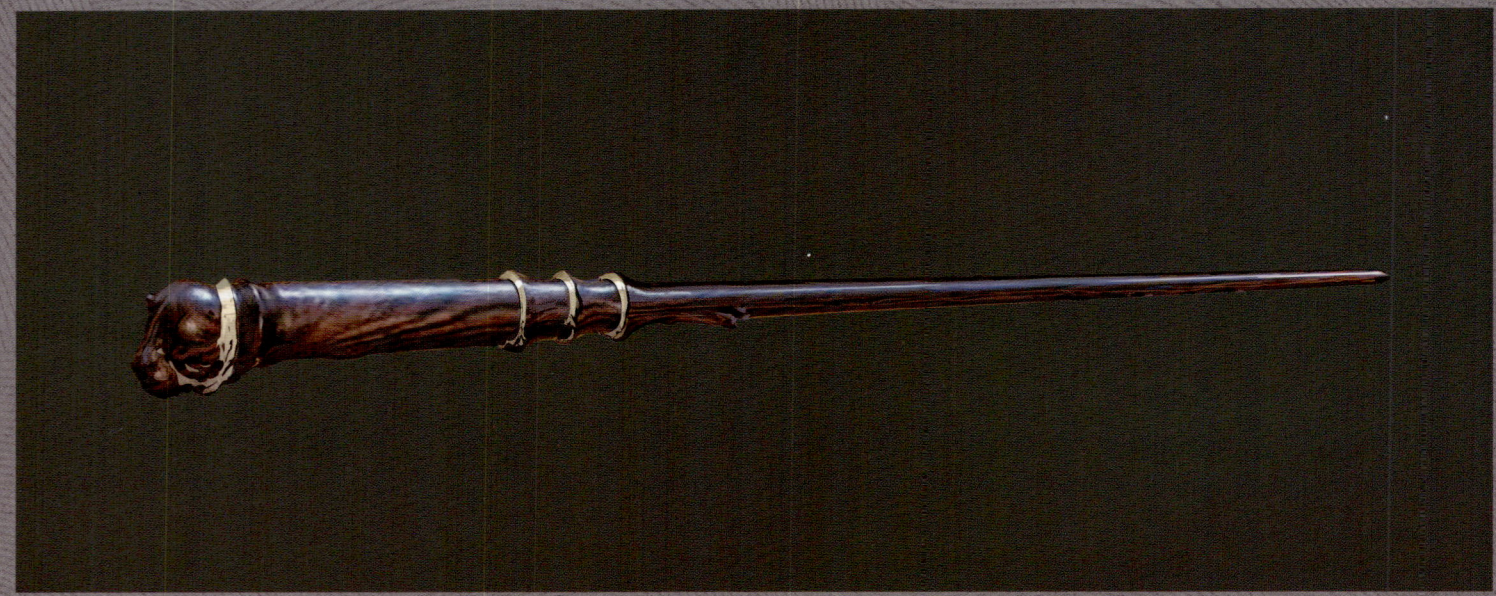

PROFESSORS AND HOGWARTS PERSONNEL

Each professor and their class provide important tools for players to use in their Hogwarts adventures. 'The professors were a blast to design,' says Sébastien Gallego. 'In a way, they are the heart of Hogwarts, and we wanted to do them justice. J.K. Rowling depicted so many colourful characters in the books and we were hoping to develop characters as rich and multifaceted as she did!' One imperative was to make them iconic at first glance. 'Professor Weasley is the strict but kind Deputy Headmistress,' he adds. 'Professor Garlick, with her long, red, braided hair and the leaf design on her clothes has her own signature look, like Mad-Eye Moody's magical eye. We tried to do this for each professor.'

Mentoring is a significant element of the Harry Potter books, and so the game makers needed the player to have their own mentor figure. In Professor Eleazar Fig, the player finds someone who can guide them through their experience at Hogwarts and through the overarching ancient magic story that occurs both within and without the castle walls.

Professor Fig was one of the first characters the team developed and perhaps the one on whom they spent the most time. Fig began as a doddering old man, but as the story of *Hogwarts Legacy* evolved during the time spent working on and developing the game, so did the character. 'Gradually, he became more of a cool old guy who has been places,' says Lybbert. 'A bit more of an Indiana Jones type of character. So what he looked like had to change – which can be painful because of the work involved, but with him being one of our more important characters, we allowed ourselves to dedicate more time and ended up having a little more fun with him.'

'Narratively, he is such a complex and fascinating character,' says Sébastien Gallego. 'A mix of grief, excitement and mentor figure, all of this was supposed to translate into his face and costume design. There's a little bit of eccentricity and world-traveller type we wanted to infuse in his costume, but without overdoing it. He is not your typical Hogwarts professor, if there's such a thing as a typical professor at Hogwarts.'

Professor Eleazar Fig, Magical Theory
[GRYFFINDOR]

Professor Eleazar Fig left behind his aspirations of working for the Ministry of Magic in order to follow his wife, Miriam, around the world as she researched the seeming disappearance of ancient magic. Fig eventually grew weary of this quest and left her to continue on her own while he took on the job of Magical Theory Professor at Hogwarts. When Miriam was killed during her travels by an as-yet-unknown assailant, Fig was devastated. He would love nothing more than to finish her work. He's generally regarded by students and faculty as driven and single-minded, even though most don't understand his passion. He doesn't suffer fools, gladly or otherwise, and he often manages to manipulate things in his favour with Headmaster Black, with whom he has a contentious relationship.

Professor Fig's passion for adventure, strong moral core and exceptional magical skill serve as aspirational forces for the player and allow them to develop their own magical skill set.

OPPOSITE TOP: Professor Eleazar Fig (3D render) by the Character Team
OPPOSITE BOTTOM: Professor Fig's Wand by Sébastien Gallego
TOP: Professor Eleazar Fig by Ben Simonsen; Portkey by Nasan Hardcastle

Professor Abraham Ronen, Charms
[SLYTHERIN]

Abraham Ronen, the jovial Charms professor, is at ease with his students. He considers the act of helping young students grow as people to be just as important as the subject of Charms itself. He was home-schooled by his father, who was a stern teacher. This resulted in Professor Ronen making a game of his studies to help him enjoy learning – a practice he incorporates into his teaching today. He particularly adores Gobstones. Abraham has a family he is devoted to.

Professor Aesop Sharp, Potions
[SLYTHERIN]

After graduating from Hogwarts, Sharp channelled his Defence Against the Dark Arts and potion-making prowess into a successful career as an Auror, until he was severely injured and his partner killed due to their failure to anticipate an ambush. The injury forced him into an early retirement from the Ministry and caused him to become even more vigilant. He applied for the position of Potions master at Hogwarts – in part hoping to use the resources at the school to treat his injury. Although he is generally respected by the students, his gruffness puts some off. While he would love to be back in the field as an Auror, he feels a sense of pride when students embrace and excel at his challenging curriculum. His lectures tend to be short as he prefers his students to learn by practical application. Sharp's face has a large scar that cuts across his left eye and he walks with a limp – both constant reminders of the reason he left the Ministry.

Professor Dinah Hecat, Defence Against the Dark Arts

[RAVENCLAW]

After graduating from Hogwarts at the top of her class, Hecat went on to have a successful career with the Ministry of Magic as an Unspeakable before becoming the Defence Against the Dark Arts professor. Strong-willed and direct, Hecat is known to be a strict but likeable teacher. Being confined to a classroom often frustrates her and so she has developed a hands-on teaching method to satiate her desire for action.

Professor Mirabel Garlick, Herbology

[HUFFLEPUFF]

Mirabel Garlick is the much-beloved Herbology Professor at Hogwarts and has a cheerful disposition that immediately sets her apart from most other teachers. Muggle-born, she developed her appreciation for magical plants when she was a student at the famed school of witchcraft and wizardry, during which time she formed a lifelong friendship with Sirona Ryan, the proprietress of the Three Broomsticks in Hogsmeade. Her sunny demeanor and 'flowery language' charm colleagues and students alike. She has yet to meet the right witch, but at present is perfectly content with her life at Hogwarts.

OPPOSITE TOP: Professor Ronen by Ryan Wood
OPPOSITE BOTTOM: Professor Sharp (3D render) by the Character Team
TOP: Professor Dinah Hecat (3D render) by the Character Team and wand by Sébastien Gallego
LEFT: Professor Mirabel Garlick by Joshua H Black and wand by Sébastien Gallego

BOTTOM: Madam Kogawa by Nasan Hardcastle; Madam Kogawa's Wand by Sébastien Gallego
OPPOSITE: Professor (and Ghost) Cuthbert Binns by Ryan Wood

Professor (and Ghost) Cuthbert Binns, History

Although not much is known about his early life, Professor Cuthbert Binns had taught at Hogwarts for decades before he died, and he has continued teaching throughout the decades since. One day, he went down to the staff room and fell asleep in a chair in front of the fire, where he died in his sleep. Then he simply got up to go to his next lecture as a ghost. Some say that he's unaware he's actually dead, yet he does typically enter and leave his classroom by floating through the blackboard.

'As a recently deceased ghost Binns has the inability to directly affect the physical world,' says **Boston Madsen, the Hogwarts Art Lead and Senior Artist, Environments**. So while designing Binns's classroom Madsen pondered just how the professor grades his students' work. 'While this may at first not seem too debilitating for a lecturing professor, it does leave interesting questions, such as just how he manages to collect and grade his students' homework or write on the blackboard. We can only hope that he has a very spectacular teacher's assistant working tirelessly away in the wings, though the lack of one could explain the disarray of his classroom and the growing stacks of unreturned assignments.'

Madam Chiyo Kogawa, Flying

[SLYTHERIN]

Madam Kogawa attended school at Mahoutokoro and eventually worked for the Japanese Ministry of Magic, which is how she met Professor Weasley and was recruited to join Hogwarts. Madam Kogawa is the sort of person who doesn't realise that her talking voice has the volume of a yell, as she's normalised projecting her voice across the Quidditch pitch. Thought to be generally affable, Chiyo becomes another person entirely when it comes to flying and and when disciplining students. A bad experience in her try-outs for the Toyohashi Tengu taught her a valuable lesson about honour and trust, both of which she values highly. Any foul sportsmanship on a student's part – blatching, blurting, bumphing, Quaffle-pocking, etc – will have them banned from the pitch quicker than you can say 'Quidditch.'

Deputy Headmistress and Professor Matilda Weasley, Transfiguration

[GRYFFINDOR]

The red-headed Professor Weasley worked for the Ministry of Magic after she graduated from Hogwarts and quickly rose through the ranks, her calm presence and extraordinary wand work making her an invaluable asset. Then, while on an assignment for the Ministry, she met a brilliant, free-spirited wizard named Paul who worked as a curse-breaker. It wasn't long before the two realised they were meant to be together, and Matilda agreed to leave the stuffy world of bureaucracy and head out to travel the globe with him as 'freelance' curse-breakers. She adored Paul, but after some time Matilda came to see that what she truly craved was stability. She missed her nephews (of whom she has many) and the camaraderie of working with a talented group of witches and wizards. Sadly, Paul had no desire to 'stop moving,' as he said. Matilda found a position at Hogwarts teaching Transfiguration, where she has become a respected mentor, despite being a stickler for rules, as she combines humour with her authority.

OPPOSITE: Professor Weasley (3D render) by the Character Team
TOP: Professor Weasley's Wand by Sébastien Gallego
BOTTOM LEFT: Professor Howin's Wand by Sébastien Gallego
BOTTOM: Professor Howin by Ryan Wood

Professor Bai Howin, Beasts

[HUFFLEPUFF]

Bai Howin has a respect for beasts, but sees them for what they are: useful to wizardkind. An encounter in her youth with an Occamy left her in awe of beasts, and she loathes poachers who would waste them for Galleons. In her mind, magical creatures are to be valued for what they can provide for wizardkind: protective clothing, potion ingredients and even wand cores. It is her mission to ensure that the next generation of witches and wizards understands this.

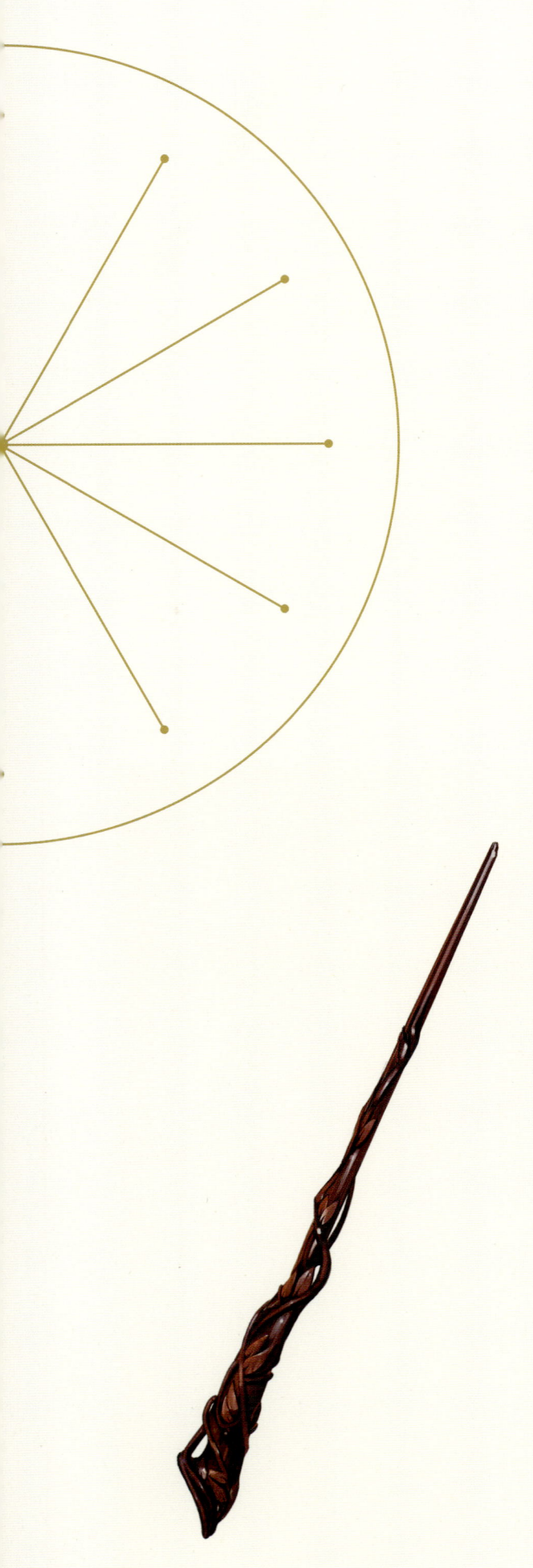

Professor Satyavati Shah, Astronomy

[RAVENCLAW]

After being raised largely in the Muggle world, Satyavati Shah took an interest in the sciences, which she carried with her into her schooling at Hogwarts. After graduating, she eventually took up a position as Professor of Astronomy and devotes herself to her subject in a way that most would find monastic and extreme. Like her scientific subject, she can come over to her pupils as a bit cold and demanding. She gets easily carried away when talking about the heavens and views many of the other Hogwarts disciplines (like Divination) as wishy-washy.

Professor Mudiwa Onai, Divination

Professor Onai taught Divination at Uagadou for a period of time before being invited by her friend Matilda Weasley to teach at Hogwarts. In an effort to leave tragic memories behind, specifically the murder of her husband, which she did not foresee, she accepted. Onai is an Animagus (an African fish eagle) but has refused to transform since her husband was murdered. She is strict and has high expectations of her students and her daughter, Natsai. While she is quite skilled with a wand like her daughter, she prefers to conjure magic with her bare hands, as is the custom in her homeland. Professor Onai is a commanding presence in any room she enters and demands respect from all with whom she interacts.

OPPOSITE TOP: Professor Satyavati Shah by Vanessa Palmer

OPPOSITE BOTTOM: Professor Shah's Wand by Sébastien Gallego

TOP: Professor Mudiwa Onai by Ben Simonsen

LEFT: Professor Mudiwa Onai Sculpt by the Character Team

Phineas Nigellus Black, Headmaster

[SLYTHERIN]

Phineas Nigellus Black is an ill-suited headmaster of Hogwarts, given his general disdain for students. Professor Black is a cantankerous, lazy and vain pure-blood who has a superior attitude and a very dim-witted view of the world. His goal is to do the least amount of work possible while minimising his actual exposure to the student body. He also fancies himself as a bit of a style icon and especially obsesses over his surgically manicured beard.

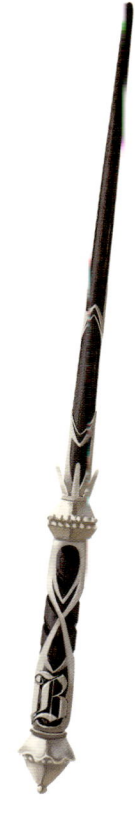

TOP: Phineas Nigellus Black sketch by Ryan Wood
LEFT: Phineas Nigellus Black by Ryan Wood
ABOVE: Professor Black's Wand by Sébastien Gallego
OPPOSITE: Phineas Nigellus Black (3D render) by the Character Team

Other Notable Personnel

Born into a Muggle family, Noreen Blainey, Hospital Matron and Hufflepuff, recently graduated from Hogwarts. The newly appointed Healer must now work to bring the hospital wing up to code while also learning the ropes of her job. What she lacks in experience, she makes up for in fortitude.

Agnes Scribner, Head Librarian, is the quintessential curator: strict about maintaining order but passionate about introducing students to literature. She is always willing to help with school projects, so long as students respect library rules and school property. Peeves is her sworn nemesis.

Gladwin Moon, Caretaker, is known for his intense self-confidence and inadequate custodial work. He was quite popular and interesting as a Hogwarts student but has failed to find success as an adult. He's comically arrogant and oblivious, has an ostentatious fashion sense and considers himself much too debonair to be a caretaker. Moon is secretly terrified of Demiguises, thanks to a childhood trauma.

The Fat Lady portrait guards the entrance to the Gryffindor common room, demanding an ever-changing password before she will open the door. 'The Fat Lady portrait was particularly fun!' says Tyler Lybbert. 'First, to be inspired by what she was like in the stories, then the films. And then to step away from those and have our own fun with that character, with her pouty facial expression and dark, bouncy curls. She is literally a ton of fun!'

However, the Fat Lady portrait proved difficult to complete. 'Who knew she could be such a difficult painting to work with!' says Boston Madsen. 'There are probably more hours behind making her portrait work – so much so, it became a phrase in many a meeting that this game won't be over until "the Pink Fat Lady sings"!'

OPPOSITE: Fat Lady Portrait by the Character Team

TOP: Librarian Portrait by Joshua H Black

BOTTOM: Gladwin Moon (3D render) by the Character Team

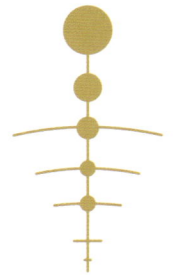

OPPOSITE TOP TO BOTTOM: Goblin Slam, Parry and Hippogriff Landing by the Animation Team

THE GHOSTS OF *HOGWARTS LEGACY*

In addition to the Hogwarts house ghosts, ghostly members of the Headless Hunt – with their own dubious histories and eternal rivalries – engage with players in Gryffindor house during a visit to the Hogsmeade graveyard.

• **Sir Patrick Delaney-Podmore**, the boisterous leader of the Headless Hunt, loves making merry and fraternising with his fellow headless ghost friends.

• **Sir Dumfrey Westland** was beheaded in a battle with goblins during a very early and nearly forgotten rebellion, but he's so slow-witted he didn't realise he was dead until the battle was long over.

• **Richard Jackdaw** was a headstrong Hogwarts student who lost his head seeking adventure in a very dangerous place. His love of adventure, in fact, was the reason for his demise and more than one broken heart.

• **Sir Nestor Amset** was executed along with a court of mutineers who were vying for power in their county. Nowhere near being a mastermind, he aligned himself with the wrong side of the dispute, and paid for it with his life. In the Headless Hunt, he's at the bottom of the pecking order.

TOP: Death Day Party by Ben Simonsen

OPPOSITE BOTTOM: Bloody Baron by Ryan Wood

LEFT: Bloody Baron by Ryan Wood

ABOVE: Headless Hunt Crest Tapestry by Ben Simonsen and BOSI

FRIENDS AND FELLOW STUDENTS

Attending Hogwarts is not just about learning to become a powerful witch or wizard. It is also about making friends with fellow students, one of the most important aspects of the experience of attending the school. Amongst the many friends the player can make in the game, three key companions help define who the player is as a wizard: Natty, who is heroic and brave; Poppy, who loves and cares for magical beasts; and Sebastian, a well-meaning Slytherin who is willing to break the rules to protect his loved ones, even if that means using Dark Magic.

'We wanted to create an interesting and diverse group of students whose stories and motivations would engage and inspire a variety of players,' says Moira Squier. Natty is a bit of an outsider, like the player, but will appeal

to those players who have a strong sense of justice. Poppy is a perfect companion to those enchanted by magical beasts. The developers also knew they wanted to have at least one character with an interest in Dark Magic for those players who wanted to delve into Dark content. Each proves themselves loyal, but each will take the player in a different direction.

'Each of their stories informs their motivations and where they will lead the player,' says Squier. 'All three have an element of tragedy in their backstories and hurdles they have had to overcome – like Harry Potter himself – and all three are determined to make the world a better place as *they see it*, whether it's improving the lives of loved ones, of beasts or of victims of crime.'

PAGES 60–61:
Hogwarts Legacy Collector's Edition Book Map by Nasan Hardcastle

OPPOSITE: Great Hall (in-game render) by the Environment Team

BOTTOM: Female Student Sketch by Ben Simonsen

Poppy Sweeting

[HUFFLEPUFF]

Poppy Sweeting is a compassionate girl with a heart for beasts. She believes they have far more redeeming values than people, an opinion she arrived at in childhood, having poacher parents and growing up in poacher camps. If given the choice she much prefers the company of beasts to people and can appear reserved as a result. She lives with her grandmother when not at school, as she is estranged from her parents and, owing to this fact, has an unmistakable air of independence about her.

In an era that has little regard for magical beasts, Poppy stands out as their champion. Although she fights a daily battle against the attitudes of the time, her more significant wars are waged against the Poacher Pack. She loathes their existence and will do everything in her power to defend beasts from them, even if it means putting herself at risk.

ABOVE: Poppy Sweeting (3D render) by the Character Team

OPPOSITE TOP TO BOTTOM: Poppy Mission Path, Poppy Sweeting Mission and Dragons Nest by Ben Simonsen

Natsai (Natty) Onai

[GRYFFINDOR]

Natty Onai is admired for her magical skill, determination and inexhaustible quest for justice. An only child, she spent her early years in Matabeleland in Africa, wandering the Matobo Hills with her father, who was a giraffe Animagus, and watching her mother, a skilled Seer, use Divination to help protect their tribe from less-than-friendly neighbours. When Natty was nine years old, her father was killed protecting her from local bandits – an event that was not foreseen by her mother – and Natty blames herself for his death.

Natty and her mother moved to Uganda, where she attended the wizarding school Uagadou and learned to become an Animagus herself, taking the form of a gazelle. Before the start of Natty's fourth year, however, her mother accepted an offer to teach Divination at Hogwarts. Natty has adjusted well to her new school, but has homed in on Victor Rookwood's gang, who remind her of the gang that killed her father, and is determined to take them down.

RIGHT: Natsai Onai (3D render) by the Character Team

OPPOSITE: Sebastian Sallow (3D render) by the Character Team

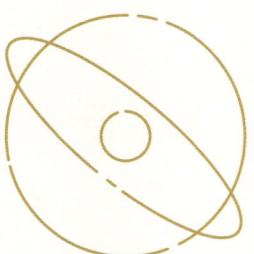

Sebastian Sallow

[SLYTHERIN]

Sebastian Sallow is a charming and driven student with many secrets. Sebastian and his sister, Anne, were raised by their uncle, Solomon Sallow, a former Auror with the Ministry of Magic. However, before their fourth year at Hogwarts, Anne was cursed during a raid on their home in Feldcroft by the goblin Ranrok and his followers. As a result, she now suffers from a magical malady that leaves her in constant pain and unable to attend school. Sebastian has taken it upon himself to find a cure for his sister and has turned to the Dark Arts to find a solution. While his aims and goals often seem well-intended, he justifies acting questionably to achieve them and uses his sister's illness as an excuse to delve into Dark Magic. Sebastian is compelled by the idea that magic is a tool, rather than something innately good or evil.

Sebastian isn't bothered by defeat and he is undaunted in pursuing his goals. Even though Sebastian's parents died, he channels their optimistic personalities and relies on his memories of them, which include being persistent and open-minded and always pursuing knowledge, to guide him.

Other Students

'Next, we tried to think of the types of general personalities that would appeal to a broad range of players and fit within the Harry Potter universe,' Squier continues, such as the prankster, the bookworm and the athlete/competitor. 'We built on all these general concepts to give each companion a very specific backstory and voice, further honing those backstories and voices during game development.'

Everett Clopton is a fun-loving fifth-year Ravenclaw who's good at breaking rules. The competitive Slytherin Imelda Reyes is known more for her broom-flying acumen than her friendliness. Garreth Weasley, a Gryffindor and Professor Weasley's nephew, tends to experiment with his own brews of magical drinks. Amit Thakkar aspires to be a famous historian – however, this Ravenclaw has developed assumptions about history and magical beings that aren't always accurate. Leander Prewett is a blustery fifth-year Gryffindor whose outward bravado masks his insecurities about living up to his house's ideals of courage and heroism.

Fifth-year student Ominis Gaunt, a descendant of Salazar Slytherin, has suffered traumatic experiences during his upbringing that have made him pessimistic, untrusting and sarcastic. However, he is best friends with Sebastian Sallow, who has been trying to enlist Ominis's aid to help his sister, Anne, by avenues involving Dark Magic with which Ominis is fiercely uncomfortable.

'All these are well-developed, appealing, distinct characters with their own histories and very different worldviews,' Squier adds. 'As in the real world, players will have different experiences depending upon the companion with whom they choose to spend time.'

LEFT: Amit Thakkar and Lenora Everleigh (3D renders) by the Character Team

OPPOSITE: Everett Clopton (3D render) by the Character Team

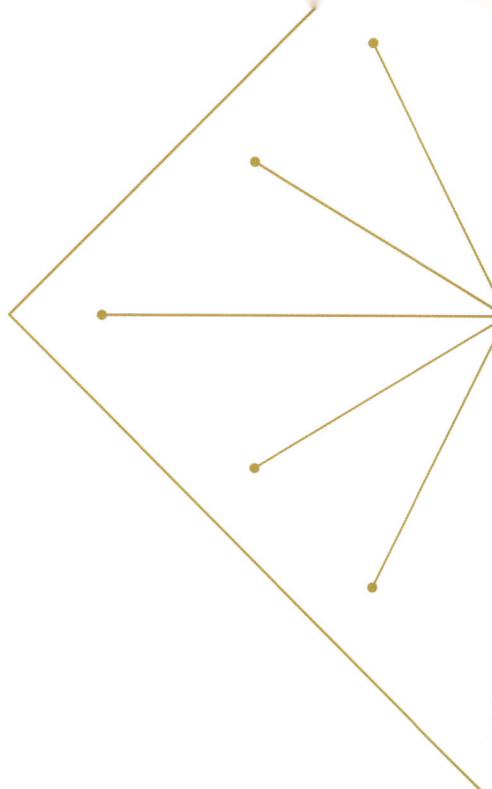

ENEMIES

There is a nefarious element actively at work around Hogwarts and within its nearby environments, including the Highlands. The enemies in *Hogwarts Legacy* include gangsters and goblins who provide challenges that become true tests of the player's abilities and character. 'Victor Rookwood, who is an ancestor of the Death Eater Augustus Rookwood we come to know in the books, is your typical Dark wizard,' says Squier. 'He's a thug, driven by a general desire for wealth and power. The goblin overlord Ranrok, on the other hand, is driven by a desire for power, to be sure, but wants to use it to rise up from under the thumb of "wand-carriers" and take over the magical world.'

By having both a Dark wizard and a goblin leader as enemies, the player must deal with two very different villains – from a combat standpoint as well as a story and lore perspective. Because their modes of combat and their motivations are so different, the player must fight and think differently when confronting them and their lackeys and henchmen.

There are witches and wizards trading spells, defending with Shield Charms and blasting each other into submission during combat in the wizarding world. 'So we made sure that these enemies use a variety of spells from lore as they try to defeat you,' explains **Combat and Enemy Design Lead, Troy Johnson**. 'On top of that there are iconic moments of conflict in existing lore that involve other kinds of creatures that we also wanted to include and properly represent, including trolls, eight-legged beasts, Inferi and more.'

Many potential enemies sound exciting on paper or in the mind of a fan, but designing an experience for those enemies that strictly adheres to lore results in difficult choices to make. 'In some cases, an enemy required such a specific spell to defeat it,' says Johnson, 'that we couldn't justify the time and effort that went into creating and teaching that spell when it would be used in only a limited way.'

'Other times, we couldn't find appropriate justification for certain creatures to fit into our world and narrative, no matter how much the combat team wanted to bring them to life,' he adds.

One of the biggest concerns in designing an individual enemy is figuring out exactly which gameplay role it should fill to stand apart from all the other enemies, whilst still staying true to lore and fan expectations. 'Audio and visual variety among the enemies is important and helpful,' Johnson says, 'but gameplay variety among them can be layered together to create deeper experiences that result in longer engagement and opportunities for a greater sense of mastery.'

Although two enemy characters – Victor Rookwood and the goblin Ranrok – stand out from the rest, a large assortment of thrilling encounters with creatures and spell casters occur. 'I personally love our assortment of Dark witches and wizards,' says Johnson. 'Defending against incoming spells and then countering with your own – and seeing their various effects and elicited reactions – is a joy that just feels right in this world. These enemies come in forms that let you feel like a powerhouse as you take on several at a time, but there are also situations where you're pitted against one daunting duellist. Fulfilling that fan fantasy is simply awesome.'

OPPOSITE: Ranrok by Ryan Wood

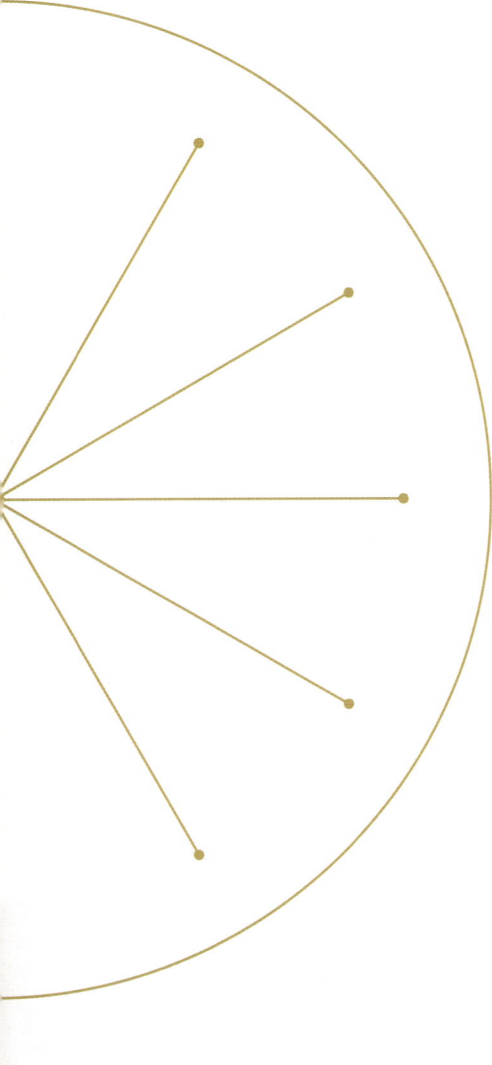

TOP AND ABOVE:
Rookwood Crest and Rookwood Wax Seal by Vanessa Palmer

OPPOSITE: Victor Rookwood by Ryan Wood

Victor Rookwood

Victor Rookwood, a Dark wizard and the brutal but cunning leader of the Rookwood Gang, took control of his father's crime ring at the young age of twenty-two after the elder Rookwood's untimely (and suspicious) death. Raised to bend the law when possible and break it when necessary, Rookwood quickly grew the business to become the most successful gang in the region. Local thieves and poachers began to take notice and found it advantageous to align with Rookwood's increasingly effective band of criminals.

Not afraid to play dirty, Rookwood soon manipulated these new partnerships, seizing complete control and increasing his stronghold to include a lucrative extortionist racket. While his sights are set on becoming Europe's most notorious underworld player, he pushes his gangs to fill his coffers by victimising residents of Hogsmeade and the surrounding villages – robbing travellers blind, smuggling rare magical beasts and selling them to the highest bidders and demanding protection payments from Hogsmeade's shopkeepers. The Ministry, for some reason, fails to take action against him. Perhaps his surname carries too much weight in the magical world – or perhaps he is really just that good at evading the law.

Although Rookwood's a bit scruffy, he's still dapper-looking, dressing in posh, expensive-looking clothes. 'We wanted Victor to have a menacing, piercing look in his eye and a rough but handsome face,' says Tyler Lybbert. 'His face is made of straight lines and sharp symmetry. His clothing is stylish for the time period, and he wears that confidence from the brim of his top hat to the toe of his boot.' Rookwood moves like a predator, the consummate sneering, gruff and distrustful villain.

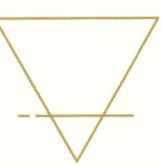

Rookwood's Gang of Dark Wizards and Poachers

Victor Rookwood's criminal gang of Dark wizards and witches – thieves and extortionists known as 'Ashwinders' and the vicious Poacher Pack – infest the Highlands. Each faction has a unique special ability: thieves can turn their teammates invisible, poacher Animagi can become wolves and extortionists can summon Inferi into the fight.

THEOPHILUS HARLOW is Rookwood's murderous, solicitous right-hand man. An unapologetic bully who thrives on cruelty, he is arrogant, condescending and entirely devoid of compassion – even for children.

ACKLEY BARNES is a prominent member of the Rookwood Gang. An intelligent and observant thief, Ackley is vengeful when he feels he's been undermined in any way.

SILVANUS SELWYN is an Ashwinder and works as a lieutenant for Rookwood. Quick-witted and fashionable, he loves the finer things in life and has a flair for the dramatic.

GWENDOLYN ZHOU, master thief, is a strong, capable and well-respected witch who used to work for the Ministry of Magic. Although she sometimes struggles with the road she now travels with Rookwood, she has come to realise that her talents are more greatly appreciated in her new role than they were at the Ministry.

CATRIN HAGGARTY is a gifted member of the Ashwinders. Her brother Pádraic is heartbroken and horrified by the turn her life has taken and suspects her of being the midnight thief terrorising the hamlet they grew up in.

IONA MORGAN and **TEMPESTE THORNE** are both particularly cruel members of Rookwood's Poacher Pack. They see beasts as commodities only and will not hesitate to take down anyone who gets in the way of their business interests.

OPPOSITE: Dark Wizard Catrin Haggarty by Jason Borne; Dark Wizard Dustin Trinity by Sébastien Gallego

TOP: Rookwood Hideout by Vanessa Palmer

LEFT: Dark Wizard Tempeste Thorne by Danny Russon

RIGHT: Dark Wizard Member of the Pack by Sébastien Gallego and BCSI

GOBLINS

'The goblins were a tricky bunch,' remembers Sébastien Gallego. 'Not so much their faces and body type, which we decided to keep close to what already existed, but the treatment of their clothes and armour.' Because of their relatively small size, it was difficult to make the goblins look menacing, and the team spent a lot of time trying to figure out armour and weapons that would have an edge to them whilst still feeling not too 'fantasy'.

'It's very easy to go all-out D&D in your design,' he explains, 'with spikes, skulls and hard edges, but this is not what the wizarding world is about. There's a certain level of sophistication and historical accuracy we were shooting for. Add to the mix the element of ancient magic, and you can see it was a design battle – no pun intended! But I'm happy with where we landed.'

OPPOSITE BOTTOM: Gringotts Guard, Arn, Belgruff, Lodgok, Loyalist Warrior and Private Banker (3D renders) by the Character Team

ABOVE: Loyalist Sentinel by Sébastien Gallego

Lodgok

Lodgok is a retired goblin metal trader, known to be friendly with Sirona Ryan, who runs the Three Broomsticks. He has a mysterious connection to Ranrok, with whom he used to be close and whom he used to follow. His experience with a particular witch who offered to share her knowledge with him turned him around about wizardkind and he is now – perhaps – willing to help stop Ranrok and his rebellious plans. He is a thoughtful and kind goblin, especially in relation to Ranrok. Lodgok is kind to humans, assuming the best in humans and goblins. He wants to be understood and find solutions, believing wizardkind and goblinkind could, one day, live in peace.

Ranrok

Ranrok is the local goblin overlord. Clever, cunning, vicious, violent and opportunistic, he is working with Victor Rookwood to amass some sort of power that he believes will help him rebel against wizardkind. He has influenced local goblins known as Loyalists to join him in a bid at overthrowing wizards. He does not hide his disdain for wizardkind and will go to any extremes to get the power he wants.

TOP: Lodgok by Ryan Wood

ABOVE: Goblin Armour (3D render), Goblin Shoulder Armour (3D render)

LEFT: Ranrok Sculpt by the Character Team

Garnuff

Garnuff is a young, softly-spoken goblin who decided to forego his family's tradition of working in Gringotts in favour of pursuing a life of activism. Although small for a goblin, and shy, he's willing to break the rules to do what is morally right. Garnuff is particularly invested in beasts' rights, believing them to be treated just as unfairly as goblins. He has a particular soft spot for Mooncalves, whom he finds to have great depth of character.

TOP: Corrupted Goblin Explorations by Danny Russon

ABOVE LEFT AND RIGHT: Ranrok and Corrupted Goblin by Ryan Wood

THE PLAYER'S CHOICES

For a heroic experience, the player's choices should make all the difference, and matter. In the books Harry Potter knew his choices mattered, and the team at Avalanche wanted players to feel this way too. Gamers like to be masters of their own destinies, which is what happens when their decisions have an actual effect in the game.

The player's first choice is in creating an avatar that best represents the wizard or witch they want to play. Players begin the game with the default school uniform, but new outfits can be purchased and found as they progress through the game.

The game's developers enabled players to express themselves and thus have a stronger connection to the game. *Hogwarts Legacy's* expressive nature goes beyond reflecting their physical identity. Branching dialogue conversations with professors, fellow students and nearby residents elicit varying options as responses from the player, allowing them to react positively and treat NPCs with respect or speak rudely to them. If an NPC asks the player to retrieve an item, the player could keep it for themselves, alienating the character further and colouring future interactions.

At Hogwarts, the player learns a variety of spells, providing multiple choices in combat approaches: Inflict damage on a troll, manipulate a group of Dark wizards with control spells or avoid combat altogether with stealth. With dozens of spells to choose from, the player can find the combination that best works for their playstyle.

Additionally, the player has the option to choose to dabble in the Dark Arts. As they follow the Dark storyline, several Dark spells can be learned, including the Unforgivable Curses, all of which can be updated with the Dark Arts talents tree. 'In addition to employing those spells' primary effects, players can choose talents to develop a unique playstyle in combat,' explains Troy Johnson. 'This grants additional power and effects when using the Dark Arts, like sucking the life force from or sharing damage amongst groups of cursed enemies.'

OPPOSITE BOTTOM: House Crest Patches by Vanessa Palmer

TOP: UI Design Exploration by the UI Team

LEFT: Dark Art Outfit by Jon Diesta and BOSI

CINEMATICS: BRINGING THE STORY TO LIFE

A cinematic, or cutscene, is a noninteractive, pre-rendered video sequence that breaks up the gameplay. 'The goal of a cinematic is to deliver critical story information that is required for establishing character and story, and for setting up future gameplay context,' explains **Cinematic Director and Manager, Nathan Hendrickson**. 'If a cinematic doesn't serve the story, or if it would work better in the hands of the player, we always lean towards player control.' Sometimes, for one reason or another, gameplay requirements cannot be achieved. This is when, Hendrickson adds, 'cinematics can hop in to help bridge the gap.'

Cinematic production is a long process, starting with story and script development. Once the story is set, storyboard artists bring the script to life with hand-drawn panels. As each panel is approved, the storyboards are then turned into a 2D animatic: a moving version of the hand-drawn panel, complemented with voice performances. 'This helps us validate the story and determine the actual runtime,' notes Hendrickson. It also allows the team to make cost-effective changes before cinematics are rendered in 3-D.

With the use of a specific 3-D tool, cutscenes are then converted to 3-D preproduction visualisation. Cameras are added to the scene to capture preferred angles, and characters are posed with models from the game. This creates 'a more fluid, exciting visualisation of the actual cutscene,' Hendrickson explains.

Once 3-D previsualisation has been approved, performance capture is completed, providing accurate body movement, facial reactions and voice performances directly from the talented actors. 'Every facial expression, body twitch and angry growl is captured as they are performed onstage and then transferred into our game,' Hendrickson says. 'From there, the animations are polished, effects are created, the scenes are lit and the sound department adds all the foley and music. It literally takes every department at the company to make great cinematics.'

The team took much of their inspiration from the Harry Potter franchise, especially the gritty and grounded camera work in the later films directed by David Yates. 'Our goal was to follow that inspiration whilst also tailoring the content for our particular time frame in the late 1800s,' explains Hendrickson. 'The goal was to keep the more dramatic turns free of too many flashy camera moves. The environments and actors speak volumes in the Harry Potter universe and we didn't want to upstage the performances. But once the action kicked in we added more energetic camera movement, as if the camera was finally free to flow wild, like some of the universe's many unique spells.'

The team experienced many challenges whilst developing the game's cinematic scenes, but with such a long production cycle, the toughest part had to be the constant change the game

OPPOSITE: Peeves (in-game cinematic) by the Environment Team

underwent. 'Gameplay must come first, and that drive to make a game great sometimes comes at the cost of cinematic rework, or even cutting completed cinematics that may be dear to our hearts,' says Hendrickson. This is expected, but as every cinematic is treated with the same amount of passion, when it is cut or altered the loss is felt throughout the studio. 'But those decisions are never done without careful thought,' he adds, 'and always towards creating compelling gameplay.'

A game that offers full character customisation presents another challenge when creating cutscenes. 'We also had to figure out how to craft our cinematic content around all the fantastical costumes the player can be wearing at any time,' Hendrickson explains. The variety of scarves, robes and hats meant much more thought had to go into camera compositions and lighting rigs than was the case with pre-rendered content. And what the player looks like in each cinematic can be surprising. 'I was watching a very serious cinematic and the player walked in with a pumpkin on his head,' Hendrickson recalls. 'While it wasn't the best look for the scene, it certainly gave me a chuckle.'

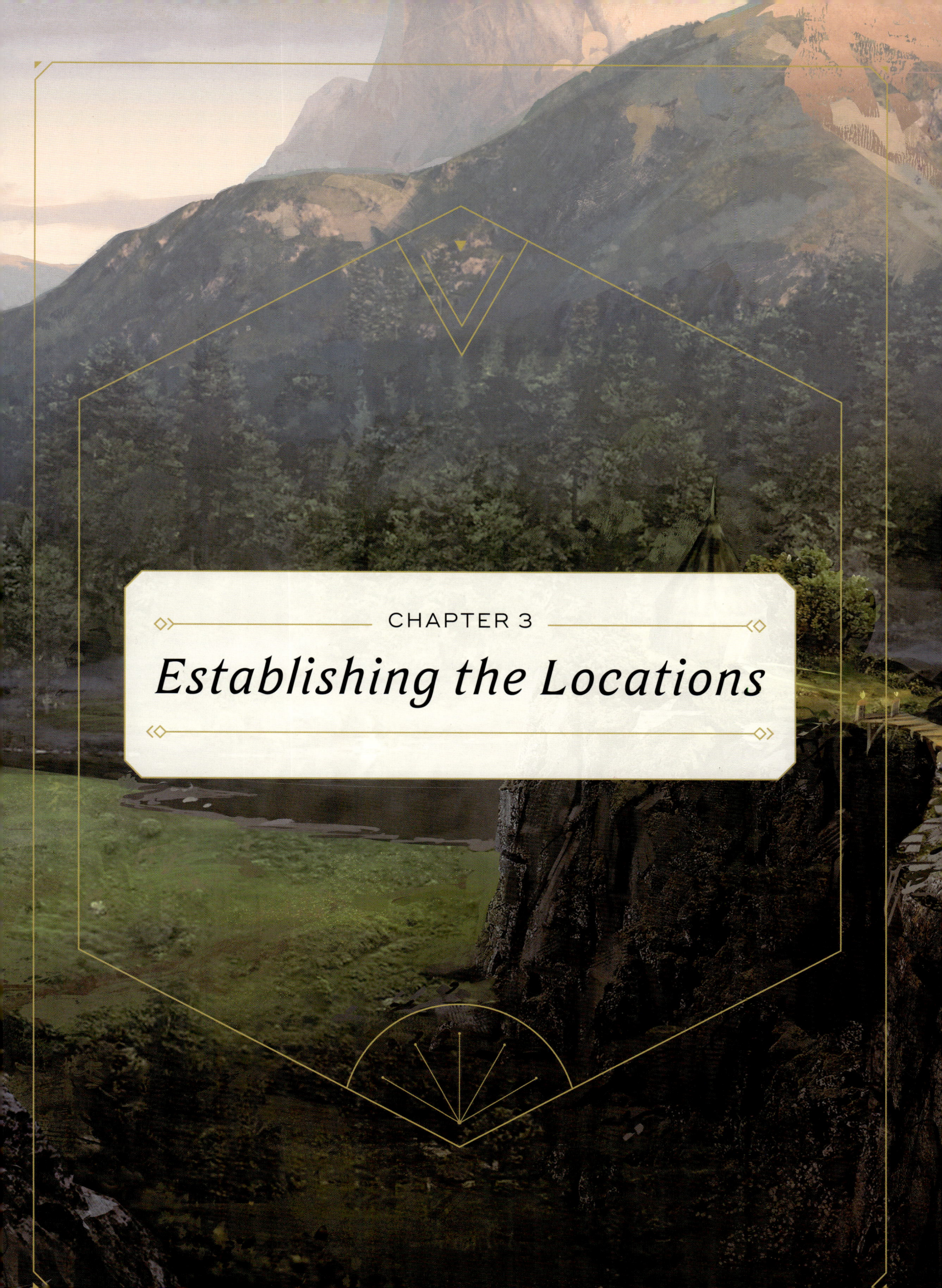

CHAPTER 3
Establishing the Locations

Hogwarts School of Witchcraft and Wizardry is not only the centre of the map for *Hogwarts Legacy* but also the centre of its world. Here, players roam familiar places like house dormitories, classrooms and the Great Hall. The shops of Hogsmeade, the Owlery and the sparkling loch beside the castle are also fairly safe, well-known and well-visited locations. However, the further one travels, the greater the possibility of danger – in the Forbidden Forest, in hamlets besieged by bandits and in the Highlands, which contains craggy hills and mountains, marshes and swamps.

Creating the locations and environments for *Hogwarts Legacy* was, without doubt, 'a bit of a challenge,' says **Dungeon Design Lead, Andrew Hayes**. 'We wanted to include a lot of the locations from the books and movies, but we couldn't risk infringing on events that happened much later than our story. The Whomping Willow wouldn't have been around at the time of our story, but perhaps there are more hidden rooms and secret passages than even Harry knew about. That's part of the premise we have to work with when building out the world.' The designers would continually ask themselves, 'What can we use that was outlined in the books and would have existed in the 1800s? And if we can't use something, can we add a similar thing without overlapping too much?'

'Fan expectations are high, and there are certainly things from the books we know people expect,' Hayes adds. 'But I think we're adding a fair number of things to the school and the world that, whilst they may not be exactly the same thing as something in Harry's time, they will provide a similar experience.'

With the game set in the late 1800s, well before the time of Harry and his beloved friends and professors, it became clear, as the title of the game indicates, that one of the most important characters would be Hogwarts itself. 'It was much more than just a location,' explains **Art Director, Jeff Bunker**. 'It needed to be alive, exuding charm and wonder, revealing mysteries with surprises and magic around every corner. Our environment artists, who are superfans themselves, were able to express their knowledge and passion for Hogwarts to their heart's content.'

PAGES 84-85: Highlands Vista by Vanessa Palmer
OPPOSITE: World Map by Nasan Hardcastle
BOTTOM: Bog by Vanessa Palmer

In his capacity of providing a vision for his team, Bunker added a few more pillars of his own. As the settings for Hogwarts and the neighbouring village of Hogsmeade are located in the Scottish Highlands, 'it should feel overcast, damp and cold,' he explains. 'Just like the films, this is translated visually with muted, somewhat monochromatic, or analogous, palettes.' Another pillar was that players should constantly be reminded that 'in spite of the bigger mystery you are caught up in, you are still attending a magical British boarding school.' And finally, 'magic is real and physical and everywhere in the wizarding world. Make it visceral, beautiful, elegant, fun and unexpected.'

'We wanted the player to be able to pull out their wand and frequently interact with the castle,' says Moira Squier. 'That's the whole point of being a wizard, after all!' However, the team felt very strongly that in having a lot of combat in the game, the castle needed to be protected against students' wild magic and would not be vulnerable to destructive spells. 'Whilst much of the outside world reacts to destructive spells, the castle is more likely to be shielded and brush off such spells, but not without giving you a dirty look,' adds **Hogwarts Art Lead, Boston Madsen**. 'Thus, a lot of thought was put into positive gameplay and puzzles and interactions that went above just breaking or blowing things up.'

It must never be forgotten that the technology used to bring the magic of Hogwarts and its diverse surrounding environments to life is true magic – and the people writing the coding and figuring out the tech are true wizards. 'I would bring my dog-eared notebook and a Harry Potter book to a conference room or Zoom call with very smart people and describe what something was supposed to look like,' says Madsen, 'and more often than not, some voice would pipe up that they had already worked out a way to make that magic happen, or someone was already knee-deep in the coding to do something like that. The magic of what this team can do is truly limitless, but the budget and memory storage is not, so naturally hard decisions had to constantly be made, but always with the player's magical experience in mind.'

TOP: Tundra Encounter by Vanessa Palmer

RIGHT: Early World Map by Sébastien Gallego

OPPOSITE BOTTOM: Hogwarts by Joshua H Black

Dark Forest and Peninsula (in-game renders) by the Environment Team

Sunrise Lighting and Irondale Hamlet (in-game renders) by the Environment Team

HOGWARTS

Hogwarts School of Witchcraft and Wizardry was founded by four great witches and wizards who wanted to pass their knowledge of magic on to younger generations. Now, in the 1800s, the school is at least nine hundred years old, and remains the standard by which all other magic schools are measured. Hogwarts is full of iconic spaces to explore, students and professors to meet and mysteries to solve.

The Avalanche art team has painstakingly constructed Hogwarts castle and its grounds, a massive part of *Hogwarts Legacy*, from both novel and film references. But, as the castle is hundreds of years old, 'we wanted to show different parts of the castle influenced by different time periods, not just the late 1800s,' says **Concept Art Lead, Sébastien Gallego**. 'The castle is timeless, but the dressing of it changes over time.'

As ancient magic is a key part of the game, the artists began by identifying which parts of the castle would have been the first built with more ancient magic, and then considered how the castle would evolve over the centuries, added onto by subsequent generations. 'The oldest part of the castle would have been the Great Hall and Grand Staircase Tower, perched on the pinnacle of the cliff,' says Boston Madsen. 'If Hogwarts was ever a "one-room school", the Great Hall would have been that one school-room. Even in modern times, it still serves as a convenient multipurpose room.'

As time and Hogwarts history progressed, the concept artists considered that students would begin to board at the school, so the next wing of the castle – the quad courtyard, which contains all four common rooms – was added onto the castle to house both the students and the increasing number of staff needed to teach them. 'Then, as the number of students attending Hogwarts grew,' she continues, 'the number of courses and classes offered at the school expanded as well, creating the addition of the entire school wing of the castle, including the Library Wing and the majestic Defence Against the Dark Arts Tower and Astronomy Tower.'

OPPOSITE: Christmas in the Great Hall by Joshua H Black

TOP: Grand Staircase Tower (in-game render) by the Environment Team

LEFT: Great Hall Door by Joshua H Black

In a true 0-1 fashion, the castle was originally built like a fully realistic school for the game. 'Every exterior window had an interior window counterpart,' Madsen explains. 'We even had secret rooms that the player would only be able to find if the outside windows were counted and compared to the inside windows – they'd notice that there was an extra window near one of the common rooms.'

Within its complex maze of stairs and corridors, the designers endeavoured to make Hogwarts castle easy to navigate and fun to play, although that proved a challenging task. First-time players are easily the equivalent of first-year wizards arriving and becoming utterly lost while trying to get to their class. It quickly became apparent that most players might not have the patience or time to become as well-acquainted with the castle as its creators were. 'As designers, we have lived between these castle walls for three to four years,' says Madsen. 'We know it so well. We know every stone because we have remade every stone multiple times.'

Therefore, measures were taken to simplify paths. 'Whereas back doors and alternative paths were once desired for stealth gameplay, the overall layout became much more linear and intuitive,' she continues. 'We are very pleased that these necessary steps were able to allow the player to feel less like a first-year, and it won't take too long for players to feel very savvy in their knowledge of the castle. It's something they should feel proud of!'

It's important that the player can move around the castle quickly when necessary, and so a system of Fast Travel allows just that. Various ideas for this were considered, including a network of toad statues the player could find and use. These statues would swallow the player and spit them out in a new location, at a new statue.

Eventually, however, the team realised that travelling via Floo powder was the best option. 'Floo powder, in lore, is a means by which witches and wizards can travel quickly by using it inside a fireplace,' explains **Kelly Murphy**. 'The final approach to this was adapted from the lore into a nod to the inventor of Floo powder, Ignatia Wildsmith.'

Fast Travel started with a Floo flames system built into the narrative, where the player would need to find a Floo flames chimney in the world and use it to travel to other Floo flames points. 'This approach prioritised presentation over player-friendliness and lore, as Floo flames in Hogwarts have strict rules,' says Murphy, 'so we decided to open up Fast Travel to anything that would appear as an icon on the map.' However, feedback obtained about this option was that it was too confusing. 'A redesign led us to the current approach,' he continues, 'which uses the Floo flames wrapper, but disassociates it from hearths where lore doesn't allow and associates it instead to a plaque of Ignatia Wildsmith.' The player unlocks Fast Travel points by discovering these plaques in the world and lighting their associated Floo flames. Once discovered, a Floo flames point can be used to Fast Travel from the map.

A visitor to Hogwarts need never go very far without being reminded that this is no ordinary castle, but a wizarding castle. Inside, they will encounter ghosts, owls, flying books and myriad other indoor 'wildlife' native to this most unique environment. The castle feels old, but is by no means dirty or crumbling – just comfortable and well broken in. Because the nature of magic makes repairs and cleaning as simple as flicking a wand, often it is not prioritised and can sometimes be overlooked. Students, in particular – and some professors as well – have a tendency to be a little sloppy. Rubble or debris or truly broken items would never be tolerated, especially by the diligent house-elf staff, yet natural wear and tear is usually overlooked and remains unfixed until absolutely necessary.

'Because we are first and foremost game makers, the castle was very carefully designed with verticality in mind to add interesting gameplay, break up long, flat paths and break long sightlines,' says Madsen. 'We didn't want players running in a straight, flat line for more than a few seconds before turning a corner or hitting stairs to break up the traversal.'

OPPOSITE: Trophy Room by BOSI

TOP: Sagittarius Constellation Drawing by Nasan Hardcastle

Classrooms

The overall layout design of Hogwarts castle features a wing specifically apportioned for classrooms. 'As the castle is huge, this would at least make the students' routes between classes at least a bit easier,' says Madsen. When first blocking out the classrooms, the developers strove to be extremely accurate to their locations in the books, with every mentioned broom closet and feature en route. 'But ultimately, we just had to accept we were dealing with a sentient castle that likes to move things around year to year,' Madsen explains. 'In the one-hundred-year span from our game's era to Harry's time, well, lots of things are going to have moved, moved back and probably moved again.' So, inevitably, the locations for the classrooms were influenced by lore, gameplay, availability or just what made sense.

The classrooms in *Hogwarts Legacy* are a mix of new and the familiar. 'The books are where it all starts,' says **Senior Producer, Brian Green**, 'but the films were also a huge inspiration for everything we did.' The architecture of the basement-set Potions classroom is largely recognisable from the films. In fact, 'the Potions class was originally positioned to perfectly duplicate a shot from the movies,' says Madsen.

Other influences from the films were the theme of gold leaf on the rough stone walls and inscriptions of Latin names for periodic elements. 'The billowy, smoke-like shapes in the room were inspired by the original graphic design of Harry's potion book from the films,' she adds, 'and are covered with potion formulas. As impossible as it sounds, we wanted the player to have a sense of smell with the Potions classroom.'

'Hopefully, the sounds, lighting and dialogue work together with the art as a kind of magic,' says Green.

The centrepiece of the Defence Against the Dark Arts classroom was made iconic in the films, with its bank of windows, curved roof trusses and most especially, the skeleton of a great winged dragon nestled in the rafters. 'It's a Hebridean Black,' Green says. As the story goes, the Defence Against the Dark Arts professor during the *Hogwarts Legacy* era, Dinah Hecat, confiscated it during the Great Poacher Raid of 1878. As each Defence Against the Dark Arts professor was inclined to decorate their classroom to reflect their tastes and interests, Hecat's is adorned with clocks. 'Without giving anything too important away, we went through various phases in which she was obsessed with timekeeping pieces and even mirrors,' says Madsen. 'And once, she even had a creepy basement full of spiders. She certainly proved to be one of the most memorable professors of *Hogwarts Legacy*.'

TOP: Quest Menu Field Guide Drawing by Nasan Hardcastle

OPPOSITE TOP TO BOTTOM: Herbology Wing, Divination Classroom and Potions Classroom (in-game renders) by the Environment Team

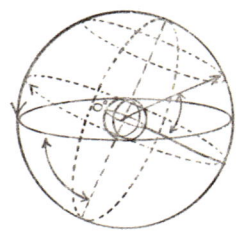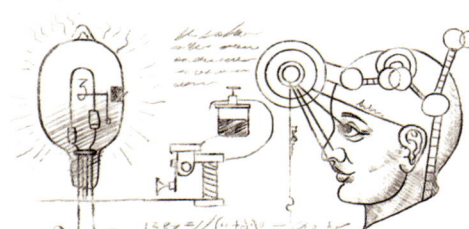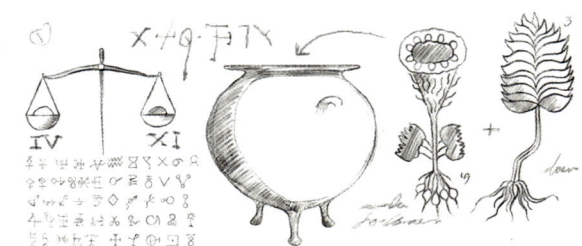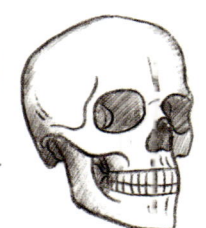

Of course, deviations from the books and films were allowable and sometimes necessary. The overall art direction for the Charms classroom came from the first movie's filming in the real-life location of Harrow School. It featured rich, dark wainscoting deeply inscribed with the graffiti of generations of students' names. 'We carried on this theme,' says Madsen, 'but instead showcased some of our favourite known charms.' As for Charms Professor Filius Flitwick's office, in the third book, *Harry Potter and the Prisoner of Azkaban*, it is located on the seventh floor of the West Tower. According to that book, when escapee Sirius Black is captured, he is incarcerated there. But in the film version, Black is held in a barred cell, high up in a dark tower.

'So, how could we make both book lore and the film details work together?' says Madsen. 'First we asked ourselves, "Why would the school keep Sirius Black in a teacher's office instead of one of the numerous dungeons we know are part of the school?" We ended up telling a story in which at some point in Hogwarts's long history, a Charms professor found it convenient to house various creatures on the balcony above his office, likely as subjects on which

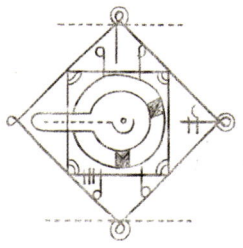

OPPOSITE TOP: Orbit Blackboard Drawing, Blackboard Diagrams and Skull Blackboard Drawing by Ben Simonsen

OPPOSITE BOTTOM: Defence Against the Dark Arts Classroom (in-game render) by the Environment Team

LEFT: Diagram Blackboard Drawing by Ben Simonsen; Charms Classroom Panel

BELOW: Scribe Wizard Library Tapestry and Astronomy Tapestries by BOSI

some of his senior students could practise experimental charms. This gave a reason for why the professor's office – or, more accurately, the cell above the professor's office – would one day be a good place to keep supposed dangerous criminals, and the balcony outside as a prime location to land a Hippogriff.'

For the Divination classroom the environment team researched symbols and creatures associated with the subject and worked them into the design of the room, along with pyramid and eye motifs, and astronomical and astrological references.

'Crows are traditionally associated with fortune-telling, so we worked them into the classroom design,' says **Kevin Keele, Senior Artist, Environments**. While the Divination classroom is small and stifling, as described in the books, there are some notable differences. 'Our Divination professor is from Uganda, so we worked to reflect her background and personality into the decor,' he continues. 'And while there are clear references to doom and death in the room, they're not quite as oppressive as the atmosphere Harry encounters in his time there.'

LEFT TOP AND BOTTOM: Hippoccmpus Statue and Fountain by Joshua H Black

OPPOSITE: Never Tickle a Sleeping Dragon Mural by Joshua H Black

The developers wanted the Herbology classroom to be a more expansive environment than had been seen in the films. 'And the books don't describe the greenhouses in too much detail,' says Keele, 'so we began by considering how a structure built to cultivate and study magical plant life might be designed. It was a great opportunity to play with a mix of organic and manufactured aesthetics, with each individual room having its own identity.' The developers supplied a range of ecosystems, including one for studying subterranean and underwater vegetation.

However, actually filling such a large space with magical plants that were appropriate for the wizarding world proved challenging. 'There's a fine line between appropriately wizarding world magical and fantastically huge or brightly coloured plants that feel like they belong in a different magical-world franchise,' Madsen explains. 'Whilst there is a large list of potion ingredients and magical plants in lore, exactly what these might and could look like led us down multiple rabbit holes, and many risked breaking the budget in desired FX or interaction.'

TOP: Greenhouse by Nasan Hardcastle

OPPOSITE: Mushroom Canopy and Giant Gourd by Nasan Hardcastle

LEFT: Dirigible Plums by Nasan Hardcastle

One guideline for Herbology was to embrace the vegetative dangers unique to Hogwarts. The enormous Herbology wing presented exciting opportunities to confront Devil's Snare, Venomous Tentacula and Mandrakes. 'Herbology Professor Mirabel Garlick is exceedingly warm, yet, at the very front of class, the player is greeted by a large and monstrous Tentacula,' says Brian Green. 'She casually feeds it a carrot and pays it no mind.'

The entrance to the Transfiguration classroom is winged by topiaries that illustrate the wonders of that discipline. Inside, the main motif of the Transfiguration classroom is depictions of animals that transfigure naturally, such as butterflies and frogs. Subtle butterfly motifs lend their shape to the classroom windows and the arches of the Transfiguration Courtyard outside. While the Courtyard is mundanely named for its position next to the Transfiguration classroom, the developers determined that it would become more memorable in 1995, 'when one Draco Malfoy was transfigured into a ferret and bounced about the courtyard, to general amusement,' says Madsen.

OPPOSITE:
Transfiguration Classroom by Joshua H Black

ABOVE AND RIGHT:
Blackboard Diagrams by Ben Simonsen

Hogwarts Black Lake by Vanessa Palmer

A Class Of Its Own

Although some other classrooms are mentioned or described in the books, they never made it to the screen, and so the designers had a fairly clean slate with which to start. The History of Magic class could easily be one of the most interesting courses taught at Hogwarts, 'if it was only taught by a different professor,' says Boston Madsen. 'But since its instructor, the late Cuthbert Binns, is a ghost teaching long past his retirement age, it looks like that is never likely to happen.' Roughly based on one of the classrooms from the films, the room is dominated by a tryptic of stunning stained-glass windows with images that depict important moments in wizarding history. 'The room has grown increasingly cluttered, as its professor is unable to do much straightening up,' says Madsen. 'His classroom and office are largely dominated by these teetering piles of unmarked essays on the goblin rebellions.'

TOP: History of Magic Tracery by Vanessa Palmer

OPPOSITE TOP: History of Magic Classroom (in-game render) by the Environment Team

OPPOSITE BOTTOM LEFT: Stained Glass by Vanessa Palmer and BOSI

OPPOSITE BOTTOM LEFT: Centaurus Constellation Drawing by Nasan Hardcastle

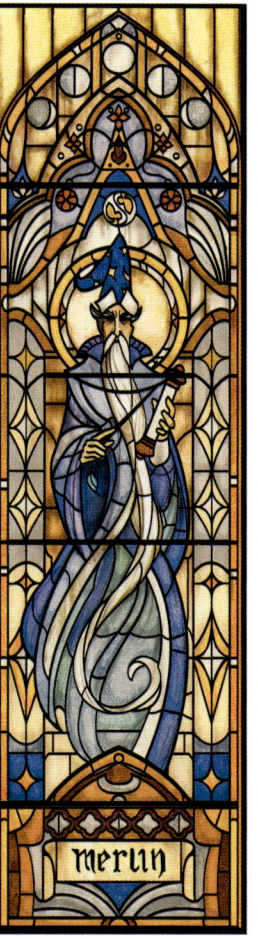

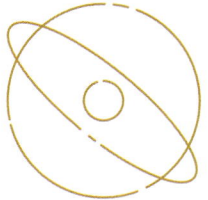

In the book *Harry Potter and the Prisoner of Azkaban*, Professor Remus Lupin teaches Harry the Patronus Charm against Dementors in the History of Magic classroom. In the film, the lesson is taught in a stripped-down Astronomy classroom. In *Hogwarts Legacy*, that room reverts to its original function and students study the wonders of the night sky. 'The Astronomy Tower is the tallest classroom in the castle,' says Madsen, 'and its main balcony is often just above the Scottish Highlands' overcast haze.' With this atmospheric height, students can work with their telescopes, or if it is too cold or overcast, they can work in a more traditional classroom just a few floors below. This wing of the castle is distinguished from other areas by its vivid blue-and-gold motifs, alluding to its astrological nature.

Another previously unvisualised room was one of Hermione Granger's favourites: the Arithmancy classroom. '[Arithmancers] also use geometric designs to help them do this,' says **Jake Black, Senior Artist, Environments**. 'In addition to having those designs drawn in chalk over the walls, we made the shape of the classroom, the layout of the floor and the design of the chandelier echo those geometric designs.' An influence that determined its location in the castle was that Hermione had to pass this classroom every day on her way to Divination. 'No wonder she was so bitter about attending her least favourite class,' says Black, 'with a clear reminder of all the fun Arithmancy homework she could be doing instead.'

According to Boston Madsen, Muggle Studies was the easiest classroom to create. 'As the most unpopular class in this time period, we thought it rather fun to consign it to the basement,' she says. Madsen describes it as more of a curio cabinet for the misunderstood curiosities of the Muggle world. 'While some items here are of ancient date, many are recent newfangled contraptions such as the electric light bulb, bicycle and sewing machine. We constantly had to double-check when items were first introduced to the Muggle world and the specific dates of our game to not get too futuristic!' Madsen's favourite feature of the Muggle Studies classroom is a set of medieval weaponry, most notably a large cannon recently pilfered by Peeves and used to create havoc and even a temporary shutdown of the school.

OPPOSITE: Astronomy Classroom by BOSI

TOP: Hydra Constellation Drawing by Nasan Hardcastle

LEFT: Astronomy Classroom (in-game render) by the Environment Team

TOP: Fig's Living Quarters by Joshua H Black and BOSI

RIGHT: Beast Studies Living Quarters by Ben Simonsen

OPPOSITE TOP TO BOTTOM: Headmaster Stair Griffin by Danny Russon; Gryffindor House Chest Collectable by Nasan Hardcastle; Goblin Instrument and Goblin Hospital Item by Nasan Hardcastle and BOSI

Their Own Room

Classrooms in Hogwarts have always been a reflection of the personality of the professor who teaches the subject. 'The students are buoyed by that professor's enthusiasm or disregard for their subject,' says Madsen, 'so even more important than the visuals is the ambience of each classroom.' Whenever possible, story prompts were used to personalise the classrooms and each professor's personal space. Some characters went through so many drafts, it was safest to stay generic in the art, adding just a few key objects to support their individualities later in production.

Not surprisingly though, 'the artists enjoyed adding little details here and there for the keen observer to help each professor at Hogwarts feel like a fully developed person with likes and dislikes,' Madsen explains. 'A favourite Honeydukes sweet, a love of cats or chess or perhaps a clue into how they like to spend their personal time, such as writing letters or playing an instrument.'

Charms Professor Abraham Ronen's personality was written to be playful and genial, with a great love for humour and games. Charmed origami birds were chosen to show this whimsical and childish playfulness, and the fluttering avians are a feature of the classroom's entrance. 'We also wanted his class to involve some sort of game with the Accio spell,' says Brian Green. 'We narrowed it down to something someone might find in a Scottish pub, something possibly related to shuffleboard. The game is much larger in scale, but it shares some of the strategies. That helped us create Summoner's Court. But because it was so big, it didn't fit in the classroom. Thankfully, Professor Ronen is just the kind of professor to take the class on a field trip, so the game is played in the Carriage Courtyard.'

As Professor Eleazar Fig rarely teaches classes, his classroom had a different focus. 'Professor Fig, as one of our main heroes, was one of the more stable professors to design around,' says Boston Madsen. 'Since his classroom was more of a front to retain his tenured position in the school, his classroom really just became a further extension of his office. The office is a bursting-at-the-seams eclectic laboratory of his passionate, decades-long research.'

Natural Classrooms

The same art team that designed the interior classrooms also worked on the classrooms for courses held in the exterior of Hogwarts castle. For Beast Studies, later to be known as Care of Magical Creatures, the designers wanted it to be familiar by paying homage to future professor Rubeus Hagrid's hut, but to also make it something new. 'Having the outside classroom under a pavilion felt appropriate for studying magical beasts,' says **Senior Artist, Environments, Jake Black**. 'It made the classroom unique, helped it feel more formal than just meeting out in the woods or grounds, and allowed the students to be near outdoor pens populated in the backyard of the hut.' Within the interior of the hut are cages, ropes, traps and other items similar to what was in Hagrid's hut, but there is also an office space and living quarters with a woman's touch for Professor Bai Howin.

For Flying class, 'while gameplay had to come first, there was thought given to just where students might first learn to fly a broom and the location of the Flying professor's office, and broom storage separate from the Quidditch pitch,' Boston Madsen explains. 'There was also once quite a debate around just how fast brooms of this era were allowed to fly and what condition the school brooms might be in. We thought it made plenty of sense, though, that a trip to the hospital wing from the flying lawns would result in the expiration of any student suffering significant injuries.'

Brian Green never thought of the classrooms as just sets: 'I see them as living things, as characters in the story. Each has its own personality and mood that is a reflection of its long history and current circumstance. The models, materials, layout, lighting, sound effects and music all work together to make each classroom an experience.'

ABOVE: Diricawl and Niffler Field Guide Drawings by Nasan Hardcastle

BELOW: Beast Studies Class Exterior by Ben Simonsen

OPPOSITE TOP: Beasts Classroom (in-game render) by the Environment Team

OPPOSITE BOTTOM: Beast Pen by Mike McCarthy

Hufflepuff Common Room by Joshua H Black

Common Rooms

The Gryffindor and Slytherin common rooms, as they appear in the 1990s, are well detailed in the books and films. In the 1890s, these beloved areas needed to be part of their own time, but it was important to the game-development team that they still feel familiar to fans. 'They shouldn't be so far from what was expected that it would feel foreign or jarring,' explains Madsen. 'We often used the mantra that if we are changing something from what the fans expect, it needs to be so much cooler so that they won't mind the change. We want our version to be so immersive and natural that the players accept it as the real thing.'

OPPOSITE: Slytherin Grand Staircase by BOSI

BELOW: Bronze Statues and Gryffindor Lion Statue by BOSI

BOTTOM: Gryffindor Fireplace and Gryffindor Common Room by Joshua H Black

Another guiding principle for them was that each house, as well as having its own colour and personality, embodies one of the four natural elements of matter, and these elements mark a centrepiece of each common room: the great fireplace in Gryffindor for fire; seemingly undulating windows and wavy features for water in Slytherin; grand windows in Ravenclaw to represent air; and hanging plants in Hufflepuff for earth. 'We began by making these elements a feature of each common room,' says Madsen. 'This wasn't hard, as it was already written into the books' descriptions.' The Gryffindor common room retains its feeling of comfort and warmth with fiery reds and golds, hanging tapestries and plush textures. But although Gryffindor does tend towards being more shabby, comfortable and cluttered, there are very tidy study tables and well-organised bookcases.

Athough the Slytherin common room was featured in the books, it was seen only briefly in the films (in *Harry Potter and the Chamber of Secrets*), and so the artists felt they had some licence to put their own take on it. 'There was much to be desired and explored in the Slytherin common room, especially from the view of Slytherin fans,' says Madsen. 'It was very important for us that, to Slytherin players, it would have the same beauty and wonder – and could feel like home base – as any of the other common rooms.'

OPPOSITE TOP AND BOTTOM: Gryffindor Common Room and Ravenclaw Common Room (in-game renders) by the Environment Team

TOP: Hufflepuff Common Room (in-game render), Slytherin Common Room (in-game render) by the Environment Team

LEFT: House Braziers (3D renders) by the Environment Team

OPPOSITE: Slytherin Snake Entrance Pattern, Gargoyle Gate and Snake Entrance Head by Nasan Hardcastle; Slytherin Common Room Entrance (in-game render) by the Environment Team; Slytherin Common Room by Joshua H Black

LEFT: Slytherin Tapestries by BOSI

TOP: Slytherin Fireplace (3D render) by the Environment Team

Having a natural element to guide them also helped make it more comfortable and magical, playing up the water motif instead of leaning too heavily towards skulls or snakes. Madsen admits that the Slytherin common room took the most iterations to find the right balance of dark mystery and cosy safety, but 'we enjoyed its challenge as we balanced both its ancient grandeur with the murkiness that naturally came from it being located beneath the lake.' Consideration was also given to personalisation within each house's common room. 'Slytherins have many talents, including music and art,' Madsen explains. 'And even though many may come from homes accustomed to more wealth, it doesn't mean they don't occasionally leave their sweet wrappers out for the house-elves to clean up, or try to train the fish outside the windows.'

Designing the Ravenclaw and Hufflepuff common rooms had to take into account the real space in which they needed to be built. 'A very talented artist figured out architecturally how to fit what was needed in the available space for the Ravenclaw common room,' explains Madsen. 'It resulted in a lot of verticality that suited the "airy perch" of the common room's personality as described.' There are comfy chairs for reading, tables for doing assignments and tall bookcases set within Gothic arches, illuminated by a huge domed window in its ceiling. 'Ravenclaw is overall more studious,' she continues, 'but those who know Ravenclaws will also know they balance this with a great sense of fun, and so they have a nice game room over their common room. They also have the best balcony in the castle, known for its raucous parties and fireworks displays that are rumoured to make every other house jealous.'

Hufflepuff is set just under the Great Hall gardens, with dorm windows that protrude from rolling grassy knolls beside the castle. This gave the designers a clue that the layout would sprawl in a flatter, wider way, unlike the other rooms. 'Hufflepuff is the best-kept secret,' says Madsen. 'They may not receive a lot of attention, but they are secure in knowing their own worth.' The light and warmth of their common room reflects this and exemplifies the creed that great depths are sometimes hidden behind a humble barrel facade. That facade is prevalent in the common room's interior, with its rounded doors and natural wood ornamentation. 'Plus, being next to the kitchens, they just may or may not have especially good food at their parties.'

Due to the climate of its Scottish location, the exterior of the castle is teeming with greenery, moss and ivy. Every corner of its grounds feels as if it has been growing vegetation for several hundred years, with only minimal efforts to keep it in check.

'Just like the true magical castle it was meant to be, Hogwarts carries hundreds of years of history with it,' adds Madsen. 'It has moved walls, grown staircases, burped out classrooms and walled off corridors to fit the yearly needs of its magical inhabitants. Does everything really make sense anymore? No, of course not, nor should it. Every quirk and crooked corridor of the castle carries a story and history that only the castle itself will ever know.'

OPPOSITE: Rowena Ravenclaw (3D render) by the Environment Team

LEFT: Humpbacked, One-eyed Witch and Ravenclaw Floor Emblem by Kevin Keele

BELOW: Ravenclaw Dorm Room (in-game render) by the Environment Team

126

Restful Rooms

'Bathrooms are a rather newfangled concept for our era,' explains Madsen. 'They're exciting new technology, so this is something students are likely to write home about to make their parents or great-aunts and -uncles jealous of the upgrade. Great pride is taken in some of Hogwarts's new plumbing, and the bathrooms tend to be some of the newest, nicest-looking areas in the school. What would one day be Moaning Myrtle's bathroom and its boys' room counterpart is probably the newest lavatory in the school!'

OPPOSITE TOP: Prefect Mermaid by Vanessa Palmer

OPPOSITE BOTTOM: Prefect Bathroom (in-game render) by the Environment Team

RIGHT: Bathroom Doorknob and Ravenclaw Toilet by BOSI

BOTTOM: Moaning Myrtle Bathroom (in-game render) by the Environment Team

THE ROOM OF REQUIREMENT

The player arrives at Hogwarts as a new fifth-year student, severely behind in their studies. The developers decided 'to provide the player a space away from Hogwarts to study, express themselves and fulfil any extra requirements they may have,' explain **Design Director, Tom Geddes** and **Lead Artist, Joe Sargent of Studio Gobo**, 'and so, just like it did for Dumbledore's Army, Hogwarts provided just what we needed: the Room of Requirement.'

After Avalanche and Studio Gobo spent time together on previous projects building a strong working relationship, Avalanche invited Studio Gobo to collaborate on *Hogwarts Legacy*. Initially, Studio Gobo's responsibilities centred around the Room of Requirement, magical beasts and the nurturing systems. 'Over time our responsibilities expanded,' explain Geddes and Sargent, 'to include the Highlands area – specifically, Hogwarts North and the Coastal Regions – missions, cinematics, extra mounts and helping with the "three C's": camera, control and character.' The partnership has additional benefits, as 'Avalanche also jokingly asked Studio Gobo to bring the "Britishness" to the game,' they add, 'to which we have more than obliged!'

The studio's philosophy with the room's design was 'Player choice, self-expression and fan fantasy,' say Geddes and Sargent. They felt that the players needed to be able to express themselves as a witch or wizard in a place they could customise around their own player identity. 'Within the Room of Hidden Things, the player decides everything,' they add, 'from which potion station they use to which ball they use to play with the magical beasts. They choose which plant to grow or which vivarium to release beasts into. It really is their own corner of the wizarding world to make their own.'

The team went through multiple concepts for the Room of Requirement, such as making the area a wizard's laboratory, with interesting plants and bubbling potions. They were also intrigued with the way Newt Scamander's suitcase played with proportions and bent space. 'The disorientation felt so weird and magical that we really wanted to get that into our Room of Requirement,' say Geddes and Sargent, 'and that is what led to the vivariums.' Jars and cases were placed all around to suggest a collection popular in the late 1800s, making the space feel like a collection of curiosities: 'strange wizarding artefacts sitting alongside each other,' they add. All these ideas helped shape what the Room of Requirement became.

Ultimately, they wanted to create a space that players could make their own. 'The Room of Requirement is perfect for that,' they remark. 'It becomes what you need. Players can express their house personalities and in one of four wizarding-inspired identities – Potions-inspired or "scientific", Herbology-inspired or "botanical", Magizoology-inspired or "eclectic", or Dark

OPPOSITE TOP: Room of Requirement Early Exploration by Damian Buzugbe

OPPOSITE BOTTOM: Room of Requirement (in-game render) by BOSI

Arts-inspired or "gothic" – via customisable crafting, nurturing and transfiguration of their own private hub or sanctuary.'

The team took inspiration not only from the books and movies but also from their own experiences – crafting a world that would fulfil a fan's fantasy of *Hogwarts Legacy* and provide something new and unique. The game takes players on a journey through the Room of Hidden Things, where they may discover many familiar sights before unlocking the space they can customise and make their own. It is here that the player meets the house-elf Deek.

The Room of Requirement is a great sanctuary for the player, allowing them to craft game-changing items with nurturing game play. Players are introduced to the main nurturing concepts in their classes: Transfiguration, Beast Studies, Potions and Herbology.

House-Elf Help

Deek the house-elf has been serving at Hogwarts for a very long time and now works with the player in the Room of Requirement. He has seen thousands of students come and go and has had a wide variety of jobs and positions throughout his years. He has always been a genuinely well-liked and sociable house-elf and, unlike most of the others serving at Hogwarts, isn't afraid to show himself to the students. Deek much prefers the outdoors and dealing with plants and beasts to the typical cooking and cleaning done by the other Hogwarts elves (although he does his fair share).

'Deek, with his long, curving ears and large, but somewhat sad, eyes, has a personality all his own,' says Tyler Lybbert. 'We obviously love to pull what we can from the descriptions of house-elves in the stories and the way they were portrayed in the films. We use all that as a jumping-off point, as we want to "find" new house-elves in the stories of our game. One look at Deek and you can see he has an outdoorsy, athletic side to him. Though quite old for a house-elf, he is quite spry, and has a youthful look on his face.'

Customising The Room

Players can customise their version of the Room of Requirement with items from 'two distinct categories,' explain Tom Geddes and Joe Sargent, 'decorative items and enchanted items, which players use to fulfil complex actions like enchanting gear or feeding beasts.'

Hundreds of novel items and architectural pieces were built based on the four wizarding identities. This allows the player 'to personalise the Room of Requirement to reflect their own personality,' they explain. 'Items range from simple chairs to an interactive frog choir!'

All of these items must be authentic to the late-Victorian era setting and the wizarding world. 'The late 1800s were an interesting time in Britain, and our research provided a lot of inspiration,' say Geddes and Sargent. 'You have the great scientific collections, Darwin and a budding conservation movement in the RSPB [the Royal Society for the Protection of Birds] and RSPCA [the Royal Society for the Prevention of Cruelty to Animals].' All these influences went into development of their Magizoologist theme. 'An interest in the occult was very fashionable in the back parlours of high society,' they add, 'which felt like a great fit for the Dark Arts. The fun comes in how you take these different themes and combine them to make something unique to your witch or wizard.'

ABOVE: Pixie's Skeleton by BOSI

OPPOSITE: Feenky and Teaque (3D renders) by the Character Team; House-elf by Ryan Wood

Enchanted items presented a bigger challenge for the team. 'Enchanted items have gameplay functions that provide a systemic quality-of-life experience for players,' they explain. 'These enrich their experiences across the game but also needed to be authentic to the wizarding world and the period.' The team's initial concepts for many of the enchanted items were strange scientific contraptions that looked amazing but did not quite fit into the franchise. 'We realised that items from the wizarding world would be everyday items enchanted to do something spectacular,' they add. 'For example, a Beast Feeder would not be a complex machine. It can be an enchanted sack of food that fills up a bucket the beasts can eat from.'

With the ability to customise the room, limits needed to be set, but at first the team did not know how this would be done. Deciding on what to keep depended on what they were most trying to achieve, as well as the user story and goal. 'Items are varied in memory budget and graphics budget,' they explain. 'Our designers, in the end, produced a simple and brilliant UI widget which visualises to the player when they have used their "item budget", flexible based on the capabilities of the device which you are playing on.'

The Room of Requirement is fully customisable, from its structural architecture to all the conjurable items. 'This was a big design, art and tech challenge to get right,' say Geddes and Sargent, 'requiring a lot of work and iteration. Combine this with a room that changes and expands with player progression – there were a lot of moving parts to consider.'

Tending To Beasts

Players gain the ability to rescue magical beasts from the wild and bring them back to the Room of Requirement, where they can be tended to. 'We wanted our players to be able to interact with the beasts and care for them,' Geddes and Sargent explain. 'There were many different ideas, but eventually we arrived at the core activities of petting, feeding, playing and breeding.'

The team needed to reward players for collecting the magical beasts, so they came up with a threefold bonus: interacting with the beasts in a completely new way, using beast by-products to improve gear and raising extremely cute baby magical beasts.

There is a variety of distinct beast types with unique locomotion – quadrupeds, flying beasts and quadrupeds that can fly – which presented its own challenges during development. The systems needed to work for all the magical beasts without requiring lots of unique animations or content. 'Luckily, we have a very smart team of animators, technical animators, programmers and character artists who rose to the challenge and delivered an amazing result,' say Geddes and Sargent. The studio is extremely proud of the outcome, they add. 'The magical beasts genuinely have their own life and personalities as they play with unique toys, come to the player for petting and navigate to the Beast Feeder to feed themselves when they are hungry.'

Lore and fan fantasy were major driving forces when selecting the beasts to include in the game. The team read creature descriptions from the Harry Potter books, scoured books about the art of the wizarding world and watched the Harry Potter and Fantastic Beasts films, paying close attention to details such as personality and behaviour. Scenes such as the Hippogriff flight across the lake and the introduction of Fawkes the phoenix are familiar to fans. The studio wanted to include magical beasts like these to give players both new and familiar experiences with them.

'We wanted every beast to provide something unique and spectacular,' explain Geddes and Sargent. Many beasts have a strong visual identity that the team did not want to stray too far from, such as the Niffler's look. Others went through many iterations of concept art, as the team worked closely with The Blair Partnership to produce a beast that is familiar yet unique to the game. 'Our creatures have male and female variations, and some of the creatures, especially the offspring, have never been seen on film or in games before.'

Much of the inspiration for these beasts was drawn from the movie *Fantastic Beasts and Where to Find Them*, say Geddes and Sargent, 'mixing flying beasts like Thestrals with smaller, cuter student pets like Puffskeins through to larger, more aggressive beasts like the Graphorn.'

The team also drew inspiration from the cinematic depiction of Newt Scamander's case, crafting four unique vivariums accessible from the Room of Requirement. The vivariums took longer to

OPPOSITE TOP: Phoenix Constellation Drawing by Nasan Hardcastle

OPPOSITE BOTTOM: Beast Offspring (3D render) by the Character Team

develop with many iterations. 'Originally, we had expansion charms that opened larger areas within the Room of Requirement itself,' say Geddes and Sargent. 'Then we investigated ideas more like the beast areas within Newt's case before finally settling upon vivariums, which start as Wardian cases before expanding into something much larger.' These vivariums represent the variety of regions that surround Hogwarts and are inspired by Scotland, where the game is based.

Brewing Potions

Potions in *Hogwarts Legacy* provide an invaluable resource in battle with the ability to heal, mitigate damage, conceal and more. By conjuring a potion station inside the Room of Requirement, players gain the ability to brew these concoctions outside of the classroom.

As the Studio Gobo team developed potions for the game, much was taken into consideration, including wizarding world lore and gameplay usage. 'From a gameplay perspective, we needed potions to empower our players,' explain Geddes and Sargent. One example is the Invisibility Potion, a more powerful stealth potion compared to the castable Disillusionment Charm. 'We also needed to balance potion usage against spell usage, resource collection and Room of Requirement crafting,' they add, 'which helped decide the number of potions required, their visuals and their effects.'

The steps required to brew these game-changing consumables create a sort of minigame, providing a fun diversion for the player. 'The design, art, visual effects and implementation all came together to deliver something very exceptional,' note Geddes and Sargent. 'Brewing potions could have been driven through a UI screen and text, but the team came together and delivered an authentic wizarding world experience, and it's one of our favourite activities.'

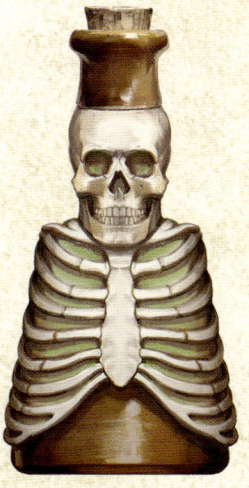

OPPOSITE, LEFT TO RIGHT: Potions Crafting Table by Mike McCarthy

TOP: Sanctuary Reveal by Damian Buzugbe

LEFT: Beautification, Ink-Shroud, Skele-Gro, Hate and Moonlight-Oil Potions by Nasan Hardcastle and BOSI

Growing Plants

The steps for growing plants are learned in Herbology class, but once a potting table has been conjured plants can be grown at any time inside the Room of Requirement. 'Herbology is particularly important to the Hogwarts school experience, and the Mandrake scene in *Chamber of Secrets* is one we wanted to recreate,' say Geddes and Sargent. 'Plants like this make for powerful tools when utilised correctly, like a Mandrake's cry being fatal to anyone that hears it.

Chinese Chomping Cabbages, Venomous Tentacula and Devil's Snare are other well-known lore plants that provide variation to combat and adventuring,' they add.

Within the Room of Requirement, the Studio Gobo team had only to provide the player with space, required conjurations and the resources to grow the plants. 'The more difficult challenge for the team was balancing them against the combat spells,' say Geddes and Sargent, 'whilst also making them feel unique and valuable enough to continually engage players in the Room of Requirement's crafting loops.'

BOTTOM: Leaping Toadstools and Honking Daffodil by Nasan Hardcastle

OPPOSITE TOP: Mandrake (3D render) by the Character Team; Venomous Tentacula by Ben Simonsen

OPPOSITE BOTTOM: Shrivelfig, Pungous Onion and Niffler's Fancy by Danny Russon and BOSI

Putting It All Together

The Studio Gobo team faced numerous challenges, such as dealing with the customisation and expansion of the space. It had to not only look beautiful but also allow for quite granular decoration and customisations. 'A player can choose one wizarding identity for a wall piece,' say Geddes and Sargent, 'then, right next to it, choose another, then, above it, another, and at some point, the whole room can expand and change shape, giving the player more space to play and express themselves. This created a three-dimensional jigsaw puzzle, and every piece was different. The team worked collaboratively and extremely hard to allow for this customisation, but not at the expense of quality.'

Numerous technical challenges presented themselves as well in the effort to ensure that this is all possible and to keep within frame budgets on the target platforms. The studio also had to ensure that the room complemented the wider game story and systems – for example, rewarding and empowering the main moment-to-moment game loops of combat, foraging, looting and exploration.

Tough decisions had to be made about which features and items to fully develop and which to scrap. Beasts, room expansions, potions, plants and even a gnome minigame ended up on the cutting-room floor due to quality or time constraints. What remains is a fully customisable room that captures the spirit of the wizarding world, whilst providing a sanctuary for the player where they may put the nurturing skills they have learned at Hogwarts to use. Studio Gobo is understandably proud of everything *Hogwarts Legacy* has to offer, but there are aspects they are especially fond of. 'I am most proud of its authenticity, its charm and, well, how magic it is,' says Joe Sargent. 'It was a joy helping bring to life magical animated Potion Stations, Beast Feeders, Dung Composters, Billywig Hives and magical expanding vivariums that grow to reveal whole new worlds for the player to nurture and care for the magical beasts. There is so much to do and see in this little space, and plenty of Easter eggs to discover, I cannot wait for the players to explore it.'

'I am proud of the whole user experience, what the room offers players and how the whole team made such a cool place,' says Tom Geddes. 'And I simply love how I can adapt the room to my own style of play. It's fun to brew potions or grow plants that help in combat and exploration, while nurturing beasts to use in gear crafting or as Highlands mounts. It all showcases the great systems the team have developed.'

'We have never seen a game deliver this kind of experience to the quality the team has achieved,' Geddes and Sargent conclude. 'We feel immensely proud and privileged to have been a part of this project and we hope that players enjoy the experience as much as we did making it.'

OPPOSITE TOP: Sanctuary customised by Damian Buzugbe
OPPOSITE BOTTOM: Terrarium Bog Entrance (in-game render paintover) by Mike McCarthy

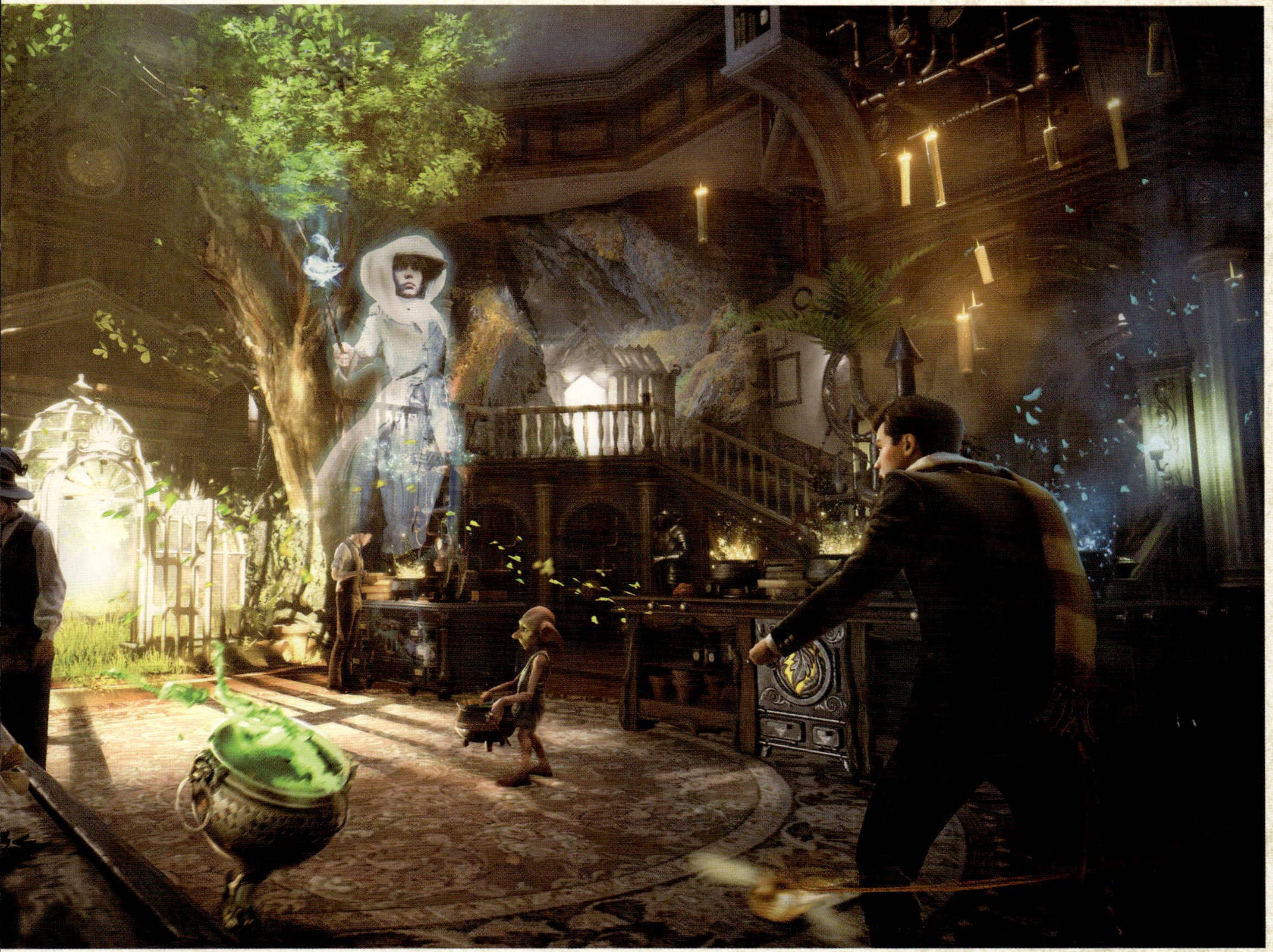

Swamp
REMEMBER!
WIPE YOUR
FEET

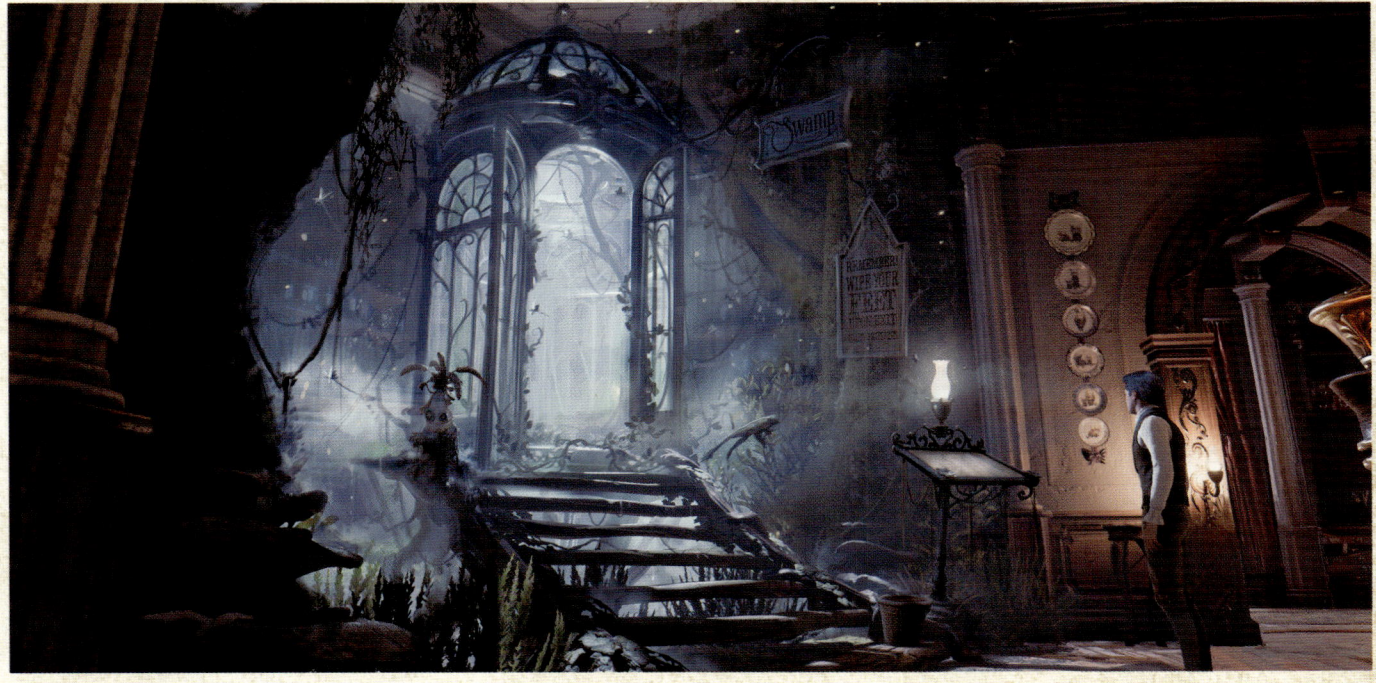

HOGSMEADE

In Hogsmeade, the player can interact with vendors of the village's shops and taverns, who offer both missions and items helpful to their quests.

More than twenty shops line the streets and side alleys of Hogsmeade, the only all-wizarding village in Britain. 'On top of the principal shops such as Honeydukes, the Hog's Head Inn, Ollivanders and the Three Broomsticks, we also have Ceridwen's Cauldrons, Gladrags Wizardwear, Dervish and Banges and so much more,' says **Jared Bastian, the Hogsmeade Art Lead**, 'fully realised and fully functional.' Some shops play a critical role in the player's game progression, and some are there just for fans to see for the first time what that shop actually looks like. 'So, as part of that, we've added a few unique shops of our own that supplement the fan favourites,' says Bastian.

Envisioning Hogsmeade for *Hogwarts Legacy* started with a whiteboard map. 'We gathered all the book descriptions we could find about Hogsmeade – where the shop locations were relative to each other – and we went to town!' says **Concept Art Lead, Sébastien Gallego**. The concept artists moved the buildings around until the map matched the book description as closely as possible. 'We knew we wanted to keep the Scottish small-town vibe,' Gallego continues, 'with a main street, a few narrower streets branching out of it, as well as making sure that the Three Broomsticks was the star of the show as you enter the town.'

OPPOSITE BOTTOM LEFT: Hogsmeade Early Map Layout by Sébastien Gallego

OPPOSITE BOTTOM RIGHT: Hogsmeade Plaza during Hallowe'en by the Environment Team

TOP: Hogsmeade Plaza by the Environment Team

LEFT: Hogsmeade during Winter (in-game renders) by the Environment Team

TOP: Owl Post Interior (in-game render) by the Environment Team; Hogsmeade Isometric View by Danny Russon

OPPOSITE: Generic House by Adam Tolman

There was another consideration to keep in mind while laying out the village. 'Since some fans are familiar more so with the films and the parks,' says Jared Bastian, 'we also wanted to create a space that felt familiar enough for them so fans coming from every reference point could feel like they were being immersed in a space they already knew and embraced.'

In keeping with the game's era, the artists needed to incorporate the long history behind Hogsmeade as well as how it would look in the 1800s. Much of Hogsmeade was built long before the 1800s, but the artists were inspired thinking about what the shops and their contents might have looked like in this previously unknown era and embraced the technology and design sense of the times.

Another idea that resonated with Bastian was a statement made by Stuart Craig, the production designer for the films. 'The general idea was that there was not a straight line or right angle found in the town,' Bastian explains. The artists embraced this concept, feeling that the wizards who designed and built the town didn't concern themselves with Muggle standards of construction. 'But they built a town full of charm and wonder whose roads were never straight and whose shop doors may be slightly off vertical.' Bastian admits one other influence to this approach: 'Maybe it was also because I had just finished building shelves for our master wardrobe, only to find out that all of my eyeballed measurements were slightly off and nothing was level or plumb in the end!'

OPPOSITE: Dogweed and Deathcap Exterior (in-game render) by the Environment Team
MIDDLE: Wizard House Interior by Danny Russon
BOTTOM: Hogsmeade stylised by Sébastien Gallego

Building a town full of crooked shapes and off-axis buildings did not lend itself well to sharing assets throughout Hogsmeade. For Hogwarts castle, a window could be reused again and again because it was designed to be uniform and straight. 'In Hogsmeade, however, windows were crooked and off-kilter, roof lines were bowed and walls were often bent and torqued to fit the feel of the town we were constructing,' says Bastian. 'It took a lot of tech and manpower to build this town!'

A small team of concept artists referenced cues from the books whenever possible, and generated several designs for each building, inside and out. These initial designs were tweaked and altered to support and enhance the gameplay planned for each shop. 'That often influenced the layout of the floor plan,' says Bastian. 'We really wanted each shop to have its own unique feel. Take Zonko's and Dogweed and Deathcap, for example. Not only would you go for different reasons, but you'd have different experiences within each shop.'

In Hogsmeade, the shops are nothing without their shopkeepers, and so each shopkeeper's personality and the purpose of their shop was woven into the design. 'We approached the design of each building, interior and exterior, as if it were a character,' says Gallego, 'and spent time designing them based on the personality of their vendors.' This is another example of the crossover between art and story for a successful and immersive visual experience. 'Some shops are more meticulously organised,' adds Bastian, 'and some are a bit rougher around the edges. Some have a more formal finish to the woodwork and the dressing of their space, and others don't care quite as much about the presentation of their shop as they do the items they sell within it.'

Hogsmeade High Street Christmas Season by Danny Russon

For the exteriors of the shops, the artists conceived that most of the buildings would be constructed of a similar set of materials from the region, 'but each shopkeeper might have a different take on aesthetics, construction style and function,' says Bastian, 'so even as you walk up the high street or a side alley, each building has its own vibe.' The designers needed to keep asking the question 'How would a wizard choose to build this?' 'That applied on a macro level to the town as a whole, as well as down to the smallest detail of construction or aesthetic design,' Bastian explains. 'What laws of physics would they embrace, and what would they choose to override with magic? Which Muggle conventions would they adopt, and which would they find silly? It was always a challenge to see how far we could push things and still feel grounded in the same world as Hogwarts and the rest of the game.'

It was decided early on that Hogsmeade would be a town dependent on foot traffic, designed for exploration and collecting things students might need throughout the game. Its tight and crooked interior spaces would contrast with the wide-open stretches of the Highlands areas and the huge, formal structured spaces found in Hogwarts. 'Students would go to Hogsmeade to let their hair down and have fun, so the space needed to reflect that,' adds Bastian.

Yet, the best of plans will change. 'While we thought we had bases covered early on for a proper home for any type of item a player might need,' Bastian explains, 'we quickly found that some gameplay items we thought would be essential were no longer going to be supported by a system of the game, and others were needed that we hadn't ever considered in the early stages.'

However, as the concept artists and game designers were in constant consultation, the shops could adjust to changes. 'There are enough nooks and crannies in all of these shops and exterior spaces that it was easy to find a home for an entrance to a dungeon here or a home for a prized possession there,' says Bastian. 'Often, we'd find that once a space had a clear game purpose, it would become inherently obvious what we needed to do as artists to support and enhance that purpose.' This sort of flexibility was necessary when game plans changed, and the first thing the player encounters in Hogsmeade became a big combat sequence. 'We didn't have a large enough space to support this originally,' says Bastian, 'but game design is always a moving target, so sometimes you just have to break a few walls to create the right experience. And we did!'

OPPOSITE: Plaza Fountain by Danny Russon

RIGHT: Plaza Fountain Sketch by Danny Russon

Hogsmeade Vendors

As each shop in Hogsmeade has its individual personality, so do the shops' vendors. 'A shopkeeper becomes the outward expression of their shop, which is also usually their passion,' says **Characters Art Lead, Tyler Lybbert**. 'Just as it's fascinating to interact with someone in the real world who has a passion for something, so, too, it will be for the players of *Hogwarts Legacy* to meet and interact with the shopkeepers of Hogsmeade. For example, Gerbold Ollivander doesn't just have a fun name, but his bald head, surrounded by fly-away grey hair and bushy sideburns, is just as entertaining!'

Ollivanders has been selling wands since 382 BCE. Gerbold Ollivander, the wand seller at the Hogsmeade branch, knows everything there is to know about wands, from wood types to cores. He's fun, enthusiastic and brings a sense of wonder to anyone who visits his shop. The Hogsmeade Ollivanders is a tighter space than the one in Diagon Alley, but it's jam-packed to the ceiling with two-storey-high displays showcasing the latest wands.

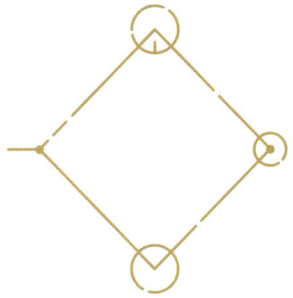

OPPOSITE: Ollivanders Interior by Danny Russon
TOP: Ollivanders Exterior by Adam Tolman
RIGHT: Ollivander Cabinet Card by Ryan Wood

The proprietor of **SCRIVENSHAFT'S QUILL SHOP**, meanwhile, is the birdlike **Ethel Wigley**, who ensures that only fallen feathers are used in the quills she stocks.

DERVISH & BANGES, run by **Thaddeus Travers**, who's a bit lazy, is the place to purchase a diversity of wizarding equipment.

Albie Weekes is the broom vendor at **SPINTWITCHES SPORTING NEEDS**. Here players can upgrade their brooms to ease travel across the Highlands.

Kits and clothing can be purchased at **GLADRAGS WIZARDWEAR**, attended to by shopkeeper and unrelenting salesman **Augustus Hill**, who has the ability to quickly put a positive spin on even the most unflattering choice of attire.

OPPOSITE TOP: Scrivenshaft's by Adam Tolman

OPPOSITE BOTTOM: Dervish & Banges Interior by Danny Russon

TOP: Spintwitches Sporting Needs (in-game render) by the Environment Team

Beatrice Green, who would be considered the 'cat lady' of plants, sells the flora at **DOGWEED AND DEATHCAP** – including some seeds that are considered dangerous. The shop, set a bit apart from the town, was built into a mountainside.

BROOD & PECK sells all sorts of products for all sorts of beasts, and the rough and tumble **Ellie Peck** is the person to see for all creature comforts.

OPPOSITE TOP:
Dogweed and Deathcap Interior and Sketches by Danny Russon

OPPOSITE BOTTOM:
Dogweed and Deathcap by Adam Tolman

ABOVE AND LEFT:
Brood & Peck Exterior, Back, and Sketch by Danny Russon; Shopkeeper Leona Peck (3D render) by the Character Team

Hog's Head Alley by Danny Russon

Parry Pippin is the potion and ingredient seller at **J. PIPPIN'S POTIONS**. He believes that there's a potion for everything, and often tries to solve even the simplest problems with complex concoctions.

BELOW: Potion Case and Potions by Nasan Hardcastle and BOSI; Leech Juice Field Guide Drawing by Vanessa Palmer; Pippin's Potions Station by Danny Russon
BOTTOM: Pippin's Potions Interior (in-game render) by the Environment Team
OPPOSITE: Pippin's Potions Exterior by Adam Tolman

TOMES AND SCROLLS, maintained by vendor **Thomas Brown**, sells not only tomes – and scrolls, of course – but also a great conjuration of recipes known as 'spellcrafts.' The proprietor of this speciality bookshop is an honourable man with a fondness for Muggle culture, particularly Christmas carols.

OPPOSITE TOP: Tomes and Scrolls Interior by Sam Nielson

OPPOSITE BOTTOM: Tomes and Scrolls and Tomes and Scrolls at Night (in-game renders) by the Environment Team

TOP: Poison Quill by Nasan Hardcastle

RIGHT: Thomas Brown Shopkeeper (3D render) by the Character Team

Calliope Snelling is the hairdresser to see at **MADAME SNELLING'S TRESS EMPORIUM**. This sophisticated resident hairdresser sees herself as a tastemaker, having lived in France for three months. In addition to her over-the-top hairstyles, she's overdressed for any occasion.

TOP LEFT: Madame Snelling's Tress Emporium Exterior by Vanessa Palmer

TOP RIGHT: Lady Bird Poster by Joshua H Black

LEFT: Magic Neep Exterior by Danry Russon

BOTTOM: Magic Neep Owner Timothy Teasdale (3D render) by the Character Team

OPPOSITE: Honeydukes Alihotsy Fudge Poster by Danny Russon

THE MAGIC NEEP is another shop to buy plant seeds, tended by **Timothy Teasdale**. Many would be surprised to find that kindly Teasdale was once an Auror.

HONEYDUKES sweet shop is a major meeting place in the town, overrun with Fizzing Whizzbees and Chocolate Frogs. It's run by **Patrick Redding** with his daughter, Olivia.

TOP SPREAD: Honeydukes Early Concept by West Studio

OPPOSITE: Honeydukes Sign Design by Ben Simonsen; Bertie Bott's Sweets by BOSI

LEFT: Fizzing Whizzbees, Chocolate Frogs, Pumpkin Fizz Drink and Strudel Pastry by BOSI

Sirona Ryan is the well-liked, quick-witted proprietress of the **THREE BROOMSTICKS**, the popular inn and pub frequented by villagers, travellers and Hogwarts staff and students in Hogsmeade. This big, iconic building is in the centre of town, so most roads lead to it or pass by it. It's usually packed with patrons inside and out with interesting stories to tell. Ryan values good company, good gossip and, above all, good Butterbeer. She is genuinely protective of her customers and has no problem standing up to the local foes like Victor Rookwood, who try to extort Hogsmeade businesses for 'protection.'

THE HOG'S HEAD INN's owner, **Jasper Trout**, is a great source of information on the latest criminal activities, and the hog's head behind the bar is a great source of drool and slobber. The drinking establishment is situated at the end of a dodgy alley where you can feel the sinister acts taking place in the shadows and around the corner. It also has a creaky dock behind it, and who knows what kinds of things move in and out of town there?

OPPOSITE TOP: Three Broomsticks Sign by Ben Simonsen
OPPOSITE BOTTOM: Butterbeer Sign by Ben Simonsen
TOP: Three Broomsticks Interior by Ben Simonsen
RIGHT: Hog's Head Sign by Ben Simonsen

THE HOGSMEADE POST OFFICE is run by **Lottie Featherbottom**, who's very connected to all the goings-on in and around Hogsmeade. She might be a bit of a know-it-all, but she loves her owls. All packaging and other supplies are ready at hand.

ZONKO'S JOKE SHOP is the place to have a bit of fun and get a good laugh, especially from its cheeky shopkeeper, who chuckles easily and is always up for a bit of fun.

TOP: Zonko's Exterior (in-game render) by the Environment Team

RIGHT: Balloons Poster by Jason Borne; Boxing Telescope Poster by Ben Simonsen; Gillyweed Tonic Poster by Danny Russon

OPPOSITE TOP: Zonko's Interior (in-game render) by the Environment Team

OPPOSITE BOTTOM: Jack-in-the-Box and its Orthographic Views, and Elephant on a Bicycle Poster by Danny Russon; Zonko's Rafters by Ben Simonsen

The owner of the **MUSIC SHOP** has a sweet musical voice, but she often seems distracted, and it's not uncommon to catch her daydreaming.

TOP: Music Shop Exterior and Interior by Nasan Hardcastle

ABOVE: Music Shop Exterior by Danny Russon

LEFT: Phonograph by BOSI

The shopkeeper of **CERIDWEN'S CAULDRONS** is suave and knowledgeable about his job, but always seems a bit bored with it, as if he'd much rather be doing something else.

LEFT: Cauldron Shop Interior by Joshua H Black
BELOW: Cauldron Shop Exterior (3D render) by the Environment Team
BOTTOM LEFT: Cauldrons by BOSI

171

STEEPLEY AND SONS TEA SHOP is run by a widow who appreciates her young customers, such as those from Hogwarts, and takes a grandmotherly approach to them all – but mind your manners! She takes no nonsense from her customers.

Hogsmeade resident **NORA TREADWELL** is an archaeologist and Merlin historian whose interest in the fabled wizard was piqued when she was at Hogwarts and her future wife gave her a book about him. Over the years, she's followed Merlin's legacy and has written a number of books about him. Nora met her wife, Priya, at Hogwarts, and the two have taken up residence in the Three Broomsticks for the duration of Nora's current expedition which involves a major discovery – trials Merlin left around Hogwarts – and while she finishes her latest book about the great wizard's schooldays.

ABOVE AND RIGHT: Hogsmeade Teashop Back and Sketches by Nasan Hardcastle

TOP RIGHT: Nora Treadwell by Vanessa Palmer

OPPOSITE: Hogsmeade Teashop Front by Nasan Hardcastle

THE HIGHLANDS

Comprised of several square miles around Hogwarts, the Highlands provides deeper explorations into familiar areas such as the Forbidden Forest and the Black Lake, and new adventures while journeying – on foot, via broom or mounted on beasts – through swamps, coastlines and Highlands. These many varied areas offer engaging experiences for the player to forage for potion ingredients and other resources, rescue beasts, combat Dark wizards and goblins and solve magical puzzles such as the Merlin Trials. There are treasure vaults to open and spider lairs to avoid. The Highlands features thirteen regions: North Ford Bog, Forbidden Forest, Hogsmeade Valley, North Hogwarts Region, South Hogwarts Region, Hogwarts Valley, Feldcroft Region, South Sea Bog, Poidsear Coast, Marunweem Lake, Manor Cape, Cragcroftshire and Clagmar Coast.

OPPOSITE: Dark Mountain Path by Vanessa Palmer
OPPOSITE TOP: Bog Biome (in-game render) by the Environment Team
TOP: Valley Castle by Vanessa Palmer

Jobberknoll Grove by Vanessa Palmer; Forbidden Forest Paintover by Mike McCarthy

Marshland Landmark and Forbidden Forest Micro Biome by Mike McCarthy

Research and reference for the environment started with compiling hundreds of images of Scotland and its Highlands. Whenever possible, the artists and designers would start with a real physical place and then grow from there. 'There's nothing better than good reference for a concept artist,' says **Concept Art Lead, Sébastien Gallego**. 'It just brings a level of authenticity you cannot get otherwise. Your imagination and memories can only go so far.' From their research, the artists could push things around, exaggerate features and add new ideas. 'When you understand your source material, it allows you to be more creative and spend your energy designing the place instead of worrying about details nature already took care of for you!' he explains. 'Grounding the visual experience of the game in the real world was key to our look.'

The team worked closely with Historic Environment Scotland, which provided reference photos of ancient castles and cairns around Scotland and provided innovative technology to produce three-dimensional scans of those historic monuments, which were utilised in environment design. 'For many of the coastlines and dungeons, we took inspiration from the shorelines of Scotland and the surrounding areas,' says **Environments and Dungeons Art Lead, Mike Thompson**. 'And, of course, we also took a significant amount of inspiration from the books and movies.'

It was very important to the team that environments were designed where players can use magic to interact with their surroundings. 'The initial ideas for each of our environments started small, with reference photos and obscure ideas,' Thompson adds. 'Through collaboration, we were able to bring those ideas to life and develop final locations where even the smallest details were accounted for.'

OPPOSITE: Coastal Region (in-game render) by the Environment Team Pellentesque

ABOVE: Brewery (in-game render) by the Environment Team

LEFT: Snidget Tree by Danny Russon

The Highlands Vendors

Throughout the Highlands, there are vendors who will sell goods to students to help them on their quests. Some have long-established shops, and others travel around. The shopkeepers and residents in these hamlets have been challenged by attacks from goblins, spiders, poachers and Ashwinders, but they fiercely defend their homes and businesses.

The vendors are a diverse group, from myriad locations and backgrounds. There are retired Aurors, world travellers looking to settle down and youthful entrepreneurs who may or may not have an idea of how to actually sell their merchandise. Indira Wolff is a quirky young woman who has taken over her father's beast-product shop in the Hamlet of Pitt-Upon-Ford. She doesn't really know what she's doing, but she tries as hard as she can to do her father's business justice.

Ewart MacQuod, who barely survived spider attacks in Aranshire Hamlet, now exclusively sells spider by-products, trying to make the most of a bad situation. Madam Fatimah Lawang manages a shop selling potions of her own expert creation. Another potion shop owner is Jalal Sehmi, who loves to share news and gossip with Hogwarts students who enter his establishment.

Some vendors and residents of the small hamlets scattered throughout the Highlands have been greatly affected by nefarious forces in their areas and are trying to do something about it. Cragcroft resident Hyacinth Oliver is a strong-willed and passionate resident of her hamlet, with a go-getter attitude and a heart for the people. She works as an activist against Rookwood and the Ashwinders and poachers.

OPPOSITE: Carnival Wagon Vendor and Colours by Ben Simonsen

TOP: Hamlet Clothing, Potion and Plant Vendors by Nasan Hardcastle

ABOVE: Carnival Wagon Vendor Posters by Ben Simonsen

TRAVERSING THE HIGHLANDS

The wizarding world is full of magical modes of transport that allow witches and wizards to easily travel between distant locations. For *Hogwarts Legacy*, developers drew on these methods of travel to provide players the means to quickly move through the game's vast, open world.

The most efficient way to move through the game is through its Fast Travel system. Numerous options for this system were proposed, such as toad statues and owl banisters, but the team settled on a system inspired by the Floo Network from the Harry Potter books. At first, players were required to find a chimney in order to travel to other points. This idea evolved into a network of Floo flames associated with plaques of the inventor of Floo powder, Ignatia Wildsmith, instead of a chimney. Found throughout the castle, Highlands and Hogsmeade, a discovered Floo flames location can be selected directly from the map, allowing the player to swiftly travel to the selected destination.

Inside Hogwarts, the team also added a series of magical shortcuts the player can use to teleport to different locations within the castle. Discovering these secrets adds to the magical charm of Hogwarts.

Broom flight, too, is a big part of the wizarding world. Witches and wizards often use enchanted broomsticks to travel between locations. Therefore, it was always planned to incorporate them into *Hogwarts Legacy*, where they play a big role. Early in the game, the player must attend Flying class to learn how to handle a broom. Then, races were added so that players could perfect their flying skill in a fun extracurricular diversion. Designers created a wide selection of brooms that provide the player with another means of character customisation.

Mounts were added as the game evolved and they were developed when the team wanted 'to include story beats and gameplay that were "greatest hits" moments for the player when they think about the wizarding world,' explains Kelly Murphy. 'Flying a Hippogriff and riding a Graphorn were two fantasies that gained traction, and two of our missions ended up being about this. Further discussion opened up the possibility for these to not just be moments in the game, but systemic mounts, which we felt created great gameplay opportunities for the player, but also something to talk about between players.'

When and how these mount options became available were 'tied to the mission flow,' Murphy says, 'where the moment of riding a Hippogriff or Graphorn precedes the unlocking of that creature as a systemic mount. When looking at all three possible mount options (broom, Hippogriff, Graphorn), we felt it was best to unlock the broom earliest, as it is a pretty core expectation of players. From there, the Graphorn became the final mount we unlock, as it is tied to a late mission in the story.'

ABOVE: Fast Travel Plaque by Danny Russon

OPPOSITE LEFT: Ignatia Wildsmith by Vanessa Palmer

OPPOSITE RIGHT: Night Dancer, Aeromancer and Moontrimmer Brooms by Nasan Hardcastle

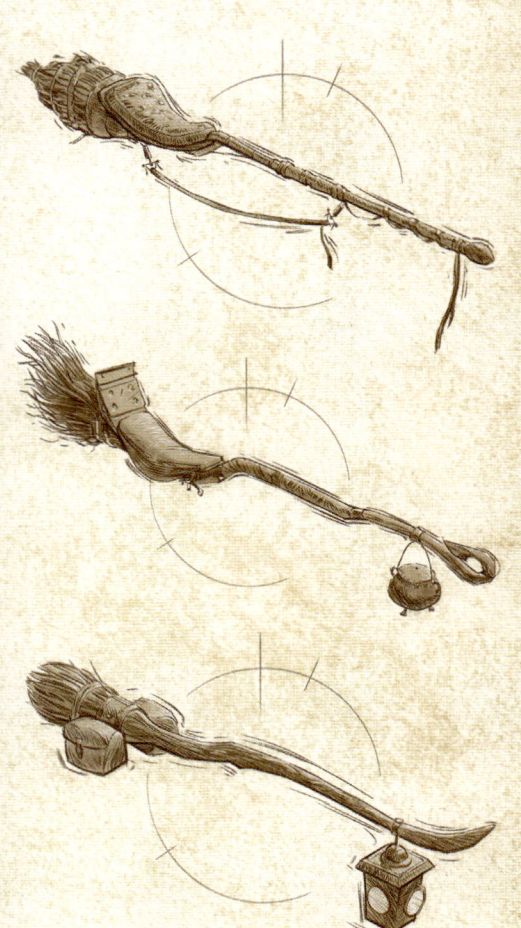

EXTRACURRICULAR ACTIVITIES

The main story, side quests and class assignments keep the player busy, but there are also plenty of extracurricular activities available for those who appreciate a good challenge or diversion. A variety of puzzles, trials and events populate the world, accessible to players that venture off the beaten path.

Creation and development of these activities can be a lengthy process as they pass through numerous iterations. Puzzle creation begins with brainstorming and a paper design. Once approved, it goes through prototyping, where it can first be played – fine-tuning until players have something fun. This may involve several prototypes, based on the complexity of the puzzle. An approved prototype is placed into a game level to be iterated on by design and art. This may also take several iterations before receiving full approval for the final game.

Level designers were encouraged from the beginning 'to explore the possibilities,' says **Dungeon Design Lead, Andrew Hayes**. 'What could they do with spells like *Accio* or *Depulso*? What objects could they find in the wizarding world to use for puzzles? For an open-world game, we were also looking for a systemic approach to magic and puzzles, creating a world that is physical, intuitive and reactive to the player's choices.'

Even after a puzzle is placed and playable in the game, there is still much to consider before it is ready to go. 'We play, watch others play and react to what we see,' says Hayes. 'Do the elements of the puzzle read to the player? Do they intuitively know what to do with them? If not, how can we make them read better? Sometimes, even if the puzzle elements are understandable, what the puzzle is asking the player to do isn't.'

Now and then, a puzzle requires too many steps to solve or a complicated button combination, or maybe the concept is tough to grasp. These may require simplification of the puzzle. Other considerations include how long a player should struggle with a puzzle, or whether the player understands how and why a puzzle is solved.

'There are limitations of controls and what the game camera can adequately communicate to the player,' explains Hayes. 'Each element needs to be worked with to help provide the information the player needs to solve the puzzle without giving away the solution from the start. Often art, audio and UI are brought in to help give the subtle push to help clarify or draw the player's eyes to a certain object or location.' It is a co-ordinated effort between many teams.

A game this large and complex requires hundreds of systems that must work together for a cohesive experience. 'Every time we started building a mechanic,' says **Senior Producer, Kelly Mondragon**, 'we needed to consider all the ripple effects it would have on other areas of the game. We also had to be careful about how we represented the wizarding world. That factored into every decision we made whilst building the game.'

TOP: Moth by Nasan Hardcastle and Vanessa Palmer

ABOVE: Moth Wall Receptacle by Nasan Hardcastle

The team was very thoughtful when deciding which gameplay elements would make the final game – as levels, gameplay mechanics and narrative elements evolve throughout development. 'Sometimes this means a puzzle no longer fits the needs of the game,' says Hayes. 'This natural selection usually allowed the best puzzles to stay and ones that didn't fit to go, but occasionally, it also meant we would move a puzzle from where it was no longer needed to somewhere else in the game.'

Review is a constant process at work. Various groups will weigh in on a variety of aspects of the puzzles, allowing for a 'broad body of feedback to assess mechanics and puzzles, see how they are coming along, how readable they are and make adjustments,' adds Hayes. 'Sometimes, the puzzle we thought was fantastic would not survive this review process, and in almost all cases, puzzles would be changed, sometimes dramatically.'

Numerous prototypes and examples were produced. 'This can, in some ways, be a rather heartbreaking process as you produce puzzle after puzzle, finding that some work great and some just don't,' says Hayes. 'Just like in any creative endeavour, the cutting-room floor is often littered with gems – possibilities for the next project.

Puzzle development is always a challenge in games,' he continues. 'Much of what you think will work on paper doesn't translate to the game world as you would expect. For the dungeons in *Hogwarts Legacy*, we very much wanted to create puzzles that would intrigue, delight and challenge the player. Even more importantly, we wanted to capture the Harry Potter sense of magic.'

Populating the world with these activities in order to find the appropriate density that would keep the player interested is an important step in any open-world game. 'We play-tested and iterated on every area of the game,' explains Kelly Mondragon. 'We made sure we felt the player would never get bored or frustrated. At the same time, we didn't want to overwhelm them with too much, so it was very difficult to strike the right balance.'

For inspiration with puzzle design, the team leaned heavily on the films and books, 'but as a team, we also tried to go outside of what was there to expand and put our own mark on the wizarding world,' says Hayes. 'There are so many things alluded to in the books or films that we could start from. For instance, we could look to the way the brick wall opened, allowing Harry to enter Diagon Alley, and ask ourselves how we could turn that into a puzzle. A fantastic presentation of a simple door opening with bricks can be turned into a mind-bending experience in a game.'

The team are also very much video game players and enjoy a wide range of games. 'Aside from those influences, we're also very lucky to have some extremely creative people on our team,' Hayes adds. 'They dream up crazy puzzles and ideas, then make them a reality in the game engine.'

There are numerous puzzles included in *Hogwarts Legacy*, although the Merlin Trials stand out from the rest. Found throughout the Highlands, these puzzles require the use of a spell to complete a specific task such as lighting a series of torches or moving blocks around to match them up. 'We wanted a set of micro puzzles in the Highlands that reinforced spell usage and took very little narrative to propagate outwards,' says Kelly Murphy. These started as 'Sphinx puzzles', 'but ultimately that lore felt out of place in Scotland and harder to explain than putting the concept behind Merlin. The team felt the famous wizard was easier to get across to the players.'

The developers also planned to incorporate three types of events in *Hogwarts Legacy*: ambient events, interactive events and enemy events that can take place anywhere in Hogwarts, Hogsmeade and the open world. 'Ambient events are mostly visual and are there to make the world feel alive,' says Mondragon. Interactive events allow the player to participate in a variety of ways. Enemy events are exactly what they sound like: encounters where the player must avoid foes – or prepare to do battle with them.

'All players expect to play in Hogwarts and Hogsmeade,' he states, 'but there are many other interesting locations and activities once players venture out to the open world. Magical beast dens, secret vaults, ancient magic ruins, hamlet communities, Dark wizard castles, astronomy tables, plant ingredients, broom activities and much more!' *Hogwarts Legacy* rewards players for exploration.

'I feel like the world is full of little touches,' Hayes shares, 'small embellishments of magic tucked into every corner. Some puzzles can surprise and delight with just the simplest premise. Using magic to open a door with Depulso or levitating a crate can be a puzzle. It gets the brain going without having to present itself as a contrived experience. Sometimes, the best puzzles are the ones the player doesn't even view as a puzzle. They just view it as exploring the wizarding world with magic.'

TOP: Merlin Trials (in-game render) by the Environment Team

OPPOSITE BOTTOM LEFT: Merlin Gazebo by Vanessa Palmer

OPPOSITE BOTTOM RIGHT: Wizard Cards by Vanessa Palmer

CHAPTER 4
The Beasts of Hogwarts Legacy

The beasts – so called in *Hogwarts Legacy* because the wizarding world wasn't quite as progressive when it came to creatures as it would become after Newt Scamander wrote his legendary book – help infuse authenticity and magic into the game. And having a place to nurture and care for beasts in the Room of Requirement allows those players with a particular affinity for beasts to focus on something they love about the franchise.

'We wanted to include a range of beasts that were iconic and also made sense to the story,' says Moira Squier. 'Clearly, we couldn't not have dragons. And what would a wizarding world game be without a phoenix or Thestrals? Beasts such as Puffskeins and Kneazles were added for fun and familiarity. And the Graphorn, a rare beast that would be very hard to find, was included for an epic moment.'

Naturally, the team's first instinct was to go to the Harry Potter books for descriptions of creatures, and, of course, the various print editions of *Fantastic Beasts and Where to Find Them*. What they learned in these books was then compared to what had been visualised in the movies. 'We discovered that there were, of course, many similarities between the two,' says **Concept Art Lead, Sébastien Gallego**, 'but also a lot of flexible space within for us to manoeuvre.'

The creation of a beast would usually start with exploration of its basic form, starting with a silhouette, and then get into the finer details. The concept artists would also do a careful study of anatomy, then mix it with creativity and enthusiasm for the fantastic. 'In the case of a video game, the player must immediately recognise what he is seeing in the distance,' says Gallego, 'especially when it is an enemy, so having a clear, strong silhouette is very important. Going big to small is always a safety net for us, the designers.' And exploring creatures that are part of the wizarding world, but haven't seen much time on screen, was particularly fun for the artists. 'I'm thinking of the Dugbog, for example,' says Gallego. 'It's a mix of giant frog and lizard, with a big mouth, big teeth and branches growing on his back: You don't design one of those every day!'

There are also the Dark beasts: Inferi, spiders, trolls and wolves. 'These, to me, are some of the most exciting to look at,' says Tyler Lybbert. 'There's a gritty realism to these that will scare you.'

The spiders were an interesting challenge, because the designers didn't want them to simply be oversized arachnids. 'Our goal was to make them look like a magical beast,' explains Gallego. 'If you take the venomous spiders, as an example, we designed them based on known venomous spiders, but mixed them up with some crab textures and design elements like the legs.'

One thing to note for Dark beasts, which can be applied to 'good' creatures too, is that the richness of their textures plays a big role in how the player perceives them. In the case of the Inferi, for example, the translucence of the skin, the thin blood vessels and the old, tattered clothes all sell the creepiness of the character.

Inspired by Newt Scamander in *Fantastic Beasts and Where to Find Them*, the player will unlock a Nab-sack, which gives them the ability to rescue magical beasts in the wild and bring them back into the shelter of vivariums that unlock in the player's sanctuary in the Room of Requirement.

Magical beasts that are tamed and cared for will help the player craft better gear within the Room of Requirement using items collected from beasts. These, like Fwooper feathers, are then brought to the Enchanted Loom, which the player can build within the Room of Requirement to improve gear. Improved and customised gear enhances combat performance.

PAGES 188-189: Ancient Graphorn by Mike McCarthy

OPPOSITE: Forest Troll Sculpt, River Troll Sculpt and Trolls (3D render) by the Character Team

TOP: Hippogriff Field Guide Drawing by Danny Russon

BEASTS

A number of magical beasts populate the wizarding world of *Hogwarts Legacy*. Some can be rescued and nurtured in the Room of Requirement, where byproducts like feathers and fur can be used to enhance gear and brew potions. Others have become quite aggressive and must be defeated in combat.

With their big eyes and shy personalities, **MOONCALVES** are as cute as they are odd. Not surprisingly, they are nocturnal by nature, and evolved so that their saucer-like eyes can only stare upwards at the moon. Similar to prairie dogs, Mooncalves live in groups.

BILLYWIGS spin as they fly, looking like bright, colourful helicopters. A Billywig's sting makes its victim giddy, and then causes levitation. Dried Billywig stingers are used in poison antidotes and hair-raising potions.

TOP LEFT: Mooncalf Early Concept by Ryan Wood

TOP RIGHT: Mooncalf Concept by Ben Simonsen

ABOVE: Billywig (3D render) by the Character Team

LEFT: Baby Mooncalf by Danny Russon

OPPOSITE: Mooncalf Den by Vanessa Palmer; Mooncalf (3D render) by the Character Team

PHOENIXES are elegant, beautiful and rare birds that possess strange and powerful magic. The loyalty of the phoenix can be won only by the most clever and great wizards. There is only one phoenix available during a beast mission.

PUFFSKEINS are round and fluffy beasts, soft enough to cuddle but tough enough to be thrown around. A Puffskein will eat almost anything, but its favourite meal is bogeys. They are common household pets for wizarding families because they are easy to maintain.

DIRICAWLS are plump, fluffy, flightless birds that have the unique ability to disappear and reappear, helpful in escaping danger. Muggles were aware of these birds at one time and called them dodos. However, Muggles now believe them to be extinct.

OPPOSITE TOP: Phoenix and Baby Phoenix by Joshua H Black
OPPOSITE BOTTOM: Phoenix Den by Vanessa Palmer
TOP: Puffskein by Sébastien Gallego; Pink and Spotted Puffskein by Mike McCarthy
RIGHT: Baby Diricawl Sketch by Damian Buzugbe; Diricawl (3D render) by the Character Team

NIFFLERS are rodentlike creatures with a long snout, covered in dark fur. They love shiny objects, whether it be a nugget of gold or a button, which they hide in a pouch on their stomach. With their single-mindedness towards acquiring anything sparkly, Nifflers can cause extensive mayhem.

The **GOLDEN SNIDGET** is a round, fat, golden bird that was used in the earliest games of Quidditch for the team to gain 150 extra points. However, as the frequent practice of catching a Golden Snidget severely reduced the species, the Golden Snitch was invented as a replacement. The Golden Snidget is now a protected beast.

A small, speckled, blue bird, the **JOBBERKNOLL** never makes any noise until the moment of its death, at which point it screams every sound it has ever heard – backwards.

CLOCKWISE FROM UPPER LEFT: Niffler Den (3D render) by the Environment Team; Baby Niffler by Mike McCarthy; Golden Snidget (3D render) by the Character Team; Baby Snidget by Sébastien Gallego; Jobberknoll by Nasan Hardcastle; Niffler by Ben Simonsen

KNEAZLES are catlike beasts that have large ears and a plumed tail. They can be aggressive, but if they like a witch or wizard, they make exceptional pets. Kneazles are highly intelligent and have an ability to detect suspicious or distrustful people.

The **HIPPOGRIFF** is a proud beast that is part eagle and part horse, so it can both fly and gallop. Hippogriffs are easily offended; it is imperative that proper etiquette is observed in any encounter, but especially the first: You must bow and wait for it to come to you. Once respect is given, Hippogriffs become loyal and useful allies.

TOP: Kneazles by Ben Simonsen
RIGHT: Baby Hippogriff by Mike McCarthy; Hippogriff by BOSI
OPPOSITE TOP TO BOTTOM: Baby Hippogriffs (3D renders) by the Character Team; Hippogriff In Flight and Hippogriff (in-game renders) by the Environment Team

199

CENTAURS, who are part human and part horse, live in herds in the forests. Highly skilled in archery, divination and astronomy, they are mistrustful of humans in general. They are particularly protective of fellow beasts and will threaten any human they believe may be associated with the Poacher Pack.

GRAPHORNS are large, mountain-dwelling creatures that have a tough hide and two sharp horns. The tentacle-like appendages on Graphorns' faces are used for capturing food or showing affection for their young. Graphorns are known for their aggressive nature, but, rarely, a witch or wizard will manage to befriend one.

TOP: Graphorn Face Concept by Ryan Wood

BOTTOM: Sitting Graphorn Cub Sculpt by the Character Team

OPPOSITE: Centaur Elek (3D render) by the Character Team

A **GIANT PURPLE TOAD** is a sizeable magical toad that produces warts useful in potion-making.

DUGBOGS live in marshes, gliding through the muck with their finned paws. When stationary, they resemble a piece of dead wood. Dugbogs prefer to eat Mandrakes with their sharp teeth, stripping them of their leaves and spoiling their potential for use in potions.

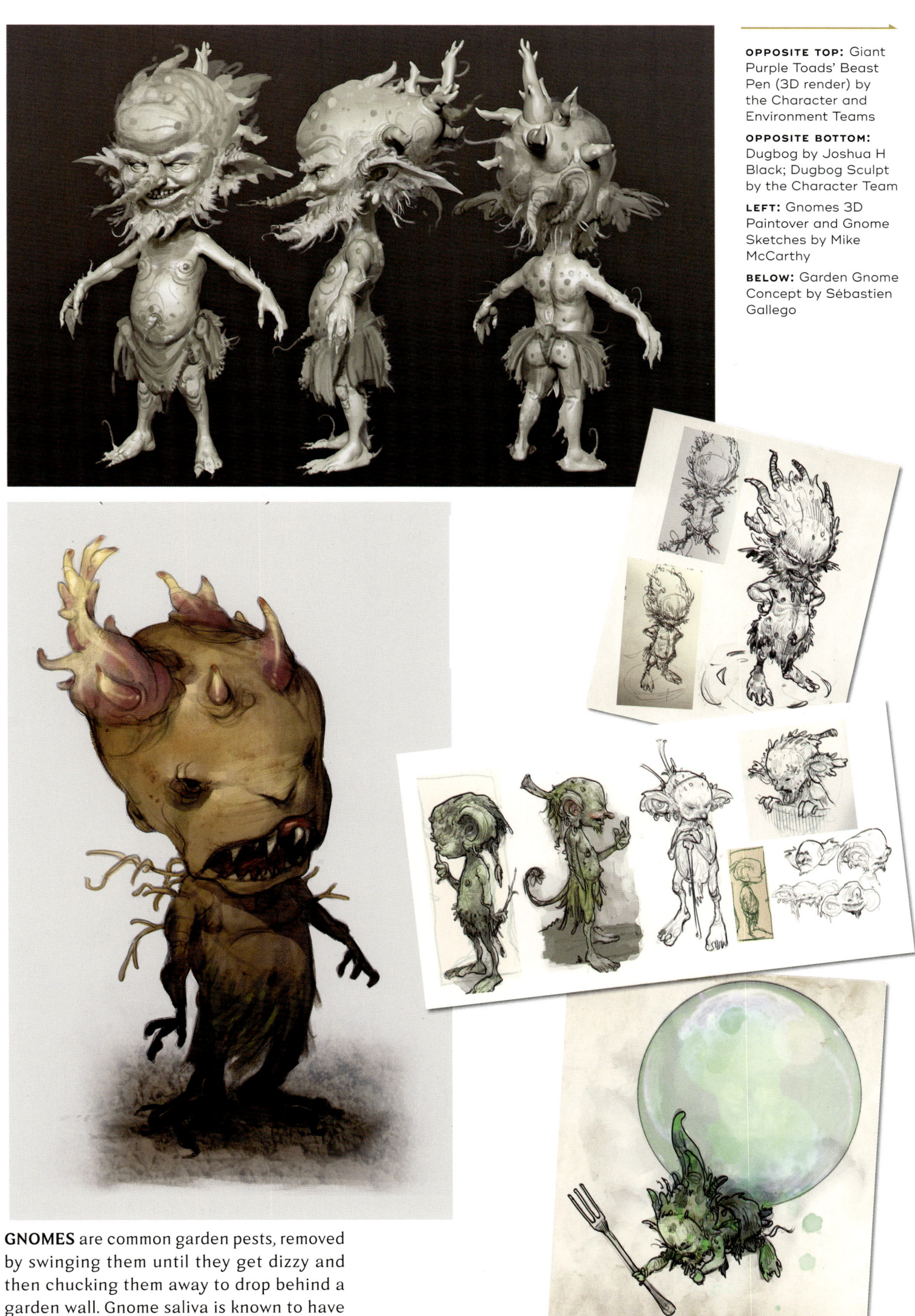

OPPOSITE TOP: Giant Purple Toads' Beast Pen (3D render) by the Character and Environment Teams

OPPOSITE BOTTOM: Dugbog by Joshua H Black; Dugbog Sculpt by the Character Team

LEFT: Gnomes 3D Paintover and Gnome Sketches by Mike McCarthy

BELOW: Garden Gnome Concept by Sébastien Gallego

GNOMES are common garden pests, removed by swinging them until they get dizzy and then chucking them away to drop behind a garden wall. Gnome saliva is known to have beneficial qualities.

203

LEFT AND BOTTOM:
Unicorn Den, Fwooper and Baby Fwoopers (3D renders) by the Character Team

OPPOSITE TOP:
Thestral Concepts by Ryan Wood

OPPOSITE MIDDLE:
Thestral Sculpts by the Character Team

OPPOSITE BOTTOM:
Baby Thestral by Joshua H Black

RARE UNICORNS are peaceful, shy and beautiful equine beasts that develop a long, spiralling horn. The foals are said to have shimmering golden coats. Unicorn blood, horn and hair are highly valuable as ingredients in magical potions.

Notable for their brightly-coloured feathers, which make excellent quills, **FWOOPERS** have a call known to drive people mad. It is helpful to have a Silencing Charm around Fwoopers.

THESTRALS are haunting, winged equine beasts visible only to those who have seen death. They may look intimidating, but they are actually quite gentle, with a cry similar to whale song. Thestrals are more often than not flown rather than ridden.

DARK BEASTS

INFERI are corpses resurrected by Dark Magic. Grotesque-looking and frightening, they are very dangerous. Inferi, found in some of the darker places in the game, are tough foes.

SPIDERS come in a variety of sizes, all the way up to the massive Acromantula, which has near-human intelligence. This eight-eyed beast can have a fifteen-foot leg span and spins its webs on the ground.

TROLLS are not particularly nice, and they are not, in most cases, particularly smart. Covered in warts, blemishes and carbuncles, these massive creatures speak in grunts. The largest and most ferocious type is the mountain troll. Taking down a troll requires just the right balance of gear, spells and potions.

TOP AND RIGHT: Wolves (3D renders) and Inferius (3D Composite) by the Character Team

OPPOSITE TOP AND BOTTOM: Thornback Biting Spider (3D Paintover) by Danny Russon; Venomous Spider Matriarch by the Concept Team; Armoured Troll (3D renders) by the Character Team

DRAGONS

Hebridean Black

The Hebridean Black has dark scales and ridges along its back that give it the appearance of a towering, craggy mountain similar to the terrain of its native land – the Hebrides Islands of Scotland. The dragon uses these physical attributes to its advantage by camouflaging itself against rocky terrain as it waits for prey. The Macfusty clan, a wizarding family native to the Hebrides, have served as guardians to the breed for centuries.

ABOVE: Hebridean Black (3D render) by the Character Team
OPPOSITE TOP: Hebridean Black Sculpt by the Character Team
OPPOSITE BOTTOM: Hebridean Black Sketch and Illustration by Danny Russon
BOTTOM: Hebridean Black Sketch by Danny Russon

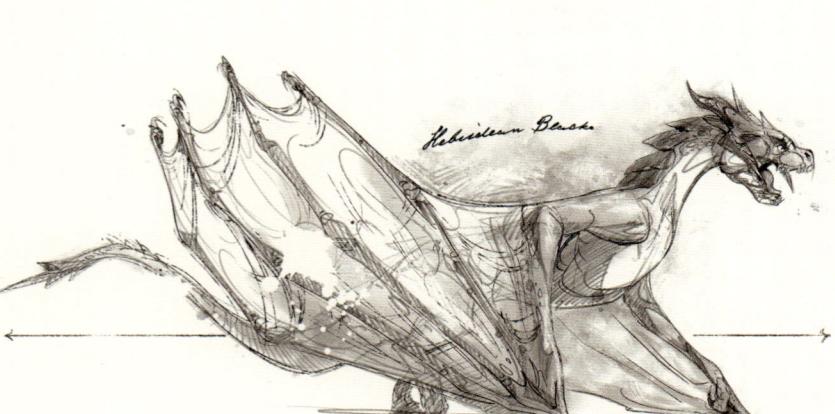

Hungarian Horntail

The Hungarian Horntail is possibly the most dangerous of dragons, with the ability to breathe fire. It has a blunt, hawklike head; huge, taloned wings; two heavily clawed legs; and a ruff of spikes that runs down to the tail, ending in a spear-shaped spike covered in smaller spikes. It is very aggressive towards humans.

Common Welsh Green

The Common Welsh Green, one of the smaller dragon breeds, prefers to avoid humans, although it will attack if provoked or startled. Its name refers to its vibrant green colour and its homeland of Wales. Its scales blend into the lush, green grass of its homeland, making it easy for it to hunt sheep, its favourite food. This dragon has a peculiar melodious roar and breathes thin jets of fire.

OPPOSITE TOP: Hungarian Horntail (3D renders) by the Character Team

OPPOSITE BOTTOM: Hungarian Horntail Colour Sketches by Nasan Hardcastle

TOP: Welsh Green by Vanessa Palmer

RIGHT: Welsh Green (3D render) by the Character Team

ANIMATING THE BEASTS

Hogwarts Legacy includes a wide range of beasts – including adorable Mooncalves, catlike Kneazles, terrifying spiders and Inferi, a majestic phoenix and, of course, powerful dragons. Every beast presented its own challenges throughout design and development, including during the animation phase, where animators put all these great creatures into motion.

The animation team first needed to understand each beast, its personality and its purpose in the game – as well as what was needed from the creature. 'After that is established, we'll do tons of research, such as finding video clips online of existing animals that may move in a similar way to the fictional creature,' explains **Enemy Animation Lead, Matt Dibb**, and 'studying the film version of a creature if it's already been in a movie.' An animator may edit the clips together to roughly create the sequence they are looking for or act out the movement to better understand how it may physically move.

Once a plan has been established, the team begins the motion-capture process, which involves digitally recording an actor's movement, which can be subsequently polished with special software. Or, in the case of most beasts, the team will begin creating their movement from scratch, 'posing the creature frame by frame, but still using as much real-world reference as possible to make them feel real and believable,' Dibb adds.

'We adopted the motion-capture process to speed up human animation asset creation,' explains **Animation Lead, Joe Percival**, 'which often put us in the suit, animating with our bodies. With advances in technology, a good mocap session can usually get us seventy to eighty percent to our target before we go in and edit by hand-keying to push or exaggerate a motion.'

While human animation is sped up with the motion-capture process, 'for beasts – due to a lack of trained dragons, Dugbogs and Thestrals – it's mostly all hand-key animation,' says Percival. 'This can be more time-consuming, especially with all those extra limbs, tails, etc., to worry about, but is often very enjoyable because it allows an animator to be creative when they are discovering and designing how a fantastic beast might act or behave.'

Sometimes, both these processes are used, as in the case of centaurs. 'We combined a human rig with a traditional horse rig,' remarks Percival. 'I say "combined", but both rigs were still somewhat independent of each other, so we could use mocap for the human portion and hand-keyed animation for the horse body. Tech and rigging figured out a way for two animations to be hooked to the one character at the same time for animating in Maya – it was a rigging feat!'

Dragons also proved to be a challenge, 'due to the number of controls and rig complexity,' says Percival, with their 'fully functioning wings, long neck and tail, etc.' With no real-world

OPPOSITE: Graphorn by the Animation Team

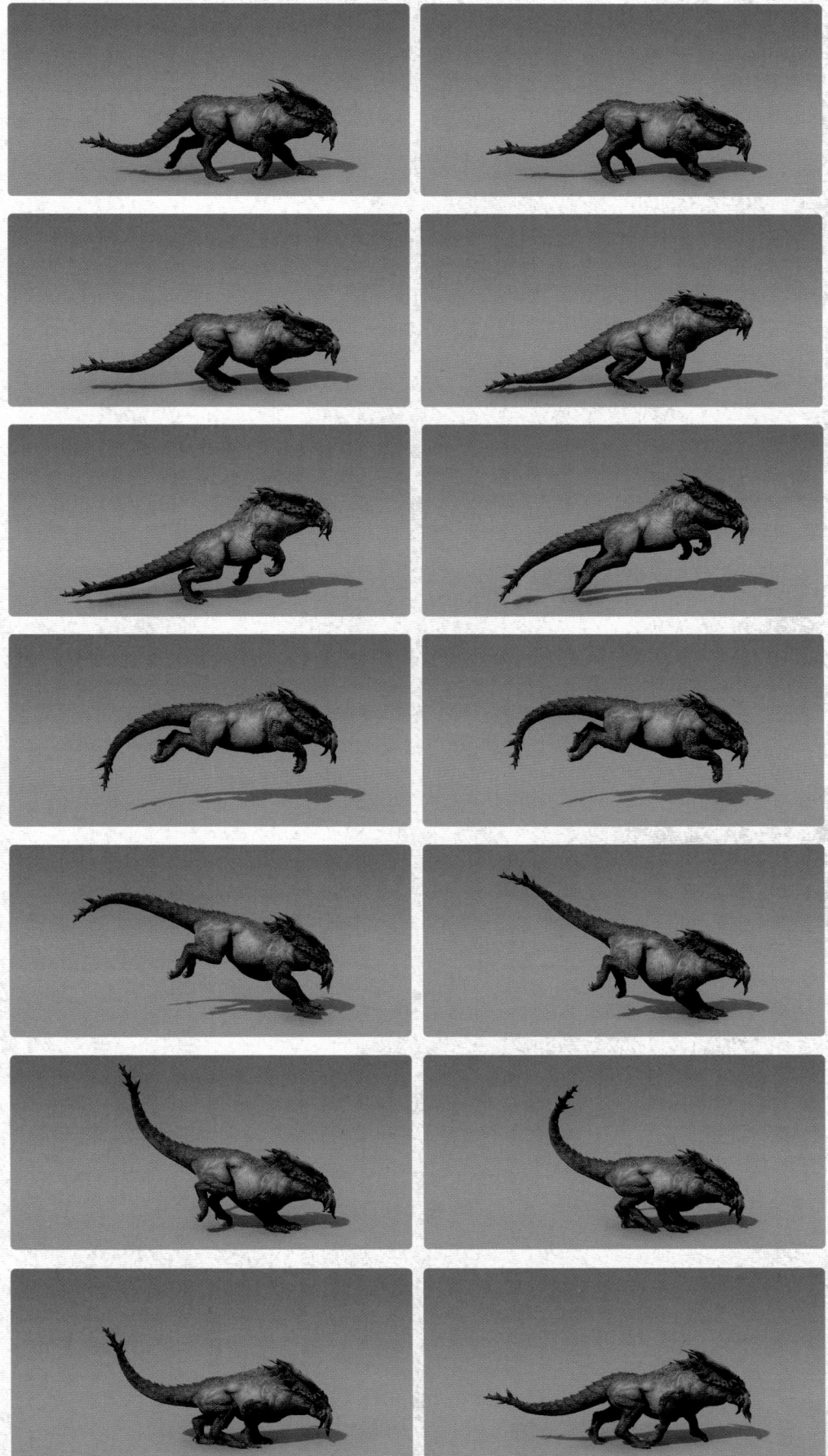

reference for a ten-ton animal that flies, moves quickly and breathes fire, the team looked at existing dragon, and even dinosaur, animation in films, games and more – as well as footage of bats, birds and elephants, amongst others. The dragon 'was also the heaviest rig we had in our game, as in, it had more controls available to the animators to manipulate than any other character,' adds Dibb.

'It often became a game of restraint and simplifying how many controls we'd use to animate it, especially early on, as it was easy to get in over your head if you tried to use too many,' he says. 'Some controls that did similar actions or were manipulated in multiple ways could be removed. Once it got into a more polished phase, we would use more controls, but using less would help the animators not lose their minds,' Dibb concludes.

Overall, the biggest challenge for the animation team, Dibb says, was 'the vast amount of animation we needed to create for this game. It took lots of planning, focus and hard work to stay on top of that mountain of animations.' There are over three thousand animations for the player's avatar alone.

'There are many challenges to game development, especially when diving into a new engine, taking on a new franchise or building a new mocap studio from scratch with a team of keyframe animators,' explains Percival. 'The biggest challenges, however, are usually those beyond our control: a change of direction, a design revamp or a character update after we've already animated it. Change can be a challenge, but we've adapted and learned to roll with it. I call it liquid development because

TOP: Death Ink FX by Vanessa Palmer

OPPOSITE: Hippogriff Flight by the Animation Team

production is always in motion, and sometimes, we need to float a different path. Change is inevitable, and most of the time those changes end up being better for the game, better for the experience, despite the bumps and difficulties, which makes it worth it.'

Despite all the hard work, the animation team was able to have some fun. 'Where I got the most laughs was probably on the mocap stage,' recalls Percival. 'We had a good time laughing at and with one another and gave several people an opportunity to act in the suit to get variety for a crowded school and find our best wizards, or best troll, and so on. When you're around one another as long as we've been, you can totally identify a colleague by how they move. We'd also superimpose the creatures over the actor in software, so the actor could see how to posture and hold their arms in a way that could work on a troll or goblin, whose proportions were quite different from the average animator. In addition to providing accurate imagery and acting ranges for the actors, this made for a lot of trial and error and some goofy, fun times.'

'I was fortunate enough to be able to put the motion-capture suit on quite a bit,' Dibb recalls, 'and one day, they were capturing me being a troll and hitting myself in the face with a club because of a spell cast by a wizard. I was using a foam stand-in for the club, but the director kept asking that I hit myself harder. Eventually, I hit myself so hard, it knocked my motion-capture cap off my head. The team was watching our monitors with the actual troll model onscreen, and his head flew off as my hat came off. It looked as if the troll decapitated himself! Thankfully, it was a digital beast – no trolls were harmed in the making of this game.'

CHAPTER 5

Golden Paths and Dark Mysteries

From a game-design perspective, 'the mission usually starts with a simple pitch,' says **Mission Design Lead, Kelly Murphy**. 'Is this a mission that introduces and/or reinforces certain mechanics, or is it more of a fantasy moment within the flow? Or is it simply a vibe/narrative mission?' Once the designer understands what role the mission is supposed to be fulfilling in the greater flow of the game, they design to that. 'And it's not mutually exclusive,' he continues. 'A mission could start out as a mission to teach a stealth mechanic, but end up being a fantasy moment where the player is escaping on a broom in a chase. So understanding which tools the player will have, how to use those tools in completing the mission, what the player has just done in the missions in front of your mission and what they will do after your mission is important in creating pace.

Co-ordinating game design and narrative elements to craft the missions took an understanding of not only the needs of the mission but also where that mission takes place in the context of the gameplay, world and narrative. As is typical with any game development, the game went through a large directional shift midway through development, which meant not only culling missions but also changing our philosophy behind them. This led to hard decisions about what to keep, what to cut and what to create from scratch. In the end, I think we've found ways of pulling some of the best concepts into what we kept or created.'

PAGES 216–217: Final Pensieve Chamber (in-game render) by the Environment Team

OPPOSITE TOP TO BOTTOM: Rookwood Castle Basement, Goblin Dungeon and Bowing to a Hippogriff (in-game renders) by the Environment Team

BELOW: Archie's Hideout by Vanessa Palmer

THE GOLDEN PATH

The Golden Path leads the player from learning the most basic of magic in classes to their discovery of their unique ability to wield ancient magic. All of these necessary acquired skills will enable them to thwart Victor Rookwood and his criminal gang and stop the goblin rebellion that threatens Hogwarts.

The Mission Design Team constantly sought a balance of authenticity with bringing something new to the wizarding world. 'Initially, we brainstormed on fan fantasies,' says Kelly Murphy. 'This was done internally among the team and through surveys and reading forums online. We wanted to understand what players most wanted and expected in an open-world wizarding world game.' From there, the team tried to identify the fantasies, locations, characters, spells and creatures that were most notable. 'We started the first versions of the Golden Path on a bunch of whiteboards in meeting rooms for weeks,' recalls Murphy. '"Fantasies" and "Expectations" each had their own mentions, as did spells, locations, etc.

We would block out missions using just conceptual words like "Pensieve Dungeon 1" or "Hippogriff Moment", then put systemic notes under them,' he adds. Throughout the process, the Golden Path constantly shifted. Whenever it was realised that the player wasn't being directed to a location in the Golden Path in a timely enough fashion, and sometimes even not at all, the narrative was adjusted along with locations that would pull the player there sooner.

SIDE MISSIONS

Side missions help define who the player is as a wizard, inspiring them to investigate locations, retrieve magical artefacts, learn secrets of Hogwarts and Hogsmeade and help fellow students solve personal dilemmas.

'Side missions tend to be more open method,' says Kelly Murphy, 'as they have fewer narrative beats we need to weave the player through. So, they are innately built with player agency in mind.' Additionally, the Missions Team wanted the player to be able to express themselves with a choice when completing the side missions. 'Do they want to be friendly and helpful,' Murphy continues, 'or would they prefer to be a bit naughty? As we move away from Hogwarts, this expression can come down to being downright evil, and characters will remember and talk about the choices the player makes in these missions.'

CLASS ASSIGNMENTS

Class assignments encourage players to explore the castle and the Highlands to find, collect and battle where needed. In creating the class assignments, the team sought a balance between which spells they wanted to use on the Golden Path and which spells would be optional, based on factors of benefits and expectations.

'From there, we tried to hit narrative and gameplay beats where we know the player will understand a certain gameplay and narrative concept at a certain point in the story,' says Murphy.

Once the world is opened for the player, it's imperative that they understand the basics of combat and shields in the game. 'We knew the player needed to cast *Incendio*, to conjure fire; *Levioso* to learn levitation; and *Accio* for summoning objects to them in encounters during combat. *Levioso* was tied to the Defence Against the Dark Arts class, and *Accio* was learned in Charms class. When it came to *Incendio*, it was decided that the charm would become an assignment,' explains Murphy, 'and should come from professors from whom you've already taken a class. So we opted to give it to Professor Hecat, who is the Defence Against the Dark Arts professor.'

OPPOSITE: Main Mission Card and Side Mission Card by Ben Simonsen

TOP: Class Assignment Side Mission Card by Ben Simonsen

RELATIONSHIP MISSIONS

Relationship missions personalise the player's experience in the wizarding world and provide the companion and friendship experience so central to the Harry Potter story in general.

'Companions each have their own unique personalities and preferences, and each has their own unique combat spells,' says Murphy. As the player plays alongside their companions, they learn how that companion feels about what the player has done or is doing, which individualises the experience for the player. Additionally, Natty, Poppy and Sebastian have their own side storylines that give the player access to locations, tools and quests that wouldn't otherwise be accessible to them without completing one or more of these missions.

In creating these missions, the developers went with what they felt was organic to Natty's, Poppy's and Sebastian's arcs. Because Natty's justice-seeking focuses on Victor Rookwood, the Dark wizard and leader of the Rookwood Gang, and his right-hand man, Theophilus Harlow, 'she and the player infiltrate only the camps and hideouts in Natty's mission that were a natural fit,' Moira Squier explains. 'Sebastian, on the other hand, has some real darkness in his storyline, so dungeons and Slytherin-related locations were a natural fit for his mission. And of course Poppy deals with beasts, so something like a dragon's lair was the perfect location for a mission with her.'

It isn't necessary to complete every relationship mission, and the player might even choose not to do any of them. 'However,' says Squier, 'they do impact the player's gameplay journey in the way that they further their relationship with the companion they chose.' While the missions unlock at certain points, they can then be completed at any point during or after the main storyline.

ABOVE: Goblin Drill Blueprint by Nasan Hardcastle

BELOW: Poor Section of the Graveyard by Joshua H Black

OPPOSITE TOP TO BOTTOM: Children's Beast Drawings by Ben Simonsen; Post Office Note by Vanessa Palmer

BEAST MISSIONS

Missions involving beasts not only teach players about the care and nurturing of these animals but also offer an added incentive. 'When rescuing beasts became a mechanic, we needed to ask, "Why?"' says Kelly Murphy. 'The answer became that beasts, when cared for, produce by-products that feed back into the gear-improvement loop.' Each beast mission was centred around two goals: Which concept did the mission need to teach around beast rescuing, nurturing and gear improvement? And then, which beasts would be the best for this mission in order to balance being aspirational and informative, but also not spoil any systemic exploration with the beast-rescue mechanic the player might enjoy?

Decisions about which beast would be used for which mission were based on the beast's role in wizarding lore, the behaviours of the particular beast and of course the aim of the mission. 'If the mission was about teaching the player to rescue beasts,' Murphy explains, 'then we wanted to make sure we started with beasts that were easy to catch and presented a non-threatening charm to the player.' For these missions, the Puffskein, the Jobberknoll and the Mooncalf were the best selections.

'If the mission was a side mission about beast rescue, we looked at where we wanted the mission to unlock in the progression of the story and the story we wanted to tell,' he continues. Based on these criteria, a beast would be picked, but opportunities were always sought to tie a unique beast to a unique mission. 'For instance, we have one quest where you need to track and rescue a particular Niffler that has been kidnapped,' says Murphy. 'This leads you to an elaborate dungeon with treasure throughout. We wanted to make sure to tie a narrative around a Niffler's penchant for finding riches.'

Certain beast missions are used as fun wrappers around tutorial moments with beasts. 'Since the player needs to learn how to rescue and care for beasts,' he continues, 'we have missions around both of those concepts. Additionally, when cared for, beasts produce materials that make the player's gear more effective in combat. Therefore, we have missions that teach this loop.' These missions often provide the player with opportunities to rescue rare and harder-to-find beasts that can produce decidedly unique materials.

It was hoped that beasts could become companion characters to the players, and be taken into the world with them, but it was quickly realised that the behaviours and the sizes of beasts were so wildly different, it added prohibitive challenges to the game. 'We wanted to bring more notable beasts like the Hippogriff or Graphorn with the player, but our environments and gameplay were not created to suit them,' says Murphy. Instead the developers opted to turn the aforementioned beasts into mounts so that the player could have an experience of playing 'with' them, while other beasts are rescued and kept as pets the player cares for and makes happy. 'This approach allowed us to circumvent the many complex issues of trying to support beast companions that are wildly different – such as a Mooncalf versus a Jobberknoll versus a unicorn – while keeping them useful and worthwhile for the player.'

PLAYING YOUR WAY

Hogwarts Legacy provides a variety of tactics to deploy in combat, allowing players to succeed no matter what their preferred playstyle. 'Our goal was to empower players to approach different combat encounters in the way that suits them best,' says **Combat and Enemy Design Lead, Troy Johnson**. Encounter areas went through countless revisions to ensure that they were accessible to as many different approaches as possible. There are still key fights that test specific skills or require the player to use a certain tactic, 'but most of the encounters are set up to allow personal expression in the path to victory,' he adds.

The Highlands and dangerous interiors, such as dungeons, can be extremely hostile, but with this kind of accessibility, the player can approach encounters in the way they are most comfortable: Confront an enemy head-on with an arsenal of powerful spells, incorporate game-changing potions and plants into a more strategic approach or avoid confrontation altogether – it is the player's choice.

'Challenges arise in this effort as you try to combine level designs that permit different playstyles with beautiful artwork and rendering that feel natural and believable for the given space,' Johnson explains. 'Certain enemies also provided a challenge, like beasts that make more sense to hide and ambush the player, rather than wander out in the open, or creatures that are naturally resistant to many spells, like trolls.'

Despite these challenges, the team has constructed a world that allows the player to play their way. 'How you survive is up to you,' Johnson says. Do you rely on your companion to relieve some of the pressure from a horde of goblins, or do you deploy a collection of Venomous Tentacula to do the dirty work for you? Those who love to practise and master direct combat will be able to sink their teeth into the combo system, finding powerful strings of spells that juggle enemies and rapidly grant additional power to finish them off as efficiently as possible.

LEFT: Death Minion Field Guide Drawing by Nasan Hardcastle

OPPOSITE TOP: Armoured Troll, Forest Troll and River Troll Drawings by Nasan Hardcastle

OPPOSITE BOTTOM: Protector Fight (in-game render) by the Character, Environment and VFX Teams

CASTING A SPELL

When it came to the combat system, the goal was 'to make sure the best ideas and implementations of what combat should feel like in the wizarding world come together in a polished, expressive, exciting experience for players,' explains Troy Johnson. 'We did a lot of R&D to discover what elements and features best invoke the fantasy of mastering witchcraft and wizardry in combat situations, and it has resulted in a system that is playful, intense and – above all – fun.'

As the player plays through the storyline and completes class assignments, they learn dozens of spells that feature numerous upgrades, as well as the ability to chain them together. These spells are used to interact with the environments during missions to move past obstacles or gain access, solve puzzles and battle enemies. There are many spells known in the wizarding world, so the team had to narrow the selection down for the game.

'The process began with intensive research through every book, movie, official site and fan-driven archive to learn about every spell that has ever been cast in the lore,' says Johnson. 'We weighed how iconic each spell is, how often it is used, whether there are fan expectations around it, how flexible or specific its use would be in a rule-based video game, whether it fit into our narrative and many more factors.' The team prototyped nearly one hundred spells during development to determine which of them would be the right fit for the game. 'With lots of time, effort and care, we ended up with the final set that is featured in *Hogwarts Legacy*,' he adds.

'One of the spells that we prototyped and that I wish we could have included was the Bat-Bogey Hex,' Johnson recalls. 'It was hilarious to make an enemy sneeze out sloppy green bats that would then randomly attack other enemies, but that spell was invented by Miranda Goshawk in the 1900s, so it wasn't something known in our game's time period.' It is this kind of attention the team paid to lore when making choices, always adhering to the pillar that everything was authentic to the wizarding world.

'That's both the challenge and the joy of working on an existing IP,' says Johnson. 'You get to bring something beloved to life in an interactive experience, but you must do it in a way that fans and gamers alike will love.'

The player learns the spells throughout the game from different sources, including classes, course assignments and the Room of Requirement, and as they progress through the storyline. 'The goal with the order and pacing of spells that the player learns was to make sure players could experience as much fun as possible as early as possible, while still having a strong thread of spell progression that extends the joy of discovery to the end of the game,' explains Johnson. 'Foundational mechanics are taught up front to let the player grasp the main gameplay loops, and certain narrative beats drive when several of the

TOP: Pensieve Colourkeys by Vanessa Palmer
OPPOSITE: Wand Link (in-game render) by the VFX Team

spells can or must be learned, but there is a fair amount of freedom in choosing when to learn much of the magical repertoire.'

The spell system works off a four-slot scheme that can be equipped with dozens of freely castable spells, allowing the player to prepare for a variety of situations. The player starts with one loadout, but a few talent upgrades provide up to three additional loadouts. An active set of four spells can be swapped to other sets with a two-button input, allowing the player to access over a dozen abilities without accessing the menu.

'Our goal with the spell system was to let players express themselves as witches and wizards who were learning and mastering a large repertoire of magic,' says Johnson. 'Some spells that are used in limited and specific ways, like the Unlocking Charm [*Alohomora*], are contextual, but whenever a spell could have multiple or discoverable uses in the world we wanted to give players the option to cast it at will and see the results of their choice. Because there are so many spells, we also wanted to give players quick access to a variety of them simultaneously so they could experiment with strings of spells in rapid succession, particularly in action-driven scenarios such as combat.'

The spell system allows for a range of combat uses: Inflict significant damage on impact with damage spells, reposition enemies with force spells or hold enemies at bay with control spells. The player can customise their playstyle to their liking. Loadouts can be further customised by spending talent points in five well-developed talent trees.

Animation of the spells presented its own challenges, going through many iterations as the game developed. 'Wand combat isn't like swinging a sword, wielding a hammer or firing a gun,' says Joe Percival. 'We started with concept drawings of poses and hand-keyed placeholder animations. That evolved to a couple of us in mocap suits twirling around and battling invisible Dark wizards. We tried single attacks, combos and several other configurations, each with its own pros and cons. We knew we wanted something flowing yet functional for casting in all directions. Each implementation of the mechanic exposed deficiencies, but as we continued to iterate and study the films, we eventually landed where we're at. It was a concerted effort with input from animators, designers and programmers.'

This massive effort by the developers resulted in a system that is simple and fun to play, but flexible enough to allow for a variety of playstyles. 'It was a huge challenge to create a system that offers power, flexibility, accessibility and depth in all the ways that we felt would satisfy our players,' Johnson explains.

It was important to the team that players feel like adept witches and wizards, but there are limits with a controller. 'We went through at least a dozen different prototypes of UI/UX and control approaches for general spellcasting alone,' Johnson adds. 'Each time, we learned something important about what we felt the system should afford and what players wanted to be able to accomplish. Beyond the UX of spellcasting, the collection of spell effects required a massive effort over several years to develop into a system of mechanics that worked well with all the gameplay scenarios we needed to achieve.'

Achieving the desired balance of wizarding world authenticity and pure fun was a daunting task. 'Duelling in lore is engaged at range, but the defensive manoeuvres and back-and-forth spellcasting feel like a form of fencing or martial arts, so taking the shooter approach didn't feel quite right,' explains Johnson. 'Many of our enemies apply close-range pressure instead of casting spells from a distance, but striking such enemies directly with wand swipes didn't hit the mark.' The idea of scripted attack patterns and combos didn't satisfy the team either. 'We landed on the term "long-range kung fu" during development,' he adds, 'and that helped guide us to a system that is responsive, expressive and impactful, whether the player is dealing with a gang of blade-wielding goblins, a sinister band of witches and wizards or a raging troll.'

The combat system doesn't stop with the spells system. Mandrakes and Chinese Chomping Cabbages can be grown in the Room of Requirement before being deployed in combat with devastating effect. A variety of potions can be brewed at potion tables in class or in the Room of Requirement and then used as a boost in combat – for example, to provide extra defence with

TOP: Repository Colour-keys by Vanessa Palmer

OPPOSITE: Reparo (in-game render) and Field Guide Intro (cinematic render) by the VFX Team

the Edurus Potion or enhanced spell power with the Maxima Potion. 'The most effective strategies come with a nice mix of spells, plants and potions,' Johnson says. 'A little extracurricular work will go a long way in dominating the battlefield.

Some players love using explosive spells to deal high damage in a single burst, but I am a fan of elegant, playful combinations that result in big damage and rapidly increasing the combo count, which grants additional benefits,' Johnson offers. 'One of my bread-and-butter combos requires swapping between sets of four spells, and it flows like this: Knockback Jinx [*Flipendo*] to flip the enemy into the air, Severing Charm [*Diffindo*] to deal initial damage, Summoning Charm [*Accio*] to pull the enemy close, Fire-Making Spell [*Incendio*] to blast them, Descendo Charm to slam them down and bounce them back up and then Banishing Charm [*Depulso*] to launch them into a destructible target or another enemy.

Pepper some low-damage, juggle-extending spells between each of those steps, and it's a fun, impressive string,' he adds. 'However, be aware that if you're fighting a group, you'll have to defend yourself from other enemies while performing extended combos, so it's not going to be a walk in the park simply because you've memorised a sequence. When you pull something like this off amongst a group of villains, it feels amazing to execute.'

DUNGEONS

As the player goes further and further from Hogwarts, their missions lead them to unknown, darker places containing harsher battles and greater danger. One of these is the dungeons.

In a grouping of Highlands ruins and subterranean locations, the dungeons include straightforward caves, Dark wizard hideouts, goblin mines, wizard tombs, ancient cairns and spectacular areas created by ancient magic. Within these environments, there are handcrafted combat encounters, puzzles to solve with magic and opportunities for exploration, looting and foraging. But beware: In these dungeons are encounters with goblin warriors, Inferi, spiders and trolls, as well as magic users that inhabit the chambers.

The philosophy for *Hogwarts Legacy* was to make everything feel magical and authentic, including the natural environment found around Hogwarts. Therefore, the Dungeon Design Team started by considering which types of locations might be found in the areas surrounding, and under, the school. They studied castle ruins for layout ideas, and ancient burial mounds to learn how rooms were shaped and chambers were connected. These ideas were then expanded on to make them feel more magical, more immersive and more interesting to navigate.

'Part of the magic of the wizarding world is that it isn't separate from the Muggle world, but with normally mundane settings, it adds the unexpected element of magic, wrapped in an authentic narrative. That's what we've tried to accomplish with each dungeon location – something tied to reality, but with a magical twist,' says **Dungeon Design Lead, Andrew Hayes**. 'In the end, we've created a variety of locations to explore, some based on real locations and architectural styles with a hint of magic, and others fully inspired by the wizarding world.'

As for every element of *Hogwarts Legacy*, a balance needed to be achieved between creating environments that would connect with the known wizarding world and those that were completely new. 'The wizarding world is full of great environments, many of them known through the books or movies,' says Hayes. 'But there are also many settings that were only hinted at, and large sections of the world around Hogwarts that have not yet been explored in the existing media. Both known and unknown locations provided us with great opportunities to create dungeons.'

TOP: Goblin Mine by the Environment Team

BOTTOM FROM LEFT TO RIGHT: Cairn Dungeon, Goblin Mine and Pensieve Dungeon (in-game renders) by the Environment Team

One already-known factor was that the Slytherin house's dormitory and the Chamber of Secrets are at the dungeon level of Hogwarts castle. At the start of their process, the Hogwarts Design Team considered whether the Chamber of Secrets could work in the game. 'Unfortunately, there were some challenges with this and it was decided not to include it,' Hayes says. 'We certainly wouldn't want the player thinking they could kill a Basilisk that needs to still be there in 1992!' The Slytherin dormitory, however, could be included, complete with views out into the Black Lake, where shadows of water creatures such as fish and squid can be seen swimming past the windows of the common room.

As some of the dungeon locations connect directly to either Hogwarts or Hogsmeade, the Dungeon Team needed to be aware of how the player would access these locations. Entrances and exits to already-familiar locations needed be believable in the known narrative canon. 'Would it make sense to find a hidden set of rooms or a cavernous expanse below Hogwarts?' asks Hayes. 'Given the history of the castle, how it was built and by whom, it certainly does make sense. What about a hidden den of Dark wizards below a tavern in Hogsmeade? The key was working with the narrative and ensuring it all was consistent with what we know about the wizarding world.'

Creating completely new locations was much more forgiving. 'Not everything is known about what lies inside the Forbidden Forest, and not much about the mountains around Hogwarts,' Hayes explains. 'So, we could largely work in what felt best for the world we were creating, the time period we were working in and the narrative of this story.'

The types of dungeons were chosen based on a few key factors, although it was an ever-evolving process during production. 'When we were deciding on which dungeons we wanted to create, we first looked at the surrounding location to see what type of dungeon would best fit that area,' explains **Environments and Dungeons Art Lead, Mike Thompson**. 'We also considered our preconfigured storylines and characters, ensuring that the dungeons would fit in with each of those aspects of the game.'

Of course, myriad ideas were brainstormed – beast dens in cavernous grottos, magical puzzle challenges left behind by a famous long-dead wizard – but as the narrative came together, it was realised that it was best to focus on wizard tombs and goblin mines and expand from there to castle ruins and caves that all became fundamental building blocks.

OPPOSITE: Goblin Mine and Cavern Dungeon (in-game renders) by the Environment Team

LEFT: Goblin Mine (in-game render) by the Environment Team

'We also had very real nefarious factions in the world that needed places to hide out or gamble – and negotiate shady deals – where the Ministry of Magic wouldn't be able to catch them,' says Hayes. 'So we added expansion tents and underground thieving dens to our tombs and mines. There are also very natural locations to be found, such as castle ruins where goblins have gathered, and burial chambers where ancient wizards were entombed, sometimes with their Dark Magic to protect their resting place.' And occasionally, there may even be a secret tunnel connecting Hogwarts itself to new or ancient locations. 'All these locations, familiar or fantastical, really came about as we tried to craft an authentic world and narrative around Hogwarts and the people who lived there,' adds Hayes.

Another factor determining what the dungeons would provide for the player was plans for what and how many enemy encounters there would be, the types of puzzles that would be used for support, what the story element was and whether that would fit the theme and the property. 'Subsequently, we blocked out the level to facilitate traversal navigation, enemy encounters, pacing and moment-to-moment interactions,' says Mike Thompson. 'We reworked areas along the way, adding and removing elements in the level until we felt it met our requirement of being both fun to play and aesthetically appealing.'

Ancient magic is featured in many of the dungeons, whether as a small addition or linked to enemies, but in some dungeons, ancient magic is the focus and part of the grander narrative. The Pensieve Chambers especially are very much crafted by ancient magic, filled with unique architecture and puzzles that can be solved by the player only by using the distinctive skills they've mastered to sense and wield ancient magic. In other dungeon settings, ancient magic is featured to solve puzzles or gain access to special rooms. 'The narrative of ancient magic is what pulls the player through many of these locations,' Hayes explains, 'and helps tie everything back to the main story.'

Each dungeon encountered challenges during production, even small ones that might serve only as a location to find a trinket. Some proved to be challenging and then disappeared as the narrative or game direction evolved, but one that stuck through the entire process was inspired by a recognisable tale known to children of the wizarding world. 'This level went through many iterations and even a handful of different level designers,' says Andrew Hayes. 'The narrative needs changed a few times, the desired feel adjusted based on feedback from game directors and even the studio head. We scoped the level larger, then smaller, then larger again, and finally landed somewhere in the middle. The level required special enemies, unique spells and even a custom visual style to immerse the player in the world. The team put in a lot of effort, felt the pain of losing parts of the level that were liked by some but not all, and in the end we hope it provides a compelling nod to a beloved part of the books and movies.'

OPPOSITE: Azkaban Prison, Percival's Dungeon and Goblin Mine (in-game renders) by the Environment Team

Level Best

Magic and combat were two of the most important elements to consider for gameplay in the dungeons. 'Many of the puzzles or magical elements in the dungeons started out in small, blocky levels we call holos or holodecks,' says Andrew Hayes. 'The mechanic would be prototyped in a very controlled environment, tested, reviewed and evaluated to see if people thought it felt magical or was intuitive, or even if it fit the property.'

Once a mechanic was decided on, it would move into a level, or a level would be built around it. As every mechanic or puzzle is different, they all came with specific setup needs or traversal requirements. 'Placing a mechanic or gameplay element in a level would invariably affect the layout,' says Hayes. 'Everything from elevation changes to the length of a hallway or room would be shaped by the needs of a given puzzle. How far does *Accio* reach when cast? What about *Lumos* – how far can you see when using it in the dark? It's a back-and-forth fitting between what the puzzle needs, what the magical mechanic is and what the setting is.'

Combat brought about some very real challenges in finalising levels. For some enemies, such as trolls, large open spaces were needed. Burial mounds, characteristically small with tight openings or corridors, were not suitable for fighting off a horde of giant spiders. 'This is where we had to sometimes stretch the bounds of reality a little,' says Hayes. 'To get the combat experience desired, we needed to enlarge certain chambers to provide enough open, flat ground for the enemies to function well, and hallways couldn't be too tight or ceilings too low.'

Everything involved in designing the dungeons is important, although some particulars can prove somewhat frustrating or downright silly. Creating large enough rooms for the needs of combat sometimes made for what felt like overly large interiors, 'which strained the realities of architecture,' Hayes says. 'Pushing the boundaries can make things more interesting and lead to a beautiful virtual environment, but within an environment, being believable is important.' One challenge in designing a dungeon level was trying to place a 140- to 200-foot-wide room in a burial mound. 'That did seem a bit silly,' he adds.

Then there was the issue of dealing with an abundance of what the team called 'toe-stubbers.' 'Our creative director, for good reason, hates anything that the player can trip on, or even looks like they can trip on,' explains Hayes. 'So, through many reviews, the predominant piece of feedback was to fix the toe-stubbers.' The term became a punchline the team used frequently.

The final elements of any game evolve over time, which proved true for dungeons. The team started with the goal of making a large number of dungeons to fill out the expansive landscape around Hogwarts. This then evolved to be more about supporting the narrative and refining the selection of levels to those that best fit the locations and story needs. 'There were a lot of levels and gameplay mechanics created by a very large team of internal and external developers, but quite a few of those levels had to be left for another time,' says Andrew Hayes. 'The process is very challenging, sometimes heartbreaking, but ultimately rewarding when we see the final product. Dungeons are locations made to support the narrative, and we hope the player enjoys them and recognises the effort and talent put into creating them.'

OPPOSITE TOP TO BOTTOM: Spider Cave Dungeon Isometric Views by Damian Buzugbe; Sanctum Dungeon Platforming and Magic Pull by Ben Simonsen

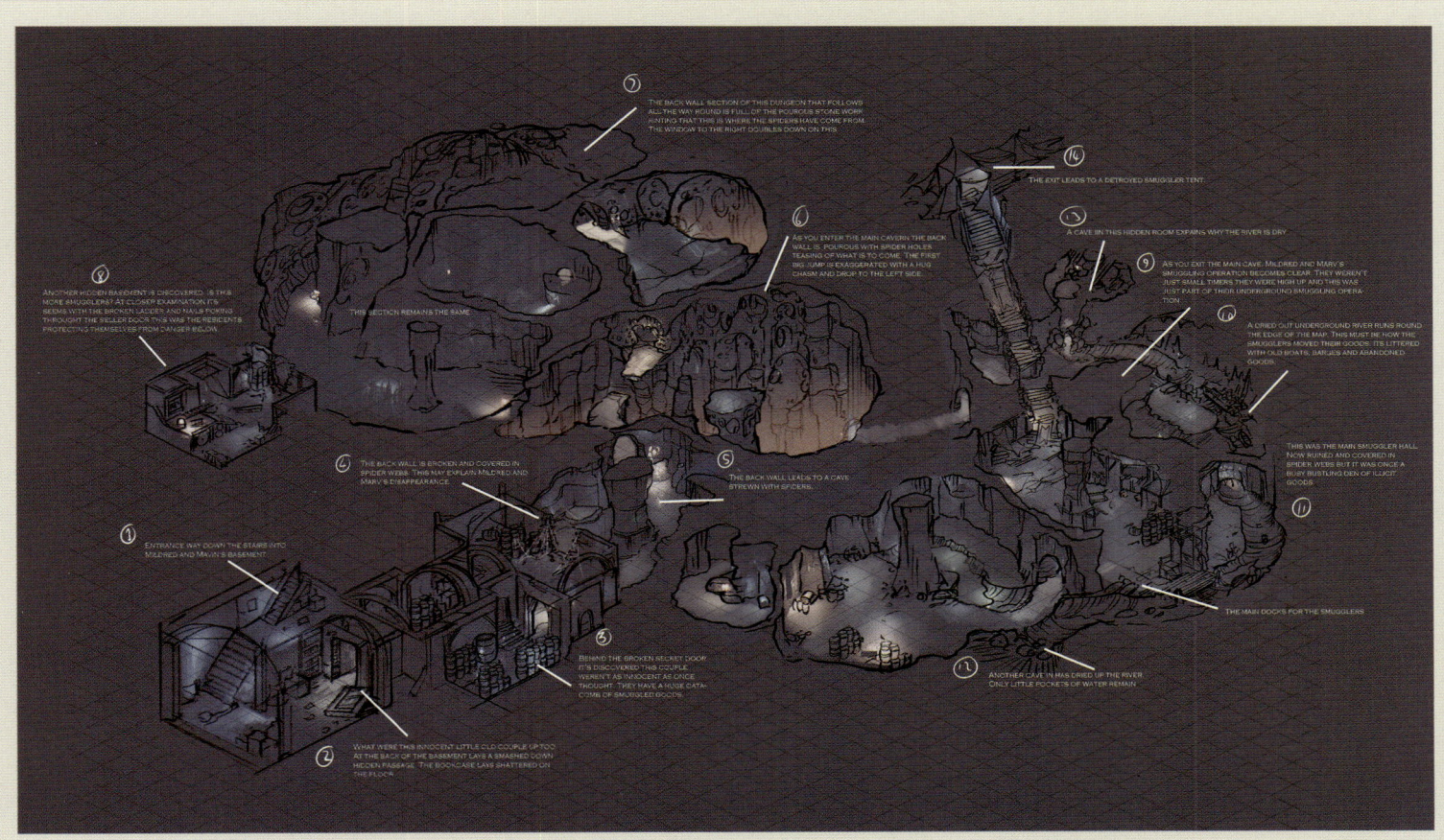

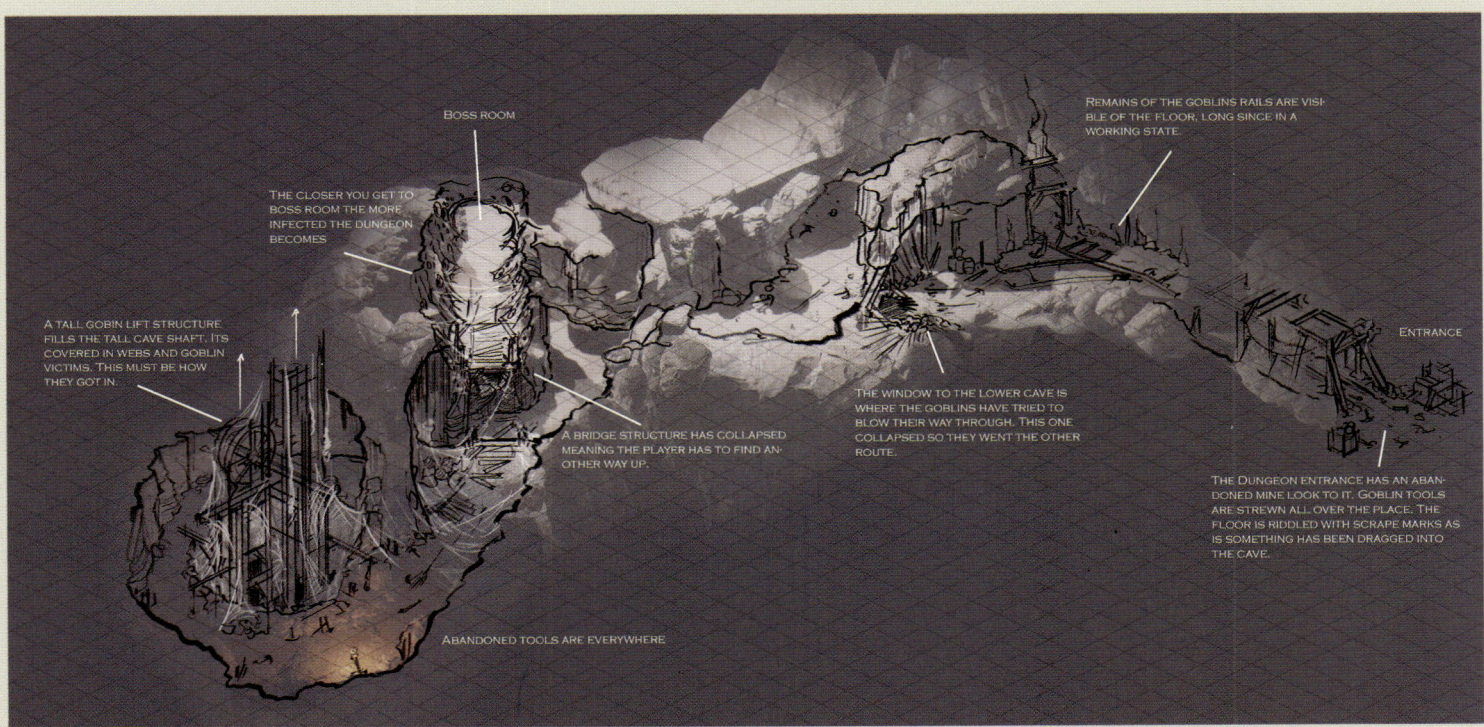

THE MAP CHAMBER

Deep below Hogwarts castle is the Map Chamber, where the player interacts with the portraits of the four guardians of ancient magic – the Keepers.

The architecture of the Map Chamber reflects the era of the Keepers, with its Tudor-style trefoil arches, reminiscent of late-medieval architecture, albeit stylised with natural, sinewy lines evoking the Art Nouveau style. Similar to the elemental assignments given to the Hogwarts houses, the Map Chamber, set deep into the earth, features a water wall and a tower of flame. A statue of an elemental being stands watch. Within a large, light-filled cavern is a Pensieve set on a podium. At its base is a silhouette of Hogwarts carved in wood.

The walls have a black, marbled texture with veins that move as if they are alive. There is polished architecture featuring natural stone, natural cave environments with sections of Sanctum architecture and areas of the Map Chamber that are returning to their natural state, including a domed ceiling, twisted columns and floating platforms that lead to the Map Chamber's entrance.

TOP: Map Chamber (in-game render) by the Environment Team
OPPOSITE TOP: Floor Map (3D render) by the Environment Team
OPPOSITE BOTTOM: Map Chamber by Ben Simonsen

THE KEEPERS

Percival Rackham

[HUFFLEPUFF]

Percival Rackham is a powerful wizard who respects intelligence and ambition. He is the leader of the Keepers, and the only Keeper able to see traces of ancient magic in the same way the avatar does. Perceiving the great potential in ancient magic, he encouraged a promising student, Isidora Morganach, to become his apprentice.

He was exceptionally skilled at Divination in his time. An elegant man, he is reserved in his movements.

San Bakar's Tower

Located in the North Ford Bog region, the tower of San Bakar, one of the Keepers, has been abandoned and run down into near ruin.

OPPOSITE: Percival Rackham by Ryan Wood

TOP: San Bakar's Tower (in-game render) by the Environment Team

ABOVE: San Bakar's Tower World Map Paper Model by Nasan Hardcastle

LEFT: Percival Rackham's Wand by Sébastien Gallego

Charles Rookwood

[SLYTHERIN]

Charles Rookwood considered himself a man of 'science' (as much as a wizard can be) and Percival Rackham's closest friend. Where Rackham is guided by an emotional intuition, however, Rookwood turns to hard facts. A loyal friend to Rackham and the other Keepers, he is also pragmatic, direct and focused. Rookwood is keenly observant and fascinated by the ways in which magic can be altered and used. He was the Transfiguration professor at Hogwarts in his day.

Niamh Fitzgerald

[RAVENCLAW]

A natural leader and protector, Niamh was the Headmistress of Hogwarts during the Keepers' era. Where Percival Rackham worried about the fate of wizardkind, Fitzgerald feared more for the individual students for whom she was responsible. She inspires courage and compassion among her colleagues and drives the group to continue the search for answers, even when the hope seems dim. Fitzgerald is even-keeled, thinks before she speaks and notices everything. She is liked and respected by her fellow Keepers, due to her grace, wisdom, kindness and confidence.

ABOVE: Charles Rookwood by Sébastien Gallego and BOSI
OPPOSITE: Niamh Fitzgerald by Ryan Wood; Charles Rookwood's Wand by Sébastien Gallego

San Bakar

[SLYTHERIN]

San Bakar left his Muggle community in Yemen when he learned of his magical abilities and eventually found his way to Hogwarts, where he completed his education and became the Beasts professor. This highly skilled wizard is compassionate and kind, and a bit of an animal whisperer – he is centred and calming, and moves carefully.

Isidora Morganach

[RAVENCLAW]

Isidora Morganach appears in the Keepers' memories. Thought not a Keeper herself, when Isidora Morganach was a child, she witnessed the Keepers reviving her drought-plagued hamlet of Feldcroft in a matter of moments. Morganach started Hogwarts as a fifth-year, similar to the player, and was taken under Percival Rackham's wing to be his apprentice and learn how to wield ancient magic – as both she and Rackham could see traces of such magic. Morganach is confident, relatable and wry, and moves gracefully and intensely. Charming and accessible, she became a popular Defence Against the Dark Arts professor at Hogwarts – until she found herself delving deeper and deeper into a never-explored Dark side of ancient magic.

OPPOSITE TOP: Graphorn's Gate by Mike McCarthy

OPPOSITE BOTTOM: San Bakar by Sébastien Gallego and BOSI

ABOVE: Isidora by Vanessa Palmer

Rookwood's Camps and Goblin Caves

The camps of Rookwood's followers can be found all over the Highlands and are occupied by Dark wizards. The camps come in all sizes: small, medium and large. The largest camps are found in old castle ruins. Additionally, there are two caves where the goblins convene.

Ranrok's Dragon

A fierce dragon imbued with ancient magic is conjured by Ranrok the goblin in his bid to overthrow wizardkind during the climactic battle of *Hogwarts Legacy*.

TOP SPREAD: Ranrok's Dragon Prison by Ben Simonsen

OPPOSITE: Ranrok's Dragon Sculpt by Character Team

TOP: Dragon Arena Entrance (in-game render) by the Environment Team

BOTTOM: Ranrok's Dragon Platform by Ben Simonsen

CONTINUE PLAY

Hogwarts Legacy expands the wizarding world not only with new locations and original characters, but by placing the player into an as yet unexplored time period, building on a lesser-known aspect of wizarding lore: ancient magic. Ancient magic is a powerful, primal and mysterious form of magic enmeshed in both the most dangerous and wonderful spells ever cast by wizardkind. Traces of this ancient magic can be found in the hides of dragons or in a spell cast unintentionally out of pure love. Even Hogwarts, built by a quartet of magical masters of the past, is a storehouse of ancient magic.

Very few witches and wizards ever gain the understanding or skill to control this spellcraft, and it is fortunate for this era that the player has the special ability to perceive traces of this unpredictable and perilous magic, which has the power to perform both the greatest good or the greatest ill. And when the player notices a connection between ancient magic and a brewing goblin rebellion, they realise that only they and their friends – with the help of a professor named Fig – can put a stop to a sinister goblin plot, the corruption of magical creatures and the schemes of Dark wizards to save Hogwarts itself from an existential threat.

Key to overcoming this new peril to the wizarding community is learning magic. And so, a spellcasting system for *Hogwarts Legacy* was created that blends fencing, parries, environment usage and counter-attacks to create a magical combat system with offensive, defensive and world interaction spells the player accumulates and masters. This wide range of spells includes *Accio*, *Levioso* and *Incendio,* and even the Unforgivable Curses if so desired. There are classes to learn about charms, herbology, potions and magical beasts. There are professors and students who have out-of-class assignments and sometimes problems that need to be resolved. The player also has their own personal and customisable space within the Room of Requirement to enhance their studies: growing plants, brewing potions, crafting gear and nurturing magical beasts and their babies, in habitats that are safe from the dangers of the world outside.

The area surrounding the Hogwarts castle grounds contains hundreds of points of interest to explore, including the well-known locations of Hogsmeade and the Forbidden Forest, to newer locations such as hamlets and dungeons peppered throughout the Highlands region that surround the castle. There are intriguing areas to traverse on foot, on brooms or other mounts; ruins to explore; and magical puzzles to solve. There are also enemies and the potential for combat with Dark wizards, specifically within the nefarious gang of Victor Rookwood, which includes poachers, thieves and extortionists, as well as goblins and dangerous creatures. Unlike most students, the player has arrived as a fifth-year at Hogwarts, but fortunately, the Hogwarts professors and the Ministry of Magic have supplied the player with a Wizard's Field Guide to quickly 'catch up' on their schooling.

'To visually create a world from words on a page, there is an infinite number of possible directions to go,' says **Art Director, Jeff Bunker**. 'With the films, those possibilities are narrowed to capture the essence of a book read over twenty-plus hours and then retell it in under three hours. Additionally, there are constraints that come naturally with the production of live-action films such as a real cast of actors and on-location environments that further narrow that vision to what you see on screen.

The films did an amazing job of casting, production design, costuming, visual FX, etc., to bring the books to life,' Bunker continues, 'and had their own visual pillars to set the appropriate tone and stage for supporting the story of each book. We obviously were heavily influenced by them. But unlike the films, which compress the stories of the books to fit the medium of film, we are expanding the wizarding world into an interactive space with a new mystery, new hero and new cast of characters to be experienced over a much longer time than the films or even the books. The ideas summed up in our pillars [authenticity, heroism and magic] were our north star in our exploration of that new territory.'

Equally important as the authentic character and personality of Hogwarts and Hogsmeade, was the development of a new mystery with a new cast of heroes and villains: professors, friends and adversaries. 'These new characters needed to become as meaningful to the player's journey as the likes of Hermione, Ron, Dumbledore and Snape were to Harry,' says Bunker. 'And the new mystery needed to reveal these new characters' motivations and backstories in compelling and engaging missions.'

But finally, Hogwarts, Hogsmeade, the Forbidden Forest and the characters and fantastic beasts that live there are not truly authentic until magic permeates everything and everyone. '*Hogwarts Legacy* is all about magic,' he continues. 'That magic needs to be beautiful, epic, playful, powerful, dangerous, unexpected, delightful, intimidating, useful and of course ... interactive. If any game ever made a visual statement about what magic should look like, it should be *Hogwarts Legacy*. That was the challenge we gave ourselves.'

'This [has been] an exciting time to develop immersive experiences,' says **Head of Story, Adrian Ropp**. 'With innovative high-definition graphics, a player can practically feel the terror of Inferi bearing down upon them, or sense the ground rumbling beneath them as a herd of angry centaurs surrounds them.'

And the biggest challenge during the creation and production of *Hogwarts Legacy*? 'J.K. Rowling's wizarding world is one of the most popular, most beloved entertainment franchises of all time,' Bunker explains. 'We felt a tremendous responsibility to pay off the fan fantasy of going to school at Hogwarts and becoming a powerful witch or wizard. To add characters, locations and stories authentic to the franchise whilst providing a new game experience appreciated by gamers and fans alike was extremely challenging ... but equally satisfying.'

Avalanche Software is justifiably proud of *Hogwarts Legacy*, with its engaging storytelling, authentic lore and unique characters. Setting the game in an exceptional and extraordinary era of the wizarding world offers fresh and innovative ways for fans to master magical skills, make friends and meet exhilarating challenges to become the witch or wizard they want to be. All that needs to be done is to press 'play.'

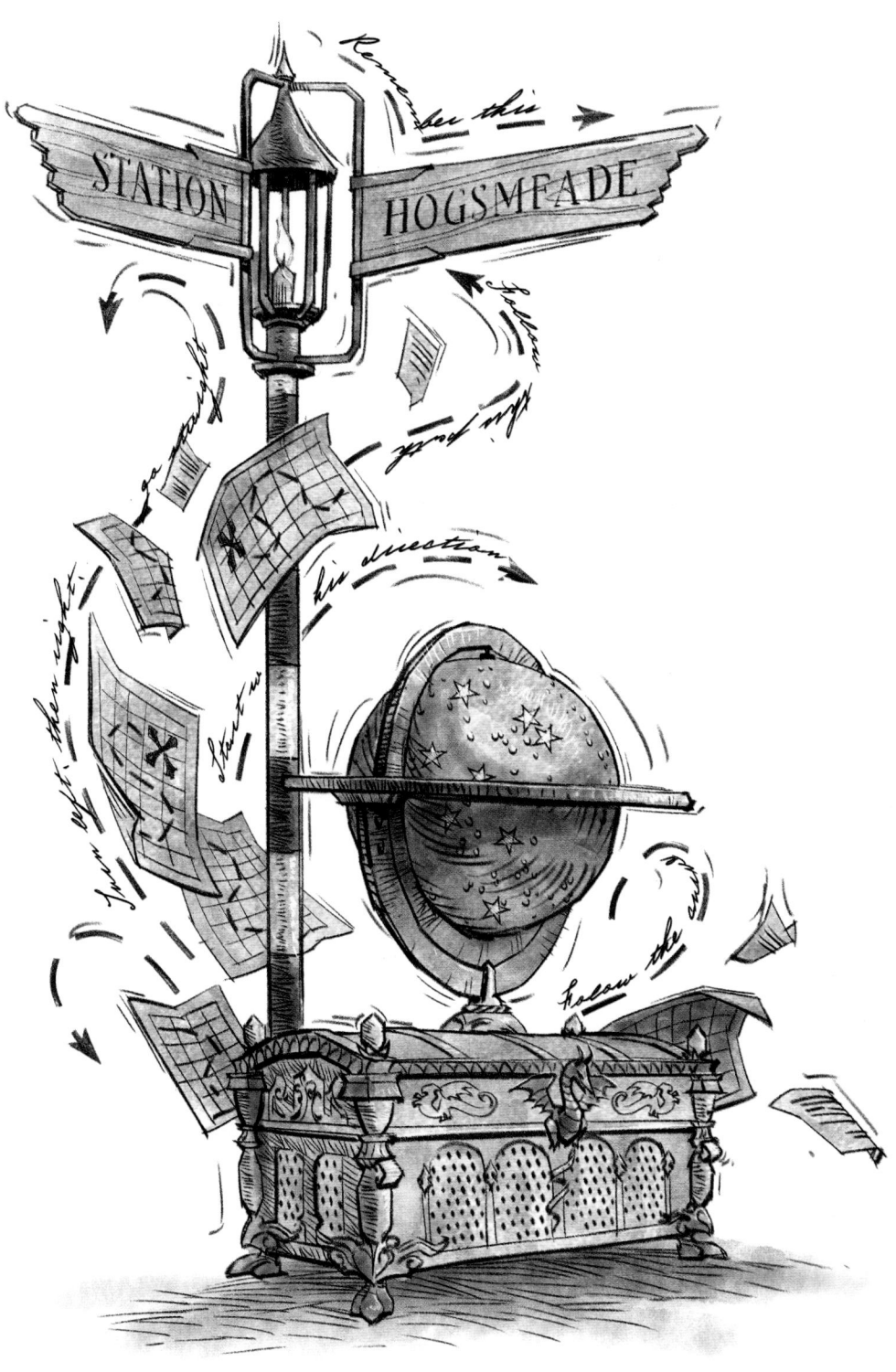

BELOW: Quest Menu Field Guide Drawing by Nasan Hardcastle

Acknowledgements

So many talented people helped bring this book to life, and we owe them a debt of gratitude. While we can't thank them all, we want to acknowledge some in particular.

The extraordinary art found in this book represents the collective creative expressions of gifted artists who used tools and features provided by programmers with the guidance and resource management of producers – a true collaboration. Many thanks go out to the entire *Hogwarts Legacy* team at Avalanche. They are incomparably talented – and good people.

A special thanks to our families who supported us through our journey to make the game and the contents of this book.

A big heartfelt thank you to our co-development partner and friends at Studio Gobo. Their stellar work on the Room of Requirement, specifically, and across the game – in general – was invaluable. They made our game, and Avalanche better.

Thank you to Jessica Paz, Kirsten Gavoni and the Warner Bros. Games production team whose effort and passion were equal to our own.

A big thank you to Ross Fraser and The Blair Partnership for their guidance and friendship.

We appreciate the staff at Insight Editions Publishing, Jennifer Sims, Sammy Holland, Sadie Lowry, Mike Degler and Lola Villanueva for helping us collect and organise our thoughts and art into such a beautiful book.

Book Contributors

Adam Tolman | Adrian Ropp | Ahmed Serbest | Alan Tew | Andrew Hayes | Ben Judd | Ben Mowson | Ben Savage | Ben Sharp | Ben Simonsen | Boston Madsen | Brandon Booth | Brett Turley | Brian Cutler | Brian Green | Brian Kohrman | Bryan Allen | Charles Pharis | Colby Acree | Dallin Haws | Dallin Jones | Damian Buzugbe | Damon Heagren | Danny Russon | Darin Beaver | Dave McClellan | David Jeka | Dillon Thompson | Duane Johnson | Emil DeGrey | Emilie Van Geel | Eric Stubbs | Ethan Hunsaker | Gabe Ford | Gavan Knowlton | Isaac Kellis | Jade Rogers | Jake Black | James Watt | Jared Bastian | Jaren Tolman | Jason Borne | Jason Price | Jason Richards | Jeff Bunker | Jeremy Hodges | Jessica Hurst Noel | Jody Eastman | Joe Cosman | Joe Patience | Joe Percival | John Blackburn | Jon Diesta | Joseph Sargent | Joshua H Black | Juan Mesa | Kalee McCollaum | Kelly Murphy | Kevin Keele | Luke Adwick | Luke Cutler | Lyle Thompson | Marcus Fisher | Marshall LeClaire | Matt Dibb | Matt Judd | Melker Berg | Michael Caldwell | Mike McCarthy | Mike Thompson | Moira Squier | Nasan Hardcastle | Nathan Hendrickson | Nick Simmons | Paul Armstrong | Rob Griffin | Rob Nelson | Ryan Kidd | Ryan Wood | Sander Vander Meiren | Sébastien Gallego | Sierra Dickey | Spencer Black | Taylor Shorten | Tom Ellis | Thomas Sincich | Tiffany Nguyen | Troy Johnson | Tyler Lybbert | Vanessa Palmer | Wei Wong | Yukun Peng-Drew

Special Thanks

WB Games Montreal | BOSI | Certain Affinity | Counterpunch Studios | d3t | Epic Games | Frame Machine | FXVille | Globant | KARAKTER Design Studio | Little Red Zombies | Monolith Productions | NetherRealm | NXA | Original Force | Passion Republic | Plastic Wax | Red Kite Games | Restar | Roaring Gate | Shiver | Sparx | Sprung | Studio Gobo | Sumo Digital | Technicolor | Traveller's Tales | Two Okes Entertainment | Ulysses Graphics | Virtuos | Waterproof Studios | West Studio

TOP: Highlands Swamp by Vanessa Palmer

LEFT: Hogsmeade Map and Hogwarts Map detail by Vanessa Palmer

PO Box 3088
San Rafael, CA 94912
www.insighteditions.com

BLOOMSBURY CHILDREN'S BOOKS
Bloomsbury Publishing Plc
50 Bedford Square, London WC1B 3DP, UK
29 Earlsfort Terrace, Dublin 2, Ireland

BLOOMSBURY, BLOOMSBURY CHILDREN'S BOOKS
and the Diana logo are trademarks of Bloomsbury Publishing Plc

HOGWARTS LEGACY software © 2023 Warner Bros. Entertainment Inc. Developed by Avalanche. WIZARDING WORLD and HARRY POTTER Publishing Rights © J.K. Rowling. PORTKEY GAMES, HOGWARTS LEGACY, WIZARDING WORLD AND HARRY POTTER characters, names and related indicia © and ™ Warner Bros. Entertainment Inc.

WARNER BROS. GAMES LOGO, WB SHIELD: ™ & © Warner Bros. Entertainment Inc. (s23)

First published in the US in 2023 by Insight Editions, San Rafael, California.

First published in Great Britain in 2023 by Bloomsbury Publishing Plc.
www.bloomsbury.com

All rights reserved. No part of this book may be reproduced, transmitted, or stored in an information retrieval system in any form or by any means, graphic, electronic, or mechanical, including photocopying, taping, and recording, without prior written permission from the publisher.

A catalogue record for this book is available from the British Library.

ISBN: 978 1 5266 5991 0

Publisher: Raoul Goff
VP of Licensing and Partnerships: Vanessa Lopez
VP of Creative: Chrissy Kwasnik
VP of Manufacturing: Alix Nicholaeff
VP, Editorial Director: Vicki Jaeger
Designer: Lola Villanueva
Senior Editor: Jennifer Sims
Editor: Samantha Holland
Assistant Editor: Sadie Lowry
Senior Production Editor: Elaine Ou
Senior Production Manager: Greg Steffen
Senior Production Manager, Subsidiary Rights: Lina s Palma-Temena
Production Associate: Kevin G. Yuen

 REPLANTED PAPER

Insight Editions, in association with Roots of Peace, will plant two trees for each tree used in the manufacturing of this book. Roots of Peace is an internationally renowned humanitarian organization dedicated to eradicating land mines worldwide and converting war-torn lands into productive farms and wildlife habitats. Roots of Peace will plant two million fruit and nut trees in Afghanistan and provide farmers there with the skills and support necessary for sustainable land use.

Manufactured in China by Insight Editions

10 9 8 7 6 5 4 3 2 1